T0049775

# FRENCH
## FOR EVERYONE
## JUNIOR
### 5 WORDS A DAY

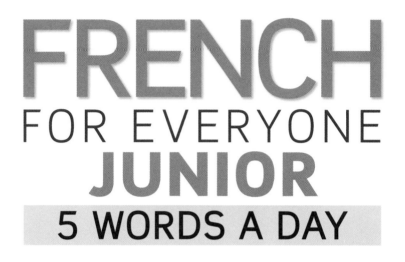

**FREE AUDIO**
website and app

**www.dk5words.com/us**

# FRENCH
## FOR EVERYONE
## JUNIOR
## 5 WORDS A DAY

**FREE AUDIO**
website and app

## www.dk5words.com/us

**DK**

For the curious

## DK LONDON

**Project Editors** Sophie Adam, Elizabeth Blakemore
**Editor** Ben Ffrancon Davies
**Project Art Editor** Anna Scully
**Designer** Annabel Schick
**Illustrators** Amy Child, Gus Scott
**Managing Editor** Christine Stroyan
**Managing Art Editor** Anna Hall
**Production Editor** Kavita Varma
**Production Controller** Samantha Cross
**Senior Jacket Designer** Suhita Dharamjit
**Jacket Design Development Manager** Sophia MTT
**Publisher** Andrew Macintyre
**Art Director** Karen Self
**Publishing Director** Jonathan Metcalf

**Translation** Andiamo! Language Services Ltd

## DK INDIA

**Pre-Production Manager** Sunil Sharma
**DTP Designers** Manish Chandra Upreti,
Umesh Singh Rawat

First American Edition, 2021
Published in the United States by DK Publishing
1745 Broadway, 20th Floor, New York, NY 10019

Copyright © 2021 Dorling Kindersley Limited
DK, a Division of Penguin Random House LLC
22 23 24 25 10 9 8 7 6 5 4 3 2
005–323272–Jul/2021

All rights reserved.
Without limiting the rights under the copyright reserved
above, no part of this publication may be reproduced,
stored in or introduced into a retrieval system,
or transmitted, in any form, or by any means (electronic,
mechanical, photocopying, recording, or otherwise),
without the prior written permission of the
copyright owner.
Published in Great Britain by
Dorling Kindersley Limited

A catalog record for this book
is available from the Library of Congress.
ISBN: 978-0-7440-3678-7
DK books are available at special discounts
when purchased in bulk for sales promotions, premiums,
fund-raising, or educational use. For details, contact:
DK Publishing Special Markets,
1745 Broadway, 20th Floor, New York, NY 10019
SpecialSales@dk.com

Printed and bound in China

**For the curious**
www.dk.com

FSC
www.fsc.org
MIX
Paper from
responsible sources
FSC™ C018179

This book was made with Forest
Stewardship Council ™ certified paper
– one small step in DK's commitment
to a sustainable future.
For more information go to
www.dk.com/our-green-pledge

# Contents

Max

Maria

# How to use this book

*French for Everyone Junior: 5 Words a Day* is a vocabulary book
for children that teaches and tests more than 1,000 French words.
Words are taught in weekly units of 5 days.

## Learning new vocabulary

On Days 1–4, the child will be presented with 20 new words, which
are taught 5 words at a time through colorful illustrations.

**1** First, listen to the words on
the audio app or website,
repeat the words out loud,
and then write them out in
the space below each word.

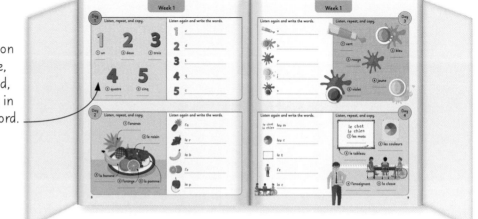

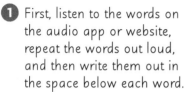

### Masculine and feminine words

In French, all nouns
(things or people) are
either masculine or
feminine. You will notice
that many words have
"le", "la", or "les" in front
of them. These all
mean "the" in English.
If a word has "le" before
it, it is masculine. If it
has "la" in front of it, it
is feminine. "Les" is used
before masculine and
feminine plurals.

**2** Next, use the book flaps to
cover the illustrations and
listen to the words again.

**3** With the words still covered,
try writing out each word
from memory.

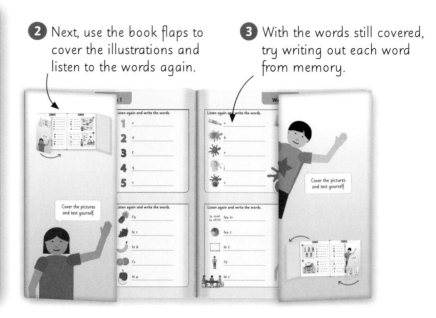

# Testing new vocabulary

On Day 5, the child can practice the 20 new words
and reinforce their learning through fun exercises.

A variety of exercises are
used to test all 20 words.

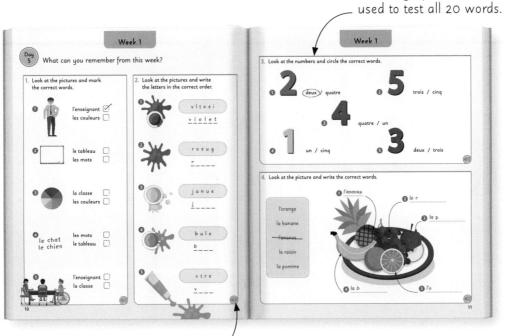

Once you have finished an exercise,
listen to the words again on the app
or website.

Answers to all the questions are
given at the back of the book.

## Audio

Pronunciation is an important aspect of learning a new language. Audio for all the
words in this book is available on the **DK 5 Words** website and app. You should
encourage your child to listen to the audio and repeat the words out loud.

Access the audio recordings for free at **www.dk5words.com/us** or download the
**DK 5 Words** app from the App Store or Google Play.

**FREE AUDIO**
website and app

## www.dk5words.com/us

## Day 1

Listen, repeat, and copy.

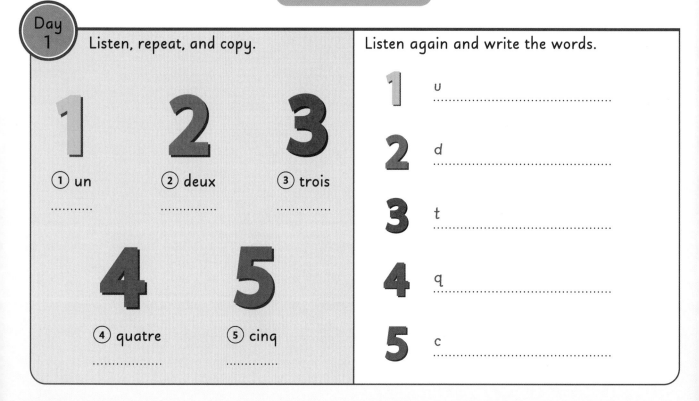

**1** ① un

**2** ② deux

**3** ③ trois

**4** ④ quatre

**5** ⑤ cinq

Listen again and write the words.

**1** u ...........................................

**2** d ...........................................

**3** t ...........................................

**4** q ...........................................

**5** c ...........................................

## Day 2

Listen, repeat, and copy.

① l'ananas

② le raisin

③ la banane

④ l'orange

⑤ la pomme

Listen again and write the words.

l'a ...........................................

le r ...........................................

la b ...........................................

l'o ...........................................

la p ...........................................

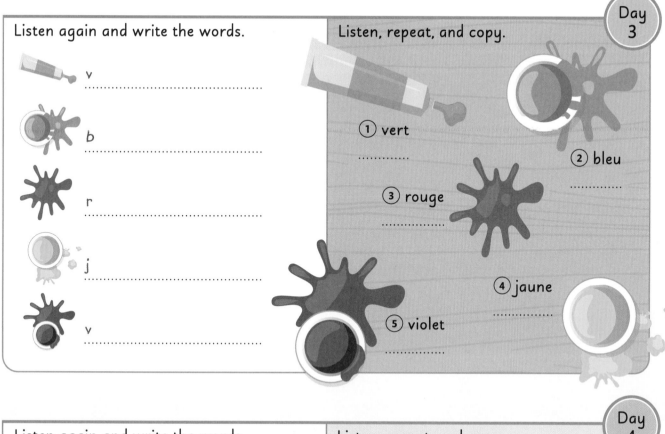

Day 3

Listen again and write the words.

v ..................................

b ..................................

r ..................................

j ..................................

v ..................................

Listen, repeat, and copy.

① vert
..............

② bleu
..............

③ rouge
..............

④ jaune
..............

⑤ violet
..............

Day 4

Listen again and write the words.

le chat
le chien
les m ..................................

les c ..................................

le t ..................................

l'e ..................................

la c ..................................

Listen, repeat, and copy.

le chat
le chien
① les mots
..............

② les couleurs
..............

③ le tableau
..............

④ l'enseignant
..............

⑤ la classe
..............

Day 5

What can you remember from this week?

**1. Look at the pictures and mark the correct words.**

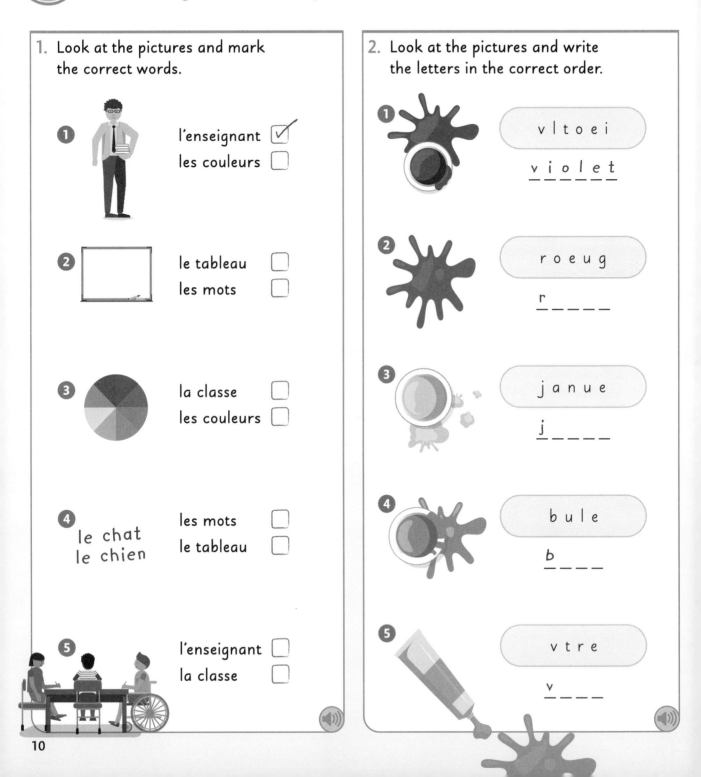

1. l'enseignant ✓
   les couleurs ☐

2. le tableau ☐
   les mots ☐

3. la classe ☐
   les couleurs ☐

4. les mots ☐
   le tableau ☐
   le chat
   le chien

5. l'enseignant ☐
   la classe ☐

**2. Look at the pictures and write the letters in the correct order.**

1. v l t o e i
   v i o l e t

2. r o e u g
   r _ _ _ _ _

3. j a n u e
   j _ _ _ _ _

4. b u l e
   b _ _ _

5. v t r e
   v _ _ _

3. Look at the numbers and circle the correct words.

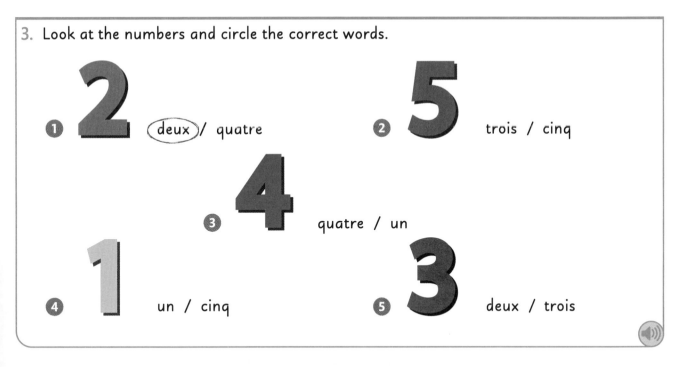

1 **2** (deux) / quatre

2 **5** trois / cinq

3 **4** quatre / un

4 **1** un / cinq

5 **3** deux / trois

4. Look at the picture and write the correct words.

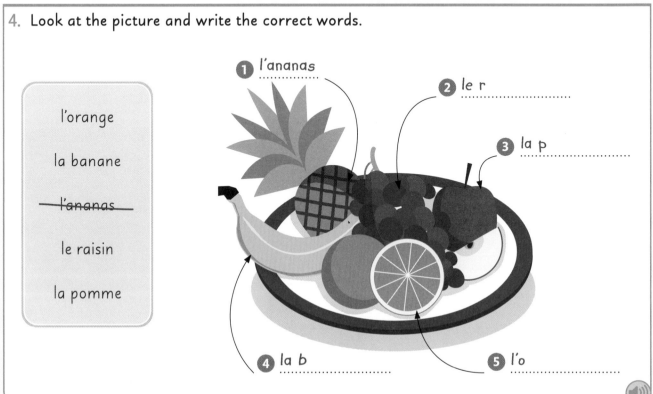

l'orange

la banane

l'ananas

le raisin

la pomme

1 l'ananas

2 le r .......................

3 la p .......................

4 la b .......................

5 l'o .......................

## Day 1

Listen, repeat, and copy.

**6** ① six
..........

**7** ② sept
..........

**8** ③ huit
..........

**9** ④ neuf
..........

**10** ⑤ dix
..........

Listen again and write the words.

**6** s ...................................

**7** s ...................................

**8** h ...................................

**9** n ...................................

**10** d ...................................

## Day 2

Listen, repeat, and copy.

12345
② les chiffres
..........

① la salle de classe
...................................

| Aa | Bb | Cc | Dd | Ee |
| Ff | Gg | Hh | Ii | Jj |
| Kk | Ll | Mm | Nn | Oo |
| Pp | Qq | Rr | Ss | Tt |
| Uu | Vv | Ww | Xx | Yy |
| Zz | | | | |

③ l'alphabet
...................................

④ les lettres
..........

⑤ la camarade
..........

Listen again and write the words.

la s ...................................

12345 les c ...................................

l'a ...................................

les l ...................................

la c ...................................

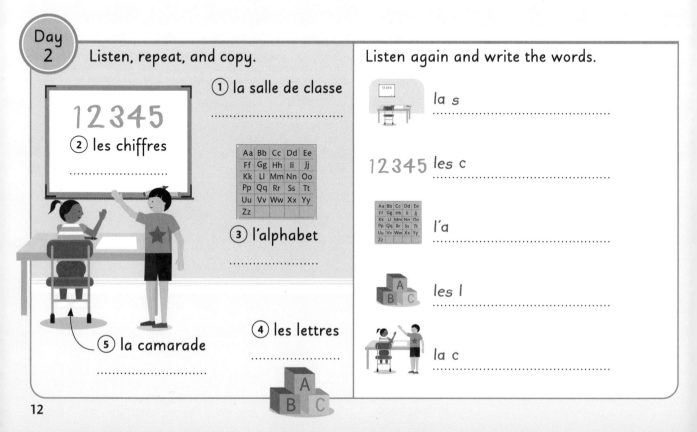

Day 3

**Listen again and write the words.**

la m .....................................

la f .....................................

le n .....................................

le j .....................................

la p .....................................

**Listen, repeat, and copy.**

① la marionnette
.....................................

② la figurine
.....................................

③ le nounours
.....................................

④ le jeu de société
.....................................

⑤ la poupée
.....................................

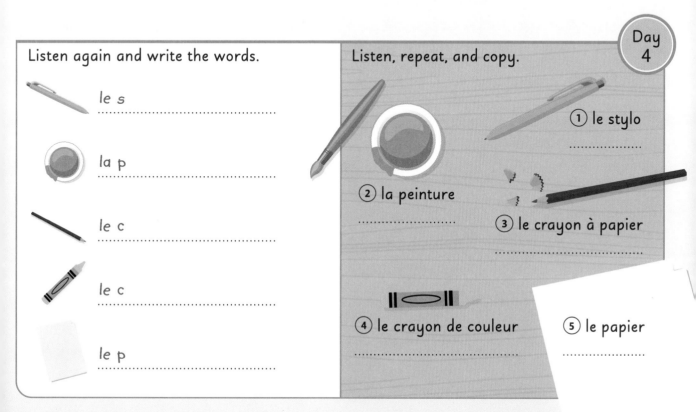

Day 4

**Listen again and write the words.**

le s .....................................

la p .....................................

le c .....................................

le c .....................................

le p .....................................

**Listen, repeat, and copy.**

① le stylo
.....................................

② la peinture
.....................................

③ le crayon à papier
.....................................

④ le crayon de couleur
.....................................

⑤ le papier
.....................................

Day 5

What can you remember from this week?

1. Look at the pictures and write the correct words.

l'alphabet    ~~les chiffres~~    la camarade    les lettres    la salle de classe

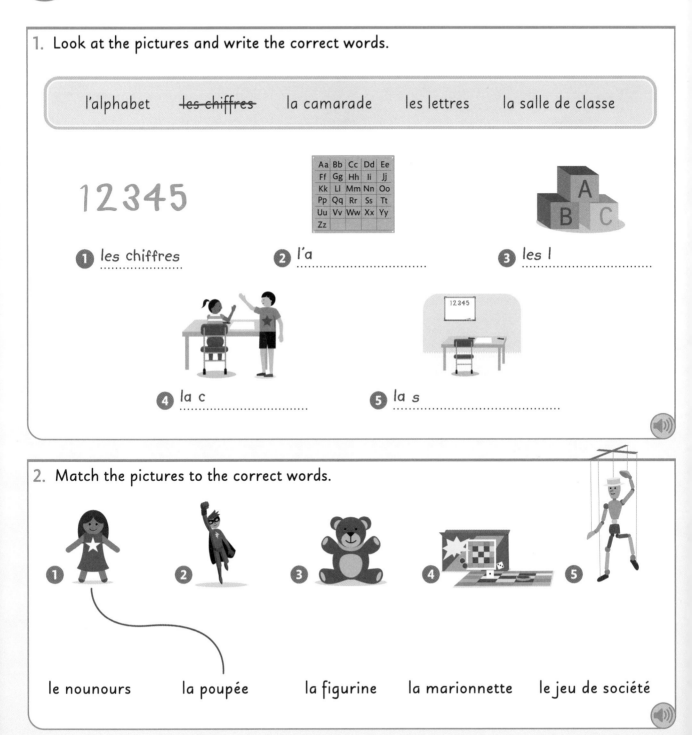

12345

| Aa | Bb | Cc | Dd | Ee |
| Ff | Gg | Hh | Ii | Jj |
| Kk | Ll | Mm | Nn | Oo |
| Pp | Qq | Rr | Ss | Tt |
| Uu | Vv | Ww | Xx | Yy |
| Zz | | | | |

1 les chiffres

2 l'a _____

3 les l _____

4 la c _____

5 la s _____

2. Match the pictures to the correct words.

1    2    3    4    5

le nounours    la poupée    la figurine    la marionnette    le jeu de société

14

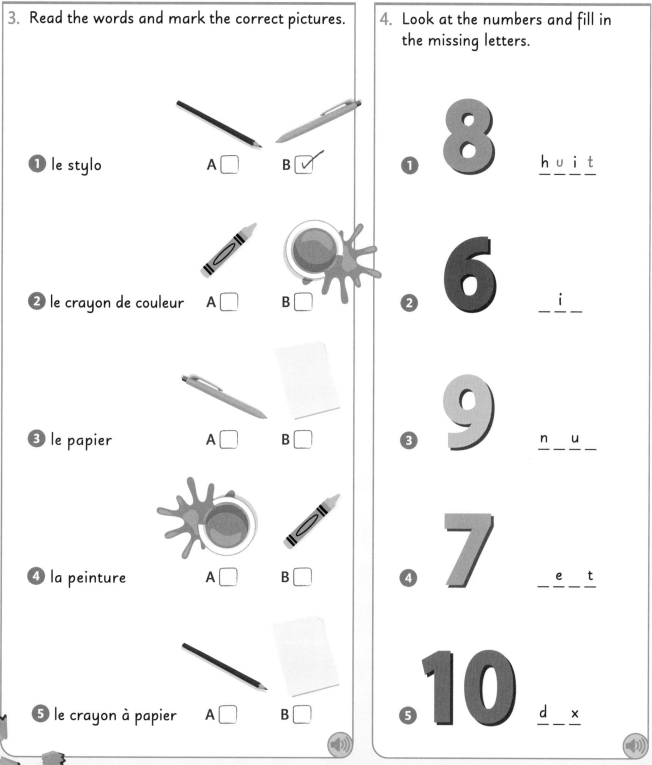

3. Read the words and mark the correct pictures.

1 le stylo  A ☐  B ☑

2 le crayon de couleur  A ☐  B ☐

3 le papier  A ☐  B ☐

4 la peinture  A ☐  B ☐

5 le crayon à papier  A ☐  B ☐

4. Look at the numbers and fill in the missing letters.

1  **8**  h u i t

2  **6**  _ i _

3  **9**  n _ _ u _

4  **7**  _ e _ t

5  **10**  d _ _ x

**Day 1**

Listen, repeat, and copy.

**11** ① onze
.............

**12** ② douze
.............

**13** ③ treize
.............

**14** ④ quatorze
.............

**15** ⑤ quinze
.............

Listen again and write the words.

**11** o .......................

**12** d .......................

**13** t .......................

**14** q .......................

**15** q .......................

**Day 2**

Listen, repeat, and copy.

① l'école
.............

② la maison
.............

③ la rue
.............

④ le parc
.............

⑤ l'aire de jeux
.............

Listen again and write the words.

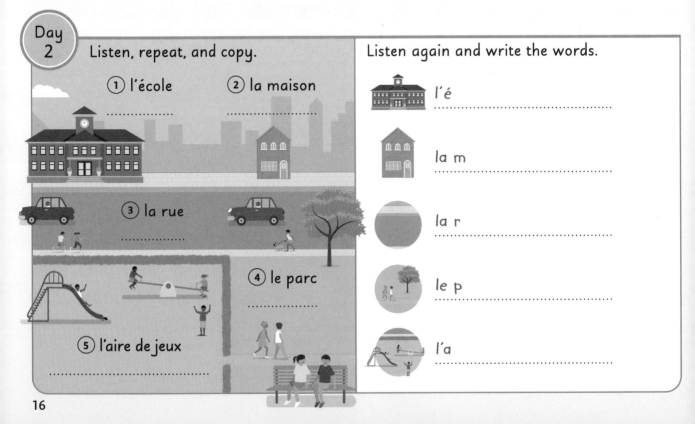

l'é .......................

la m .......................

la r .......................

le p .......................

l'a .......................

16

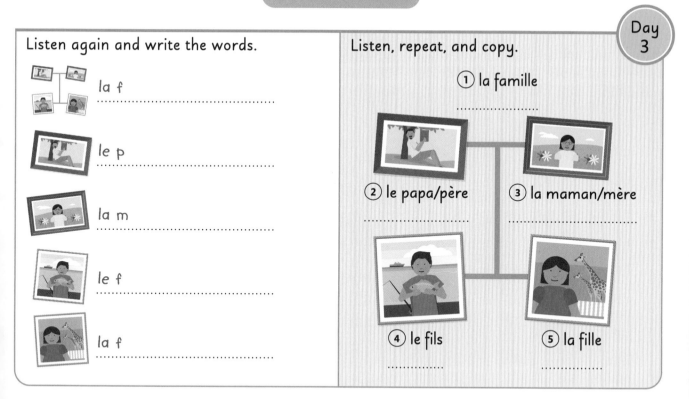

Day 3

**Listen again and write the words.**

la f .................................................

le p .................................................

la m .................................................

le f .................................................

la f .................................................

**Listen, repeat, and copy.**

1 la famille
.........................

2 le papa/père
.........................

3 la maman/mère
.........................

4 le fils
.........................

5 la fille
.........................

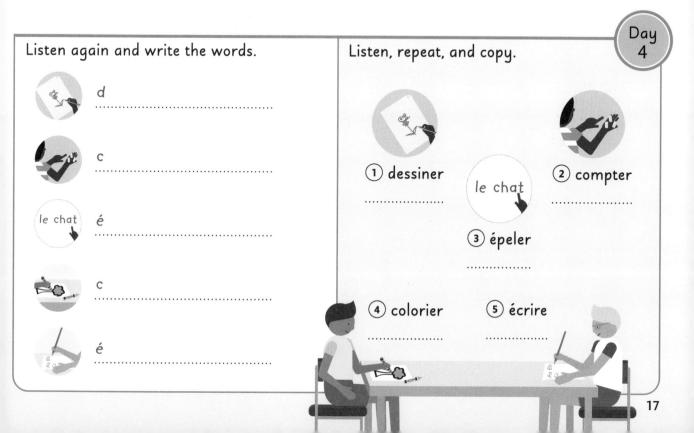

Day 4

**Listen again and write the words.**

d .................................................

c .................................................

le chat  é .................................................

c .................................................

é .................................................

**Listen, repeat, and copy.**

1 dessiner
.........................

le chat

2 compter
.........................

3 épeler
.........................

4 colorier
.........................

5 écrire
.........................

Day 5

What can you remember from this week?

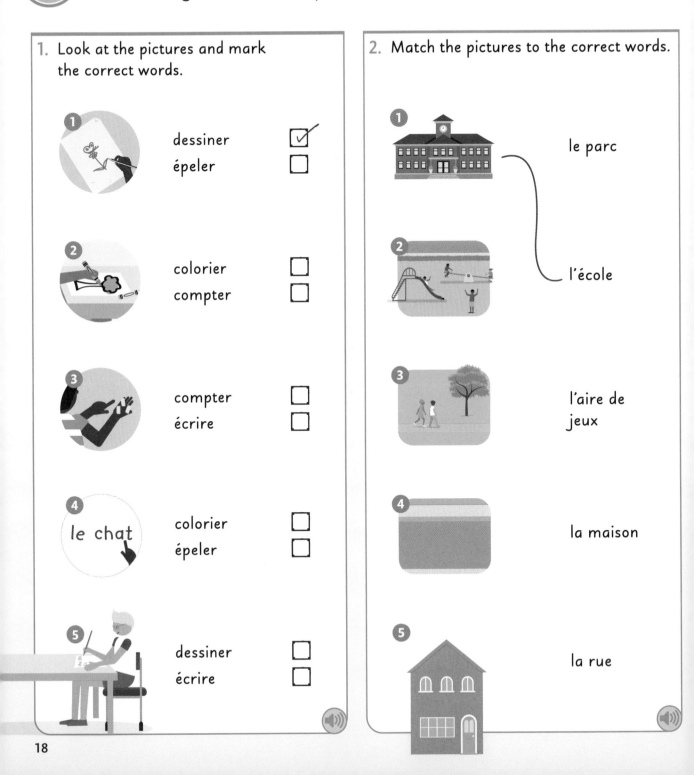

1. Look at the pictures and mark the correct words.

1. dessiner ✓
   épeler ☐

2. colorier ☐
   compter ☐

3. compter ☐
   écrire ☐

4. le chat
   colorier ☐
   épeler ☐

5. dessiner ☐
   écrire ☐

2. Match the pictures to the correct words.

1. le parc

2. l'école

3. l'aire de jeux

4. la maison

5. la rue

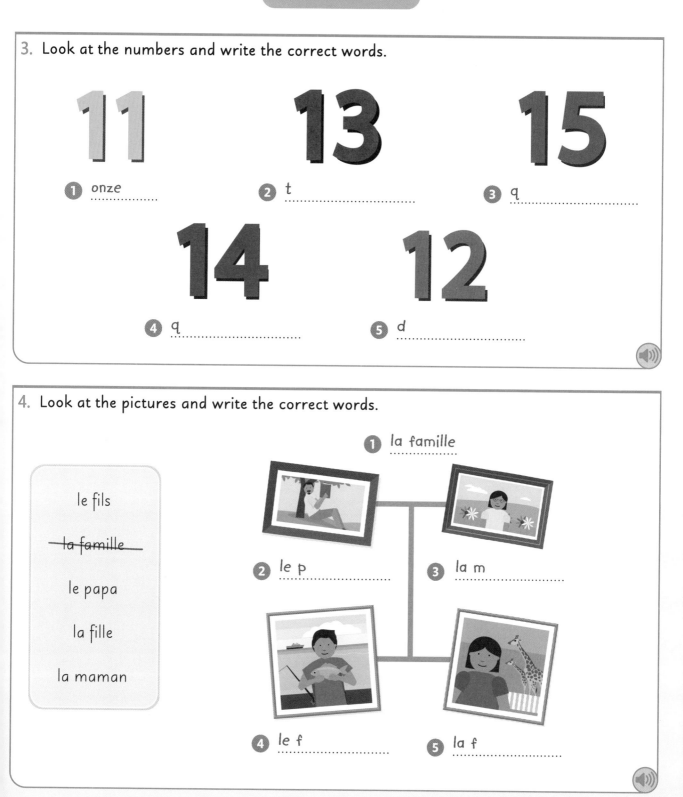

**3.** Look at the numbers and write the correct words.

**11**

① onze

**13**

② t

**15**

③ q

**14**

④ q

**12**

⑤ d

**4.** Look at the pictures and write the correct words.

① la famille

le fils

~~la famille~~

le papa

la fille

la maman

② le p

③ la m

④ le f

⑤ la f

**Day 1**

Listen, repeat, and copy.

**16** ① seize

**17** ② dix-sept

**18** ③ dix-huit

**19** ④ dix-neuf

**20** ⑤ vingt

Listen again and write the words.

**16** s ............................

**17** d ............................

**18** d ............................

**19** d ............................

**20** v ............................

**Day 2**

Listen, repeat, and copy.

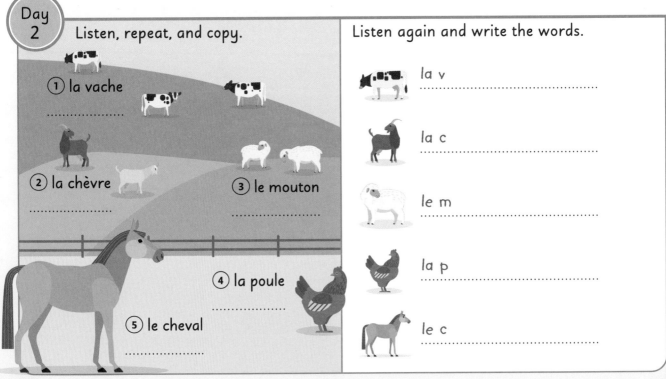

① la vache

② la chèvre

③ le mouton

④ la poule

⑤ le cheval

Listen again and write the words.

la v ............................

la c ............................

le m ............................

la p ............................

le c ............................

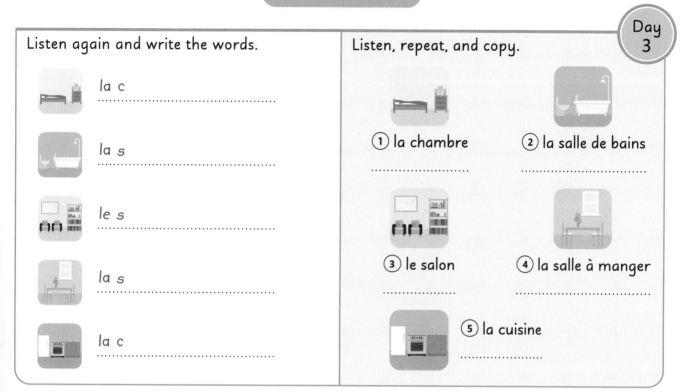

## Day 3

**Listen again and write the words.**

la c .................................................

la s .................................................

le s .................................................

la s .................................................

la c .................................................

**Listen, repeat, and copy.**

① la chambre
.......................

② la salle de bains
.......................

③ le salon
.......................

④ la salle à manger
.......................

⑤ la cuisine
.......................

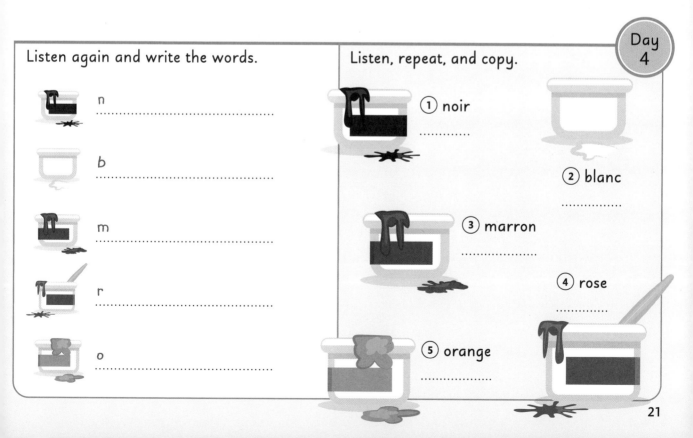

## Day 4

**Listen again and write the words.**

n .................................................

b .................................................

m .................................................

r .................................................

o .................................................

**Listen, repeat, and copy.**

① noir
..........

② blanc
..........

③ marron
..........

④ rose
..........

⑤ orange
..........

**Day 5**

What can you remember from this week?

1. Look at the pictures and fill in the missing letters.

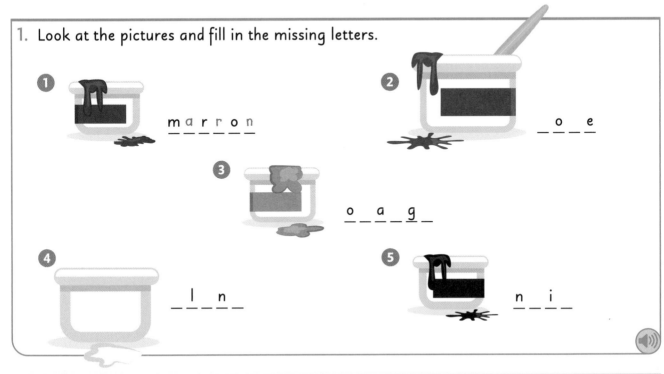

① m a r r o n

② _ _ o _ e

③ o _ a _ g _

④ _ _ l _ n _

⑤ _ n _ i _

2. Read the words and mark the correct pictures.

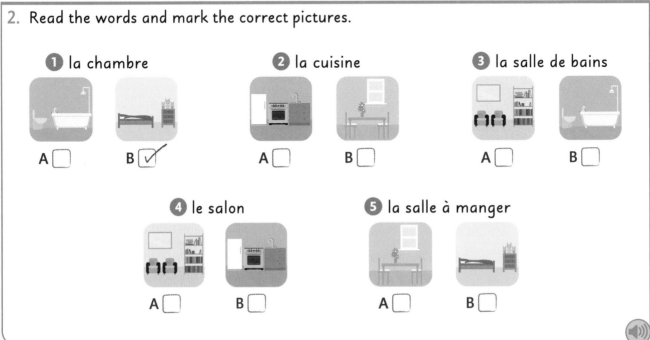

① la chambre    A ☐    B ☑

② la cuisine    A ☐    B ☐

③ la salle de bains    A ☐    B ☐

④ le salon    A ☐    B ☐

⑤ la salle à manger    A ☐    B ☐

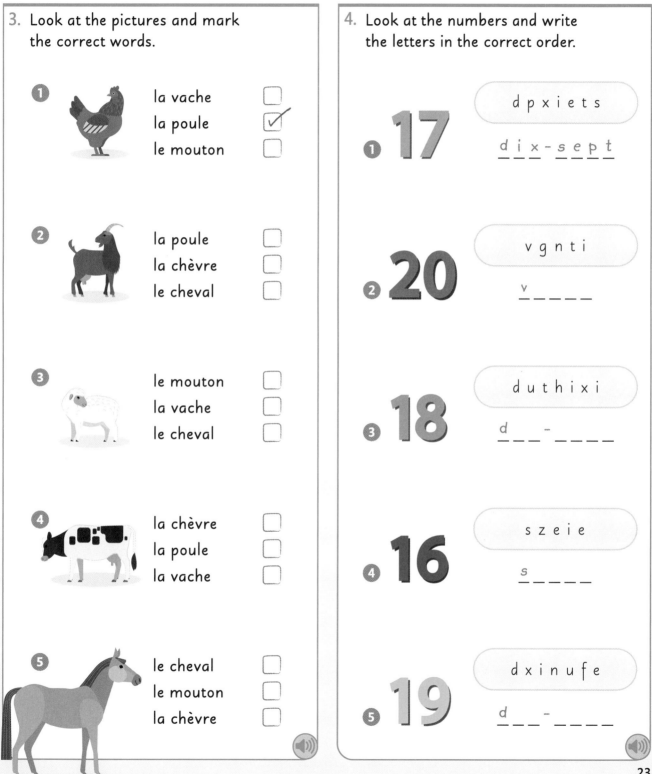

3. Look at the pictures and mark the correct words.

1. la vache ☐
   la poule ☑
   le mouton ☐

2. la poule ☐
   la chèvre ☐
   le cheval ☐

3. le mouton ☐
   la vache ☐
   le cheval ☐

4. la chèvre ☐
   la poule ☐
   la vache ☐

5. le cheval ☐
   le mouton ☐
   la chèvre ☐

4. Look at the numbers and write the letters in the correct order.

1. **17**
   d p x i e t s
   d i x - s e p t

2. **20**
   v g n t i
   v _ _ _ _ _

3. **18**
   d u t h i x i
   d _ _ _ - _ _ _ _

4. **16**
   s z e i e
   s _ _ _ _ _

5. **19**
   d x i n u f e
   d _ _ _ - _ _ _ _

23

**Day 1**

Listen, repeat, and copy.

① le zèbre

......................

② la girafe

......................

③ le lion

......................

④ l'hippopotame

......................

⑤ l'éléphant

......................

Listen again and write the words.

le z

......................

la g

......................

le l

......................

l'h

......................

l'é

......................

**Day 2**

Listen, repeat, and copy.

① la gomme

......................

② les ciseaux

......................

③ la règle

......................

④ le livre

......................

⑤ le sac à dos

......................

Listen again and write the words.

la g

......................

les c

......................

la r

......................

le l

......................

le s

......................

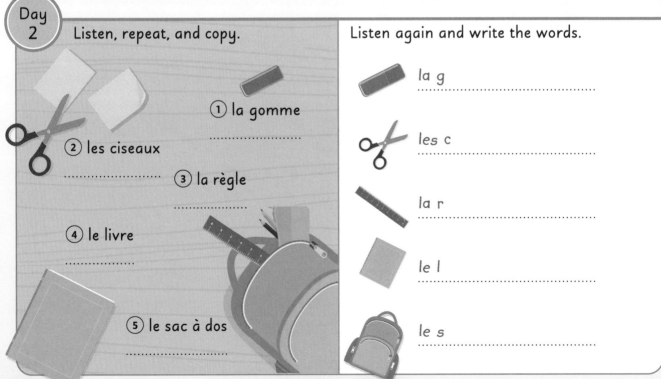

# Week 5

## Listen again and write the words.

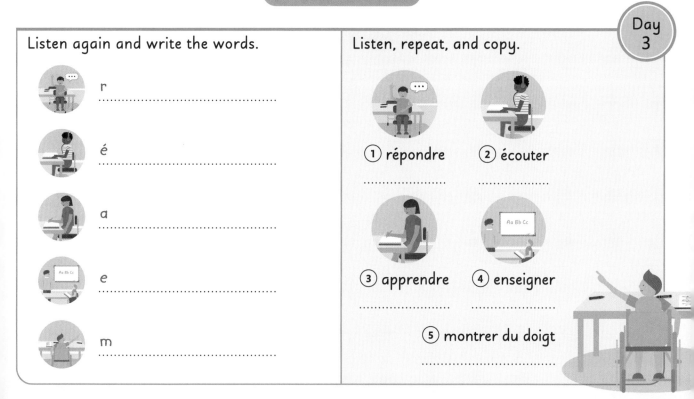

r
.............................

é
.............................

a
.............................

e
.............................

m
.............................

## Listen, repeat, and copy.

① répondre
.........................

② écouter
.........................

③ apprendre
.........................

④ enseigner
.........................

⑤ montrer du doigt
.........................

## Listen again and write the words.

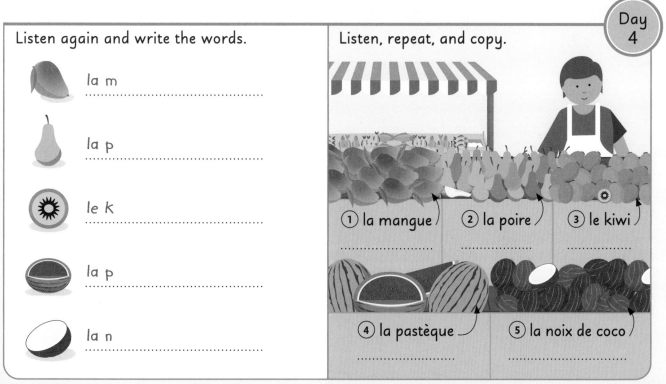

la m
.............................

la p
.............................

le k
.............................

la p
.............................

la n
.............................

## Listen, repeat, and copy.

① la mangue
.........................

② la poire
.........................

③ le kiwi
.........................

④ la pastèque
.........................

⑤ la noix de coco
.........................

**Day 5**

## What can you remember from this week?

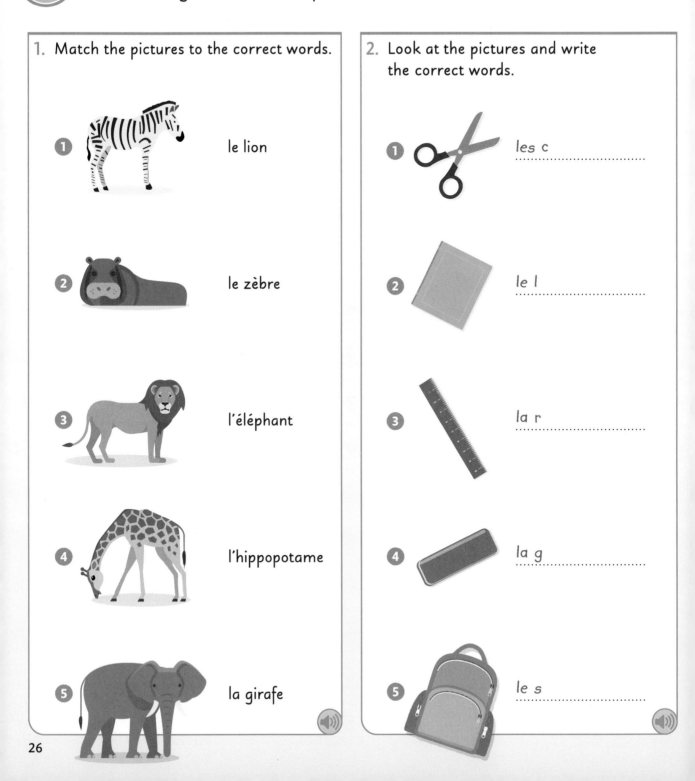

1. Match the pictures to the correct words.

1    le lion

2    le zèbre

3    l'éléphant

4    l'hippopotame

5    la girafe

2. Look at the pictures and write the correct words.

1    les c ............................

2    le l ............................

3    la r ............................

4    la g ............................

5    le s ............................

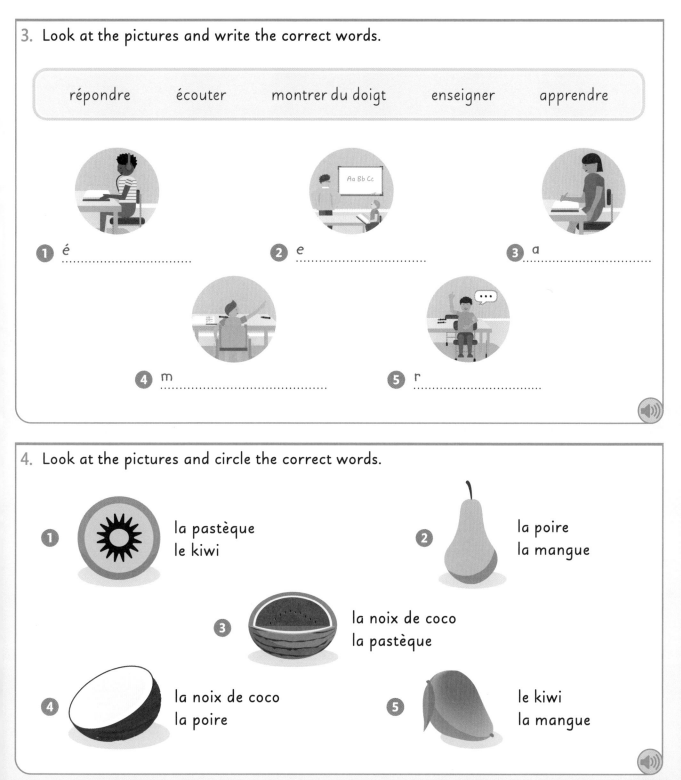

# Week 5

**3.** Look at the pictures and write the correct words.

répondre    écouter    montrer du doigt    enseigner    apprendre

① é .................................
② e .................................
③ a .................................
④ m .................................
⑤ r .................................

**4.** Look at the pictures and circle the correct words.

① la pastèque / le kiwi
② la poire / la mangue
③ la noix de coco / la pastèque
④ la noix de coco / la poire
⑤ le kiwi / la mangue

27

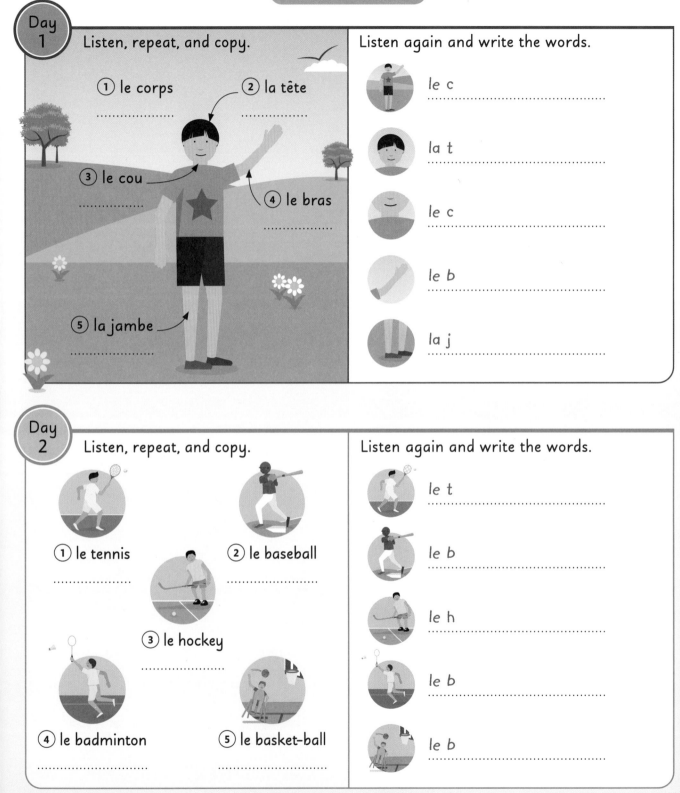

# Week 6

## Day 1

Listen, repeat, and copy.

① le corps

② la tête

③ le cou

④ le bras

⑤ la jambe

Listen again and write the words.

le c ......................................

la t ......................................

le c ......................................

le b ......................................

la j ......................................

## Day 2

Listen, repeat, and copy.

① le tennis

② le baseball

③ le hockey

④ le badminton

⑤ le basket-ball

Listen again and write the words.

le t ......................................

le b ......................................

le h ......................................

le b ......................................

le b ......................................

Day 3

**Listen again and write the words.**

la m ........................

le c ........................

le n ........................

la m ........................

la b ........................

**Listen, repeat, and copy.**

1 la mouette ........................

2 le cerf-volant ........................

3 le navire ........................

4 la mer ........................

5 la balle ........................

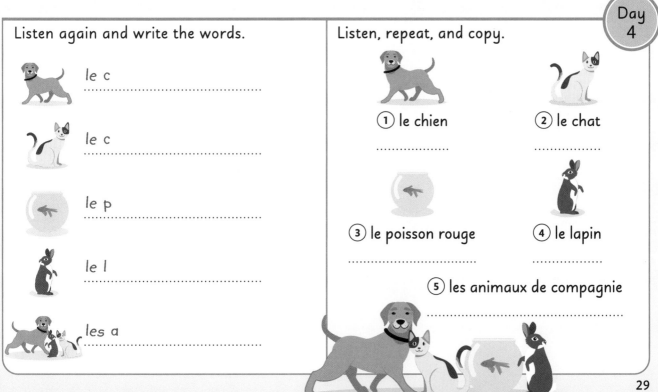

Day 4

**Listen again and write the words.**

le c ........................

le c ........................

le p ........................

le l ........................

les a ........................

**Listen, repeat, and copy.**

1 le chien ........................

2 le chat ........................

3 le poisson rouge ........................

4 le lapin ........................

5 les animaux de compagnie ........................

**Day 5**  What can you remember from this week?

1. Read the words and mark the correct pictures.

① le chat       ② le lapin       ③ le chien

A ☐   B ☐       A ☐   B ☐       A ☐   B ☐

④ les animaux de compagnie       ⑤ le poisson rouge

A ☐   B ☐       A ☐   B ☐

2. Look at the pictures and fill in the missing letters.

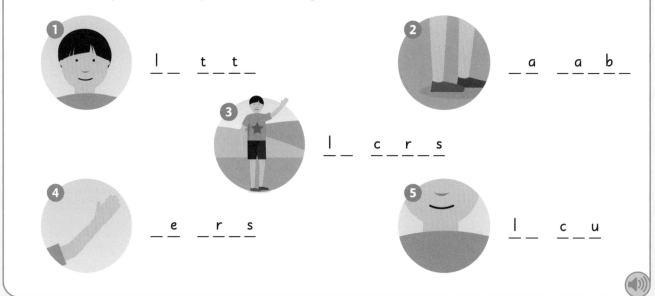

1. l _ _  t  _  t _

2. _ a  _ _ a _ b _

3. l _ _  c  _ r _ _ _ s

4. _ _  e  _  _ r _  s

5. l _  _  c _ u

3. Look at the pictures and mark
the correct words.

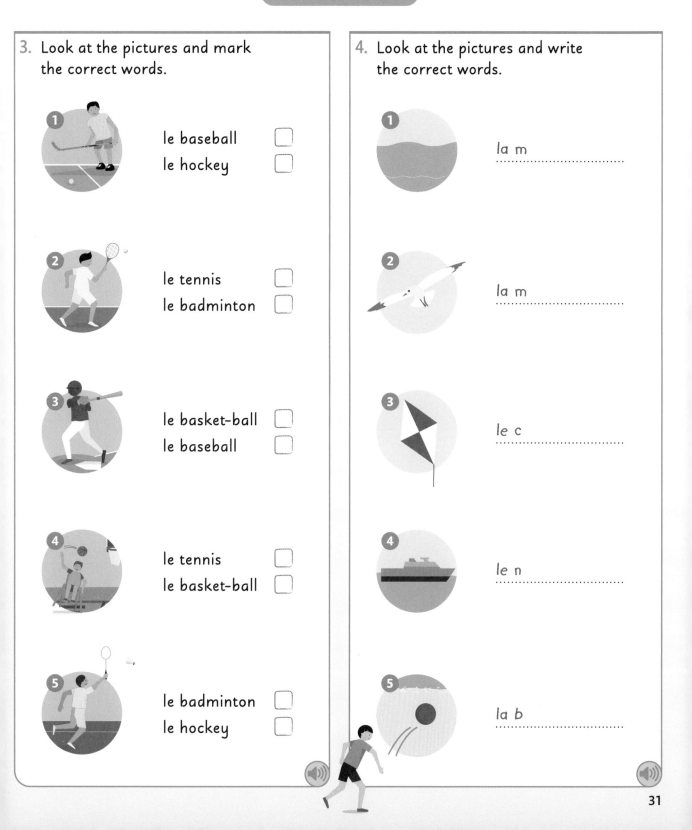

1. le baseball ☐
   le hockey ☐

2. le tennis ☐
   le badminton ☐

3. le basket-ball ☐
   le baseball ☐

4. le tennis ☐
   le basket-ball ☐

5. le badminton ☐
   le hockey ☐

4. Look at the pictures and write
the correct words.

1. la m .........................

2. la m .........................

3. le c .........................

4. le n .........................

5. la b .........................

# Week 7

## Day 1

**Listen, repeat, and copy.**

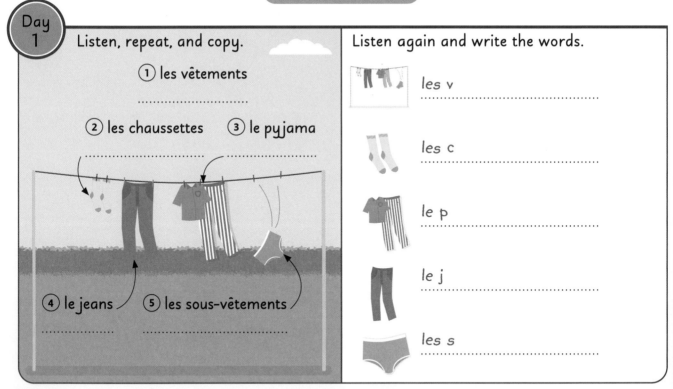

① les vêtements

....................

② les chaussettes   ③ le pyjama

....................

④ le jeans   ⑤ les sous-vêtements

....................

**Listen again and write the words.**

les v ....................

les c ....................

le p ....................

le j ....................

les s ....................

## Day 2

**Listen, repeat, and copy.**

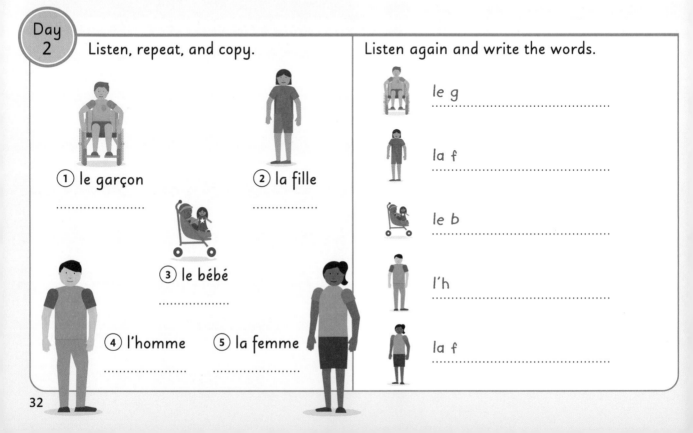

① le garçon

....................

② la fille

....................

③ le bébé

....................

④ l'homme   ⑤ la femme

....................

**Listen again and write the words.**

le g ....................

la f ....................

le b ....................

l'h ....................

la f ....................

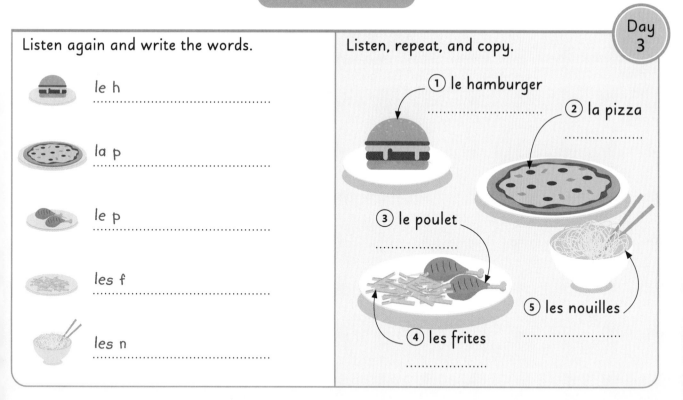

**Day 3**

Listen again and write the words.

le h
................................

la p
................................

le p
................................

les f
................................

les n
................................

Listen, repeat, and copy.

① le hamburger
................................

② la pizza
..................

③ le poulet
..................

⑤ les nouilles
..................

④ les frites
..................

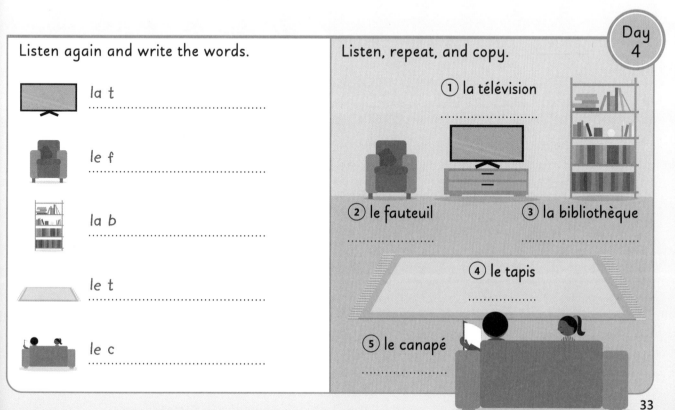

**Day 4**

Listen again and write the words.

la t
................................

le f
................................

la b
................................

le t
................................

le c
................................

Listen, repeat, and copy.

① la télévision
..................

② le fauteuil
..................

③ la bibliothèque
..................

④ le tapis
..................

⑤ le canapé
..................

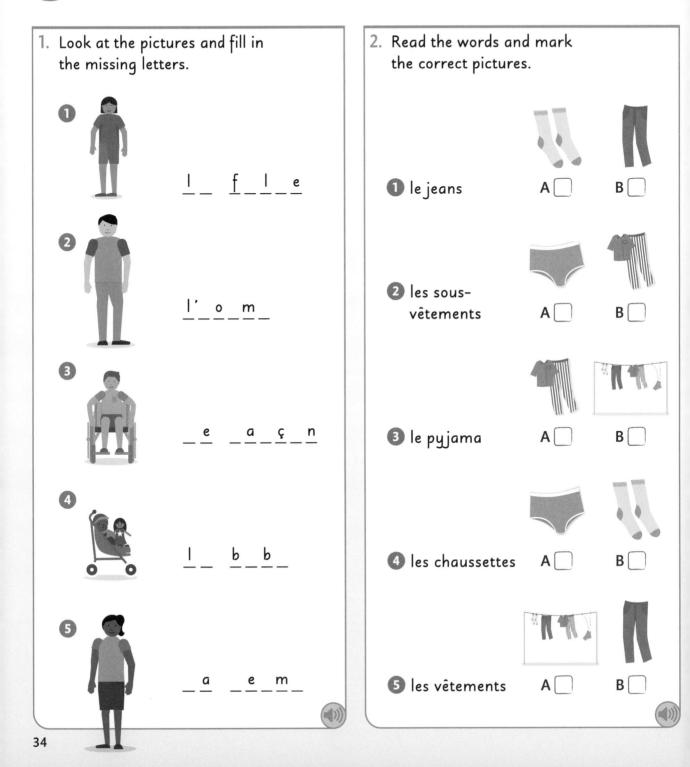

Day 5

What can you remember from this week?

1. Look at the pictures and fill in the missing letters.

1 l _ f _ _ l _ e

2 l' _ o _ m _

3 _ e _ _ a _ ç _ n

4 l _ b _ b _

5 _ a _ e _ m _

2. Read the words and mark the correct pictures.

1 le jeans    A ☐    B ☐

2 les sous-vêtements    A ☐    B ☐

3 le pyjama    A ☐    B ☐

4 les chaussettes    A ☐    B ☐

5 les vêtements    A ☐    B ☐

3. Look at the pictures and write the correct words.

| le tapis | le canapé | la télévision | la bibliothèque | le fauteuil |

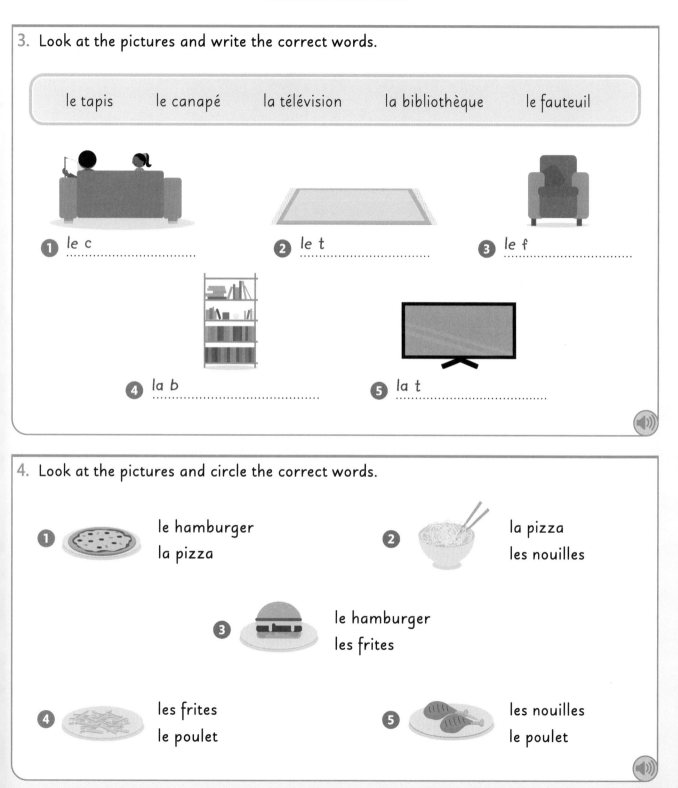

**1** le c
.................................

**2** le t
.................................

**3** le f
.................................

**4** la b
.................................

**5** la t
.................................

4. Look at the pictures and circle the correct words.

**1** le hamburger
la pizza

**2** la pizza
les nouilles

**3** le hamburger
les frites

**4** les frites
le poulet

**5** les nouilles
le poulet

**Day 1**

Listen, repeat, and copy.

① le calendrier

② le poster

③ le lit

④ les jouets

⑤ le coffre à jouets

Listen again and write the words.

le c ...................................

le p ...................................

le l ...................................

les j ...................................

le c ...................................

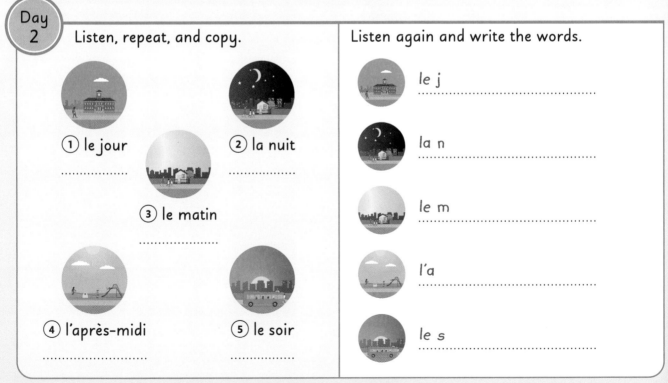

**Day 2**

Listen, repeat, and copy.

① le jour

② la nuit

③ le matin

④ l'après-midi

⑤ le soir

Listen again and write the words.

le j ...................................

la n ...................................

le m ...................................

l'a ...................................

le s ...................................

# Week 8

## Listen again and write the words.

o ...................................

f ...................................

r ...................................

s' ...................................

s ...................................

## Listen, repeat, and copy.

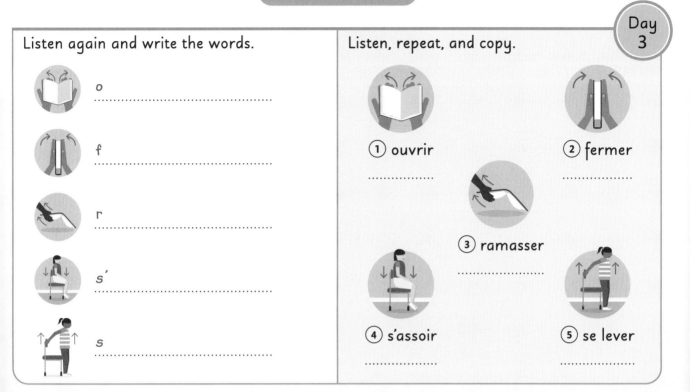

① ouvrir

② fermer

③ ramasser

④ s'assoir

⑤ se lever

## Listen again and write the words.

la j ...................................

le s ...................................

le t ...................................

l'o ...................................

la g ...................................

## Listen, repeat, and copy.

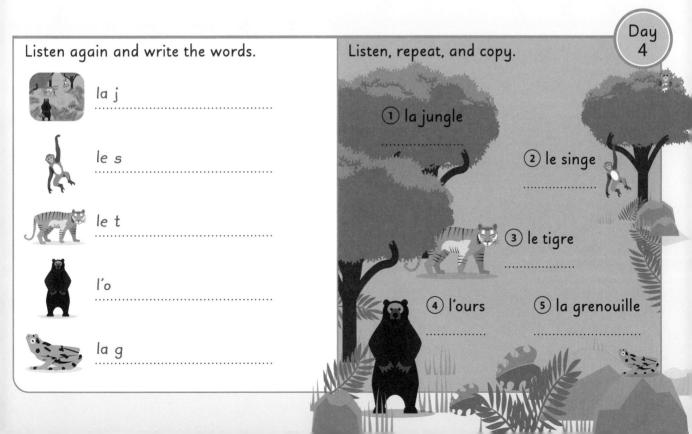

① la jungle

② le singe

③ le tigre

④ l'ours

⑤ la grenouille

Day 5

What can you remember from this week?

1. Look at the pictures and write the correct words.

1  le t ..................................

2  la g ..................................

3  le s ..................................

4  la j ..................................

5  l'o ..................................

2. Read the words and mark the correct pictures.

1  le poster
A ☐   B ☐

2  le calendrier
A ☐   B ☐

3  le lit
A ☐   B ☐

4  le coffre à jouets
A ☐   B ☐

5  les jouets
A ☐   B ☐

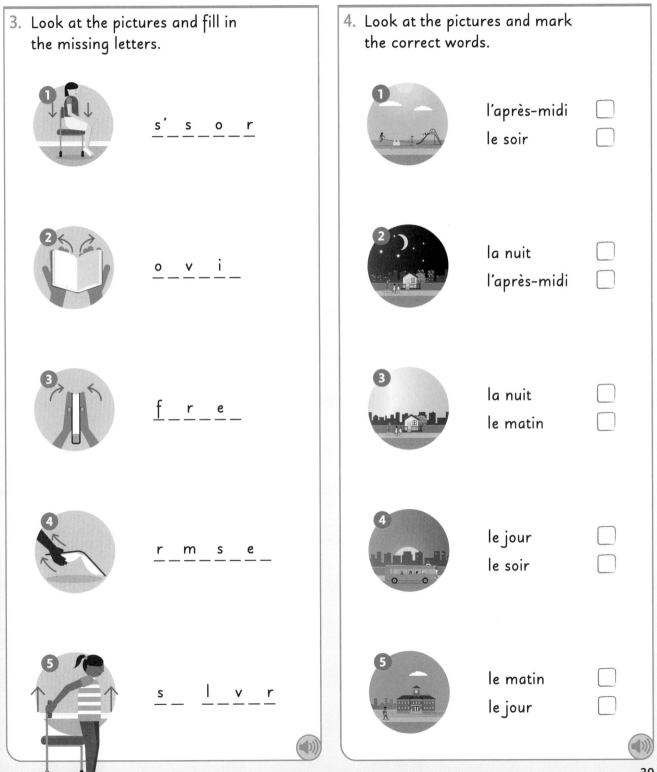

3. Look at the pictures and fill in the missing letters.

1. s ' _ s _ o _ r
2. o _ v _ i _ _
3. f _ r _ e _
4. r _ m _ s _ e _
5. s _ _ l _ v _ r

4. Look at the pictures and mark the correct words.

1. l'après-midi ☐
   le soir ☐

2. la nuit ☐
   l'après-midi ☐

3. la nuit ☐
   le matin ☐

4. le jour ☐
   le soir ☐

5. le matin ☐
   le jour ☐

# Week 9

## Day 1

### Listen, repeat, and copy.

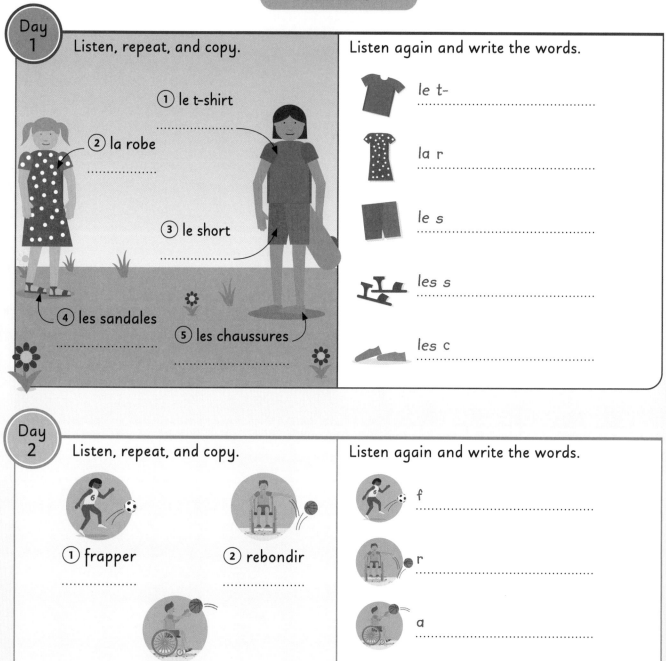

① le t-shirt
...................

② la robe
...................

③ le short
...................

④ les sandales
...................

⑤ les chaussures
...................

### Listen again and write the words.

le t-
...................

la r
...................

le s
...................

les s
...................

les c
...................

## Day 2

### Listen, repeat, and copy.

① frapper
...................

② rebondir
...................

③ attraper
...................

④ lancer
...................

⑤ taper
...................

### Listen again and write the words.

f
...................

r
...................

a
...................

l
...................

t
...................

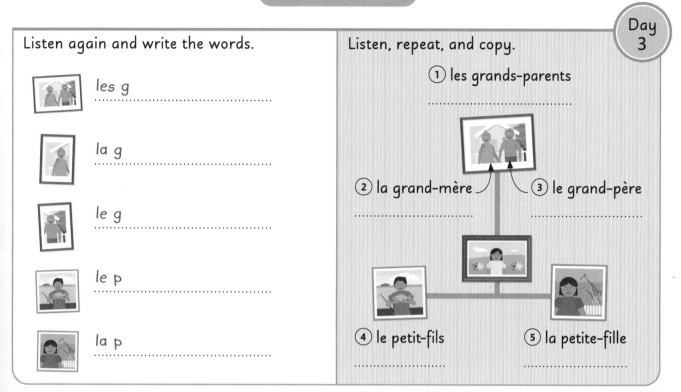

**Day 3**

### Listen again and write the words.

les g ...................................

la g ...................................

le g ...................................

le p ...................................

la p ...................................

### Listen, repeat, and copy.

① les grands-parents
...................................

② la grand-mère .................

③ le grand-père .................

④ le petit-fils .................

⑤ la petite-fille .................

**Day 4**

### Listen again and write the words.

j ...................................

j ...................................

â ...................................

g ...................................

e ...................................

### Listen, repeat, and copy.

① joli
..........

② jeune .................

③ âgé .................

④ gentil .................

⑤ effrayant .................

**Day 5**

What can you remember from this week?

1. Look at the pictures and write the correct words.

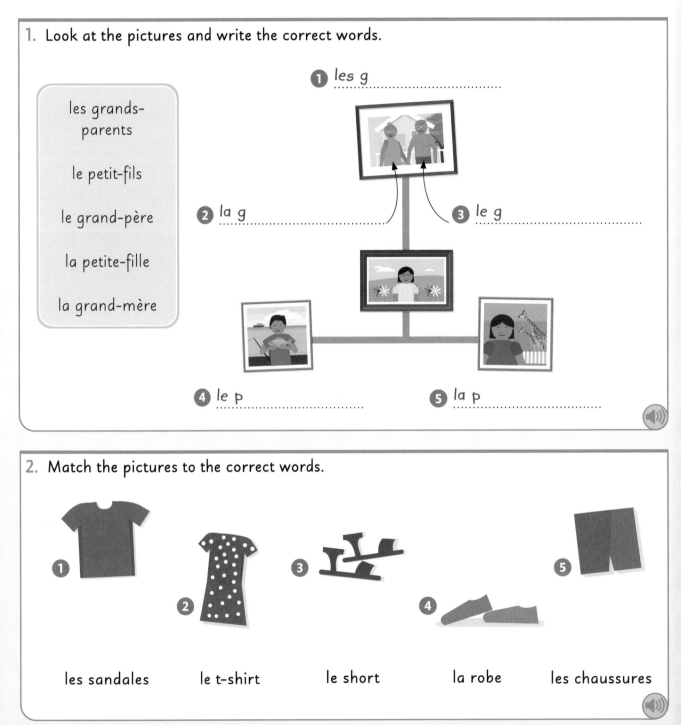

les grands-parents

le petit-fils

le grand-père

la petite-fille

la grand-mère

**1** les g ...............................

**2** la g ...............................

**3** le g ...............................

**4** le p ...............................

**5** la p ...............................

2. Match the pictures to the correct words.

**1**  **2**  **3**  **4**  **5**

les sandales    le t-shirt    le short    la robe    les chaussures

3. Look at the pictures and mark the correct words.

1. joli ☐
   âgé ☐

2. effrayant ☐
   âgé ☐

3. effrayant ☐
   gentil ☐

4. joli ☐
   jeune ☐

5. gentil ☐
   jeune ☐

4. Look at the pictures and write the correct words.

| frapper | attraper | taper |
| lancer | rebondir | |

1. a ...............................

2. t ...............................

3. f ...............................

4. l ...............................

5. r ...............................

**Day 1**

Listen, repeat, and copy.

① la ferme

② le tracteur

③ les animaux

④ le champ

⑤ la grange

Listen again and write the words.

la f .....................................

le t .....................................

les a .....................................

le c .....................................

la g .....................................

**Day 2**

Listen, repeat, and copy.

① le monstre

② le dinosaure

③ le robot

④ le skateboard

⑤ le jeu vidéo

Listen again and write the words.

le m .....................................

le d .....................................

le r .....................................

le s .....................................

le j .....................................

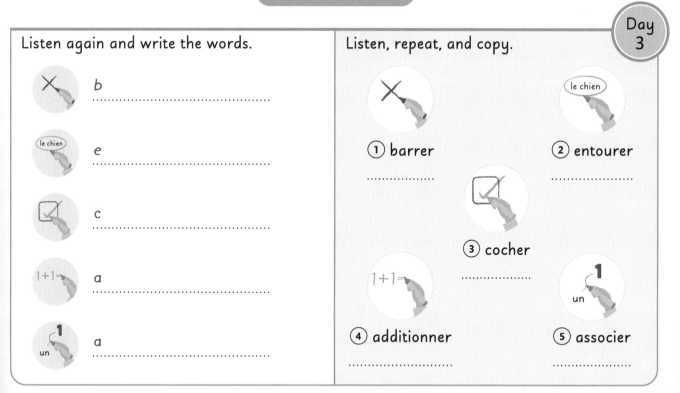

**Day 3**

Listen again and write the words.

b ..........................

le chien — e ..........................

c ..........................

1+1= — a ..........................

un 1 — a ..........................

Listen, repeat, and copy.

① barrer ..........................

② entourer ..........................

③ cocher ..........................

④ additionner ..........................

⑤ associer ..........................

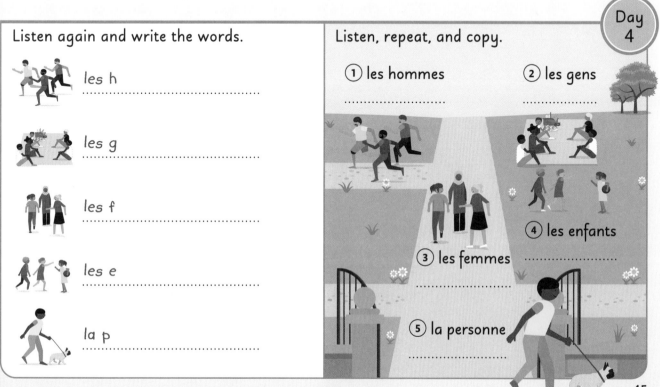

**Day 4**

Listen again and write the words.

les h ..........................

les g ..........................

les f ..........................

les e ..........................

la p ..........................

Listen, repeat, and copy.

① les hommes ..........................

② les gens ..........................

③ les femmes ..........................

④ les enfants ..........................

⑤ la personne ..........................

## What can you remember from this week?

**1.** Look at the pictures and write the letters in the correct order.

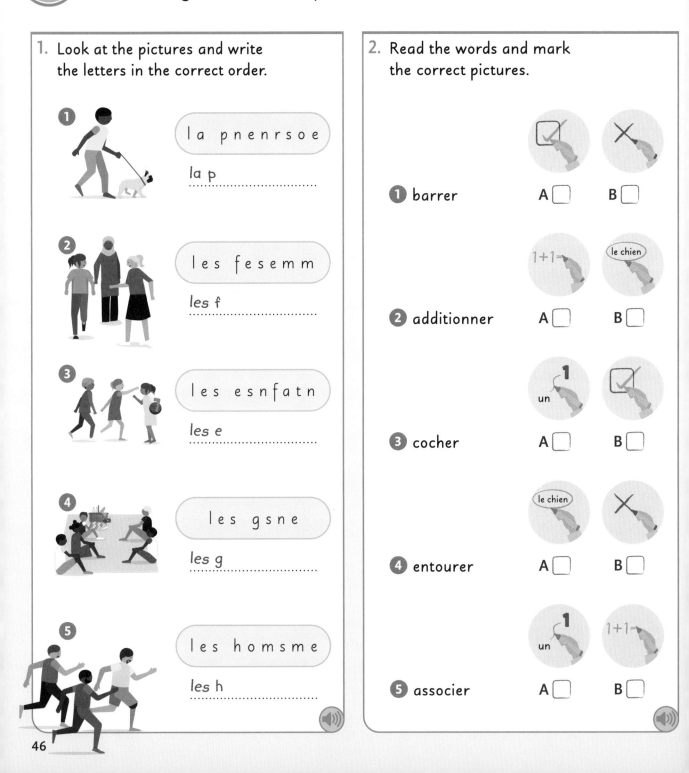

1. la p n e n r s o e

   la p ......................................

2. les f e s e m m

   les f ......................................

3. les e s n f a t n

   les e ......................................

4. les g s n e

   les g ......................................

5. les h o m s m e

   les h ......................................

**2.** Read the words and mark the correct pictures.

1. barrer    A ☐    B ☐

2. additionner    A ☐    B ☐

3. cocher    A ☐    B ☐

4. entourer    A ☐    B ☐

5. associer    A ☐    B ☐

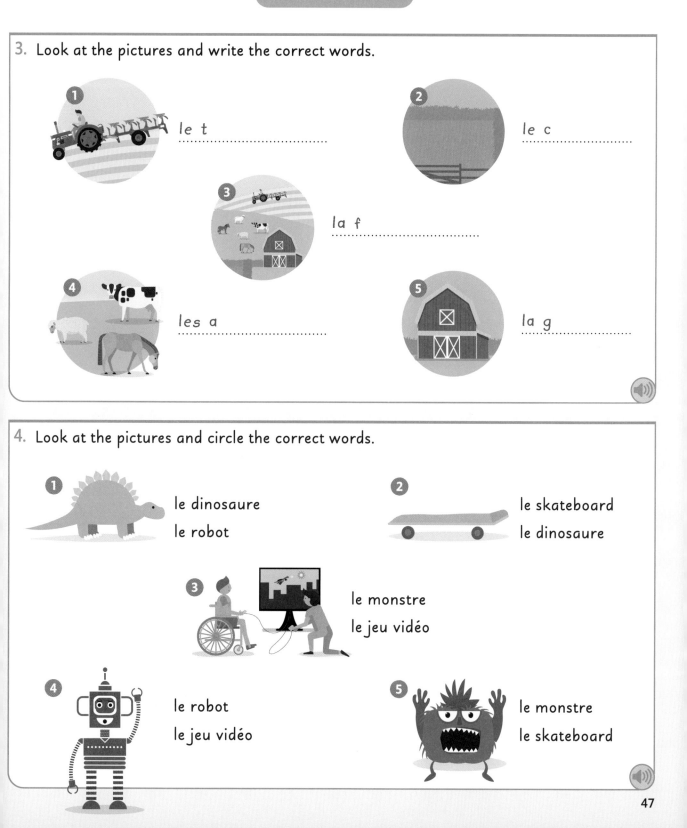

3. Look at the pictures and write the correct words.

1   le t .....................

2   le c .....................

3   la f .....................

4   les a .....................

5   la g .....................

4. Look at the pictures and circle the correct words.

1   le dinosaure
    le robot

2   le skateboard
    le dinosaure

3   le monstre
    le jeu vidéo

4   le robot
    le jeu vidéo

5   le monstre
    le skateboard

## Day 1

### Listen, repeat, and copy.

① chanter

..................

② danser

..................

③ jouer du piano

..................

④ jouer de la guitare

..................

⑤ prendre une photo

..................

### Listen again and write the words.

c ...................................

d ...................................

j ...................................

j ...................................

p ...................................

## Day 2

### Listen, repeat, and copy.

① propre

..................

② sale

..................

③ beau

..................

④ grand

..................

⑤ petit

..................

### Listen again and write the words.

p ...................................

s ...................................

b ...................................

g ...................................

p ...................................

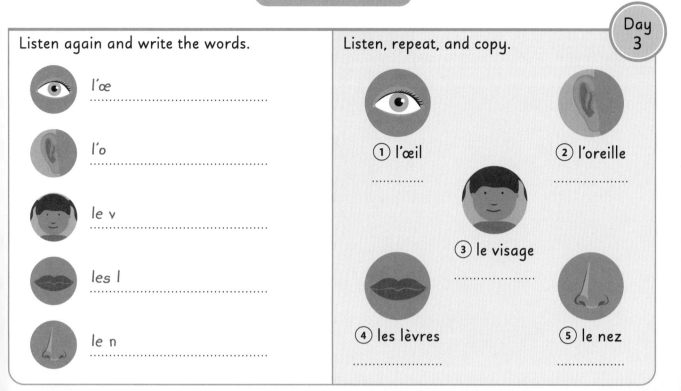

**Day 3**

Listen again and write the words.

l'œ
.................................................

l'o
.................................................

le v
.................................................

les l
.................................................

le n
.................................................

Listen, repeat, and copy.

① l'œil

② l'oreille
.................

③ le visage
.................

④ les lèvres
.................

⑤ le nez
.................

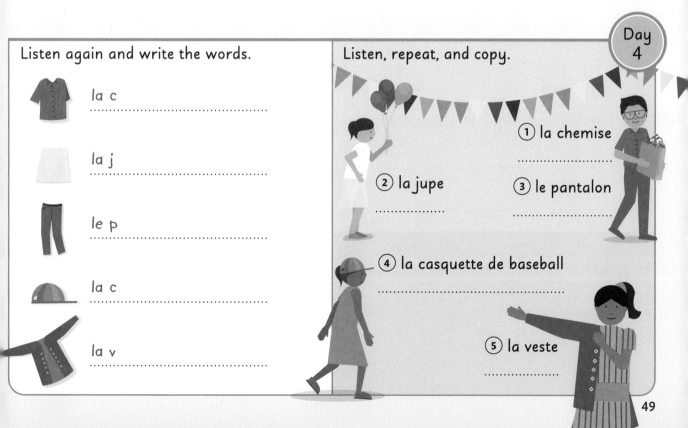

**Day 4**

Listen again and write the words.

la c
.................................................

la j
.................................................

le p
.................................................

la c
.................................................

la v
.................................................

Listen, repeat, and copy.

① la chemise
.................

② la jupe
.................

③ le pantalon
.................

④ la casquette de baseball
.................

⑤ la veste
.................

Day 5

What can you remember from this week?

1. Look at the pictures and write the correct words.

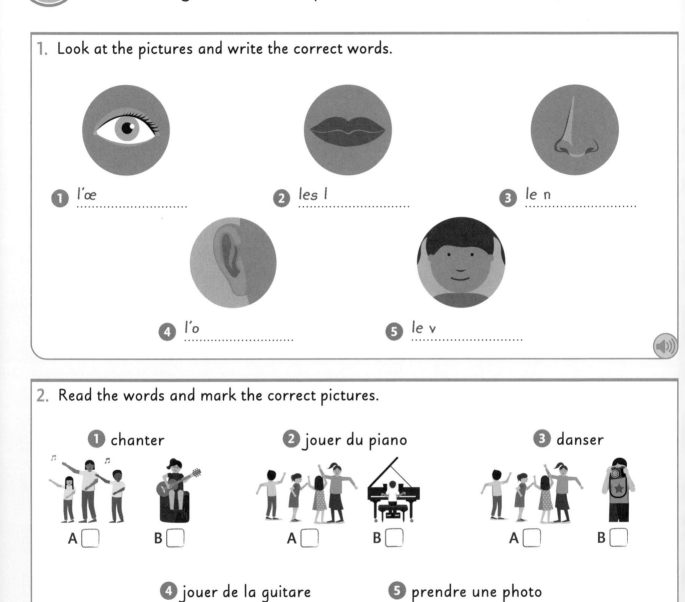

1 l'œ ...........................

2 les l ...........................

3 le n ...........................

4 l'o ...........................

5 le v ...........................

2. Read the words and mark the correct pictures.

1 chanter
A ☐   B ☐

2 jouer du piano
A ☐   B ☐

3 danser
A ☐   B ☐

4 jouer de la guitare
A ☐   B ☐

5 prendre une photo
A ☐   B ☐

# Week 11

3. Look at the pictures and write the letters in the correct order.

1. b u e a

   b _ _ _ _

2. p r o e p r

   p _ _ _ _ _

3. p t e i t

   p _ _ _ _

4. s l e a

   s _ _ _

5. g a d r n

   g _ _ _ _

4. Match the pictures to the correct words.

1. 

2. 

3. 

4. 

5. 

la jupe

la chemise

la casquette
de baseball

la veste

le pantalon

## Day 1

Listen, repeat, and copy.

① le petit déjeuner

...................................

② l'œuf

...................

③ les céréales

...................................

④ la saucisse

...................................

⑤ la crêpe

...................

Listen again and write the words.

le p ...................................

l'œ ...................................

les c ...................................

la s ...................................

la c ...................................

## Day 2

Listen, repeat, and copy.

① joyeux

...................

② triste

...................

③ en colère

...................

④ apeuré

...................

⑤ surprise

...................

Listen again and write the words.

j ...................................

t ...................................

e ...................................

a ...................................

s ...................................

# Week 12

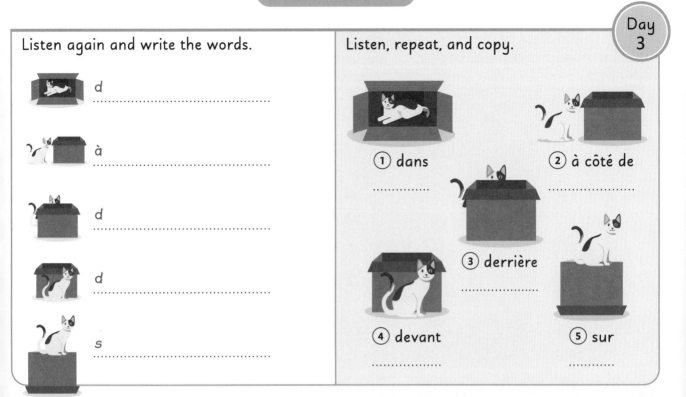

Listen again and write the words.

d ...................................

à ...................................

d ...................................

d ...................................

s ...................................

Listen, repeat, and copy.

① dans
...............

② à côté de
.......................

③ derrière
.................

④ devant
.................

⑤ sur
..........

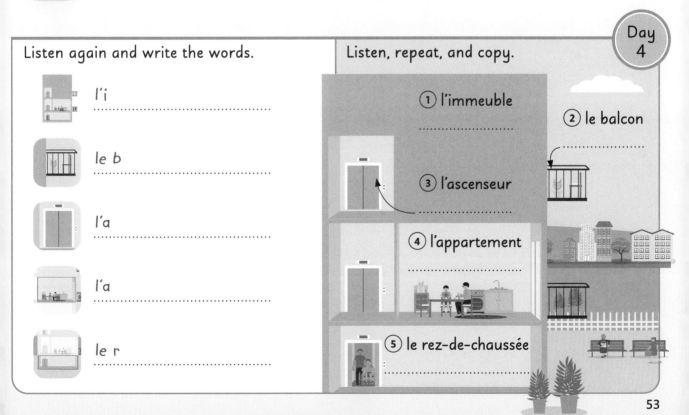

Listen again and write the words.

l'i ...................................

le b ...................................

l'a ...................................

l'a ...................................

le r ...................................

Listen, repeat, and copy.

① l'immeuble
.......................

② le balcon
.......................

③ l'ascenseur
.......................

④ l'appartement
.......................

⑤ le rez-de-chaussée
.......................

Day 5

# What can you remember from this week?

**1.** Look at the pictures and write the correct words.

| dans | derrière | sur |
|---|---|---|
| devant | à côté de | |

**1** d ................................

**2** d ................................

**3** d ................................

**4** à ................................

**5** s ................................

**2.** Look at the pictures and mark the correct words.

**1**
les céréales ☐
l'œuf ☐

**2**
la crêpe ☐
le petit déjeuner ☐

**3**
l'œuf ☐
la saucisse ☐

**4**
la crêpe ☐
les céréales ☐

**5**
le petit déjeuner ☐
la saucisse ☐

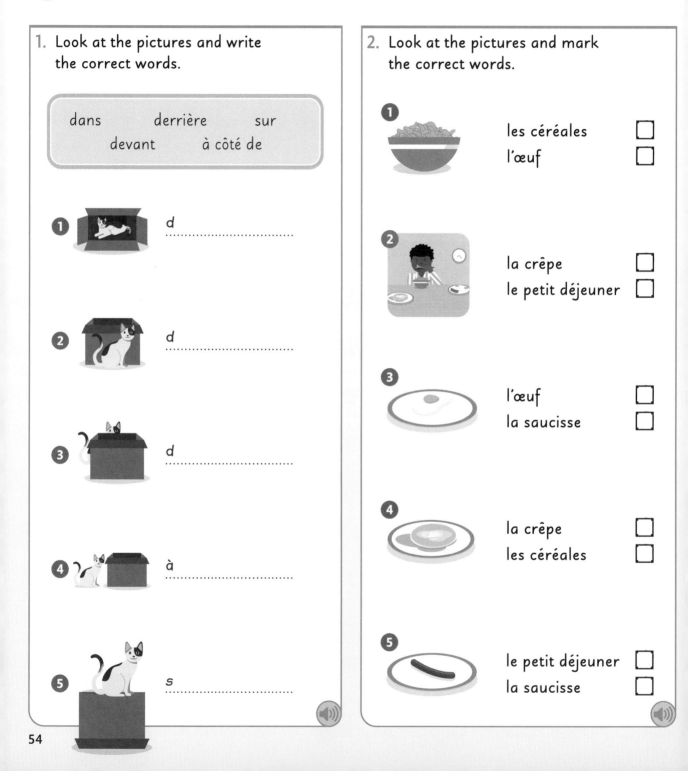

3. Look at the pictures and circle the correct words.

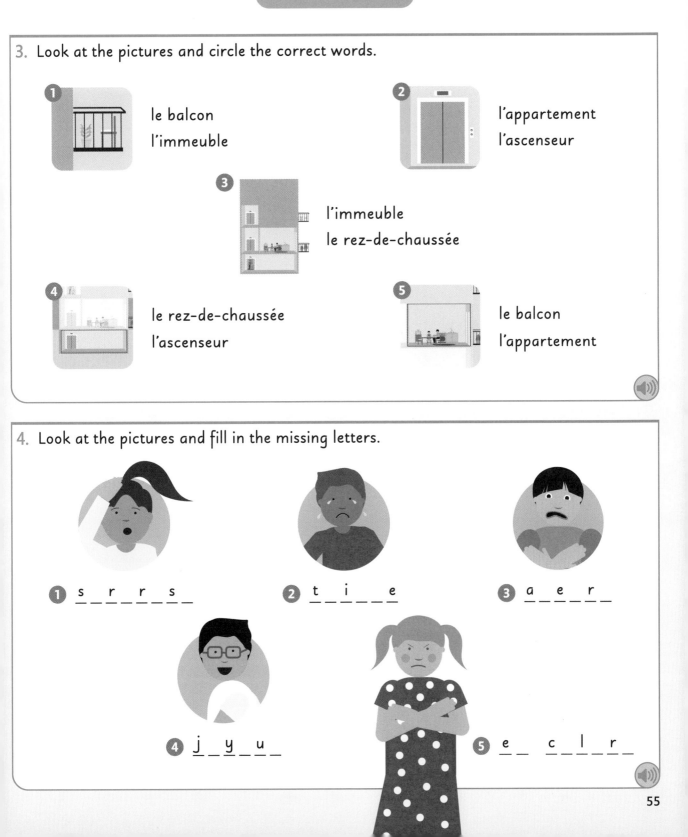

1. le balcon
   l'immeuble

2. l'appartement
   l'ascenseur

3. l'immeuble
   le rez-de-chaussée

4. le rez-de-chaussée
   l'ascenseur

5. le balcon
   l'appartement

4. Look at the pictures and fill in the missing letters.

1. s _ r _ r _ s _

2. _ t _ i _ _ e

3. a _ _ e _ r _

4. _ j _ _ y _ u _

5. e _ _ c _ l _ r _

**Day 1**

Listen, repeat, and copy.

① le déjeuner

② le sandwich   ③ l'en-cas

④ le yaourt   ⑤ les fruits

Listen again and write the words.

le d ...................

le s ...................

l'e ...................

le y ...................

les f ...................

**Day 2**

Listen, repeat, and copy.

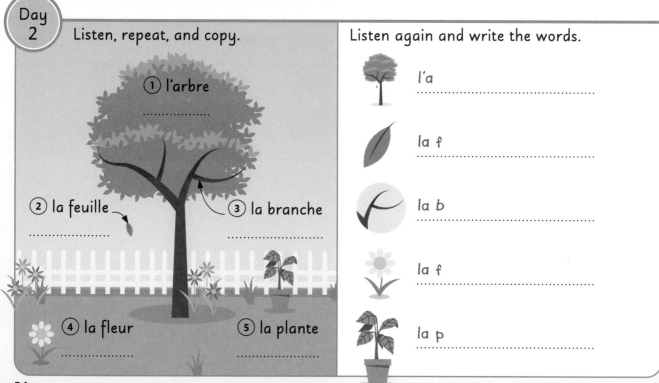

① l'arbre

② la feuille   ③ la branche

④ la fleur   ⑤ la plante

Listen again and write the words.

l'a ...................

la f ...................

la b ...................

la f ...................

la p ...................

# Week 13

## Listen again and write the words.

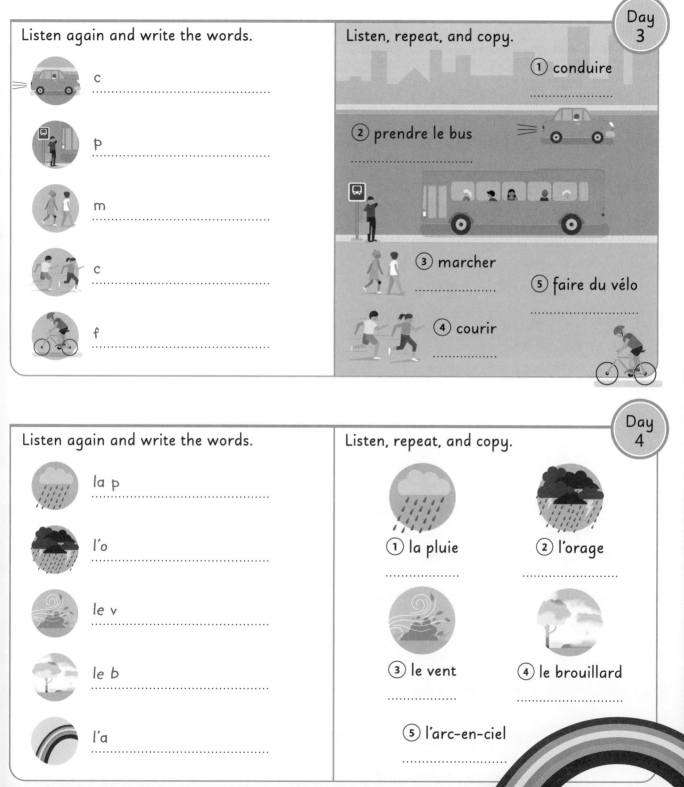

c ............................

p ............................

m ............................

c ............................

f ............................

## Listen, repeat, and copy.

① conduire
............................

② prendre le bus
............................

③ marcher
............................

④ courir
............................

⑤ faire du vélo
............................

## Listen again and write the words.

la p ............................

l'o ............................

le v ............................

le b ............................

l'a ............................

## Listen, repeat, and copy.

① la pluie
............................

② l'orage
............................

③ le vent
............................

④ le brouillard
............................

⑤ l'arc-en-ciel
............................

57

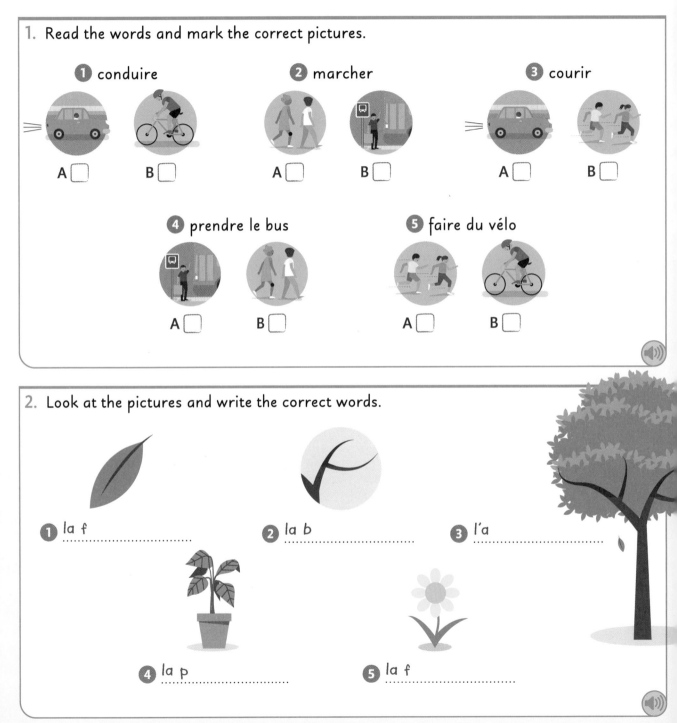

Day 5    What can you remember from this week?

1.  Read the words and mark the correct pictures.

1  conduire

A ☐    B ☐

2  marcher

A ☐    B ☐

3  courir

A ☐    B ☐

4  prendre le bus

A ☐    B ☐

5  faire du vélo

A ☐    B ☐

2.  Look at the pictures and write the correct words.

1  la f ............................

2  la b ............................

3  l'a ............................

4  la p ............................

5  la f ............................

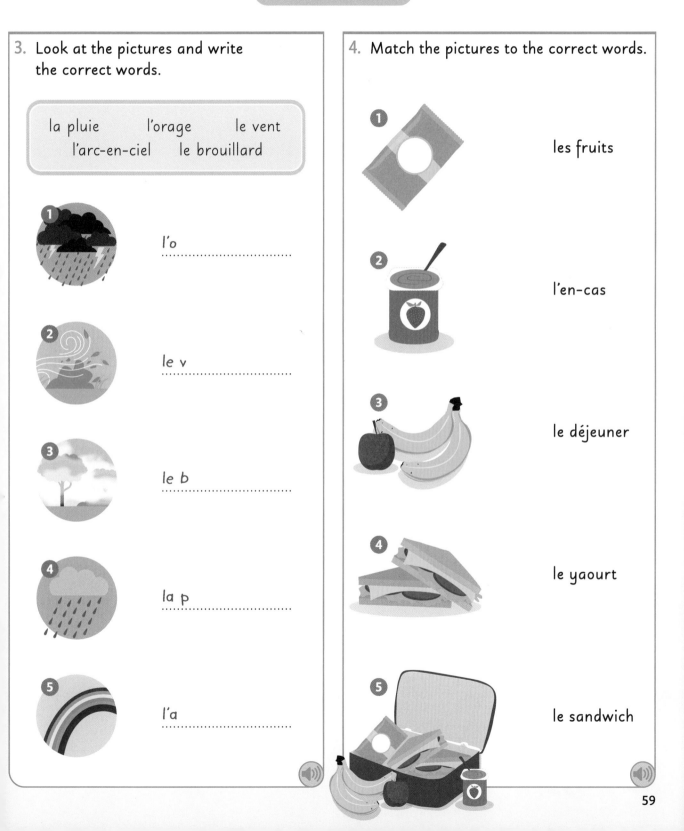

3. Look at the pictures and write the correct words.

la pluie      l'orage      le vent
l'arc-en-ciel      le brouillard

1. l'o ...........................................

2. le v ...........................................

3. le b ...........................................

4. la p ...........................................

5. l'a ...........................................

4. Match the pictures to the correct words.

1      les fruits

2      l'en-cas

3      le déjeuner

4      le yaourt

5      le sandwich

# Week 14

## Day 1

Listen, repeat, and copy.

1. le dîner

2. les pâtes

3. la sauce

4. le pain

5. les boulettes de viande

Listen again and write the words.

le d ....................

les p ....................

la s ....................

le p ....................

les b ....................

## Day 2

Listen, repeat, and copy.

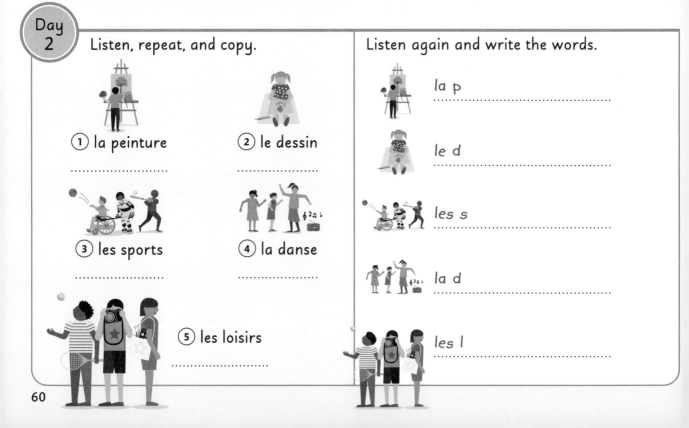

1. la peinture

2. le dessin

3. les sports

4. la danse

5. les loisirs

Listen again and write the words.

la p ....................

le d ....................

les s ....................

la d ....................

les l ....................

# Week 14

Listen again and write the words.

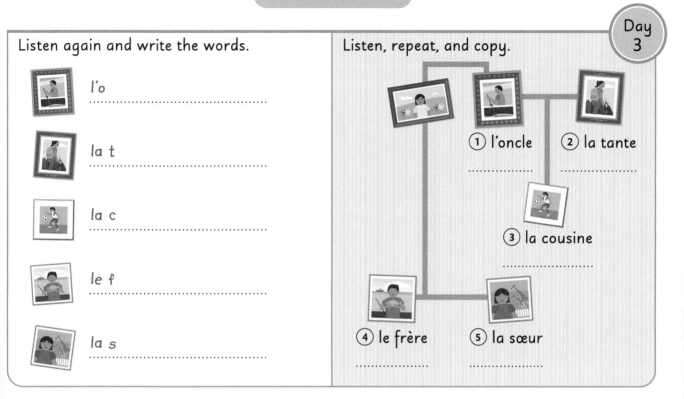

l'o
.................................

la t
.................................

la c
.................................

le f
.................................

la s
.................................

Listen, repeat, and copy.

① l'oncle　　② la tante
.................　.................

③ la cousine
.................

④ le frère　　⑤ la sœur
.................　.................

Listen again and write the words.

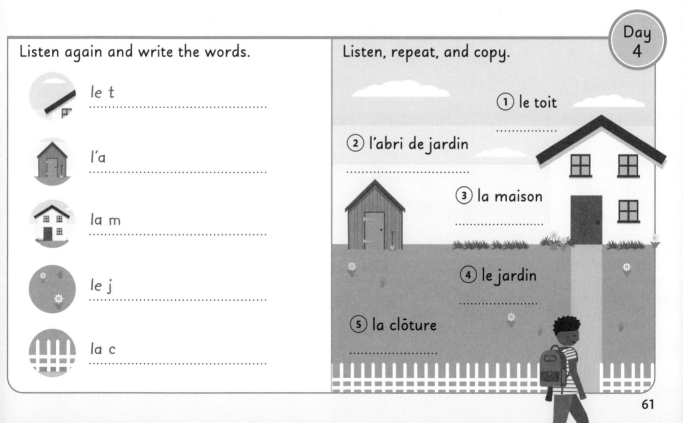

le t
.................................

l'a
.................................

la m
.................................

le j
.................................

la c
.................................

Listen, repeat, and copy.

① le toit
.................

② l'abri de jardin
.........................

③ la maison
.................

④ le jardin
.................

⑤ la clôture
.................

Day 5

What can you remember from this week?

**1.** Look at the pictures and circle the correct words.

1. le toit

   le jardin

2. l'abri de jardin

   la clôture

3. le jardin

   la maison

4. le toit

   l'abri de jardin

5. la maison

   la clôture

**2.** Look at the pictures and write the letters in the correct order.

1. le dsiesn

   le d ..................................

2. la dnsea

   la d ..................................

3. la pnetirue

   la p ..................................

4. les sotpsr

   les s ..................................

5. les lisiros

   les l ..................................

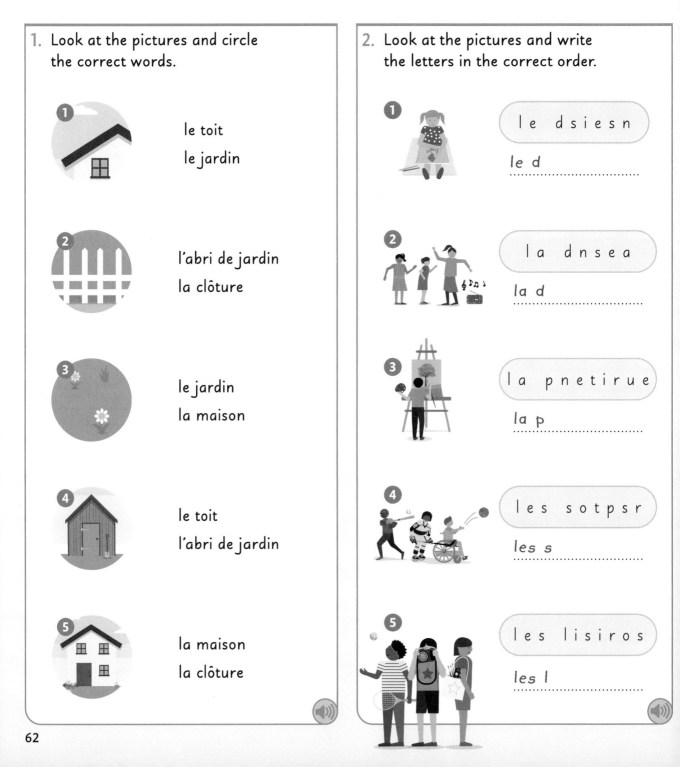

3. Look at the pictures and write the correct words.

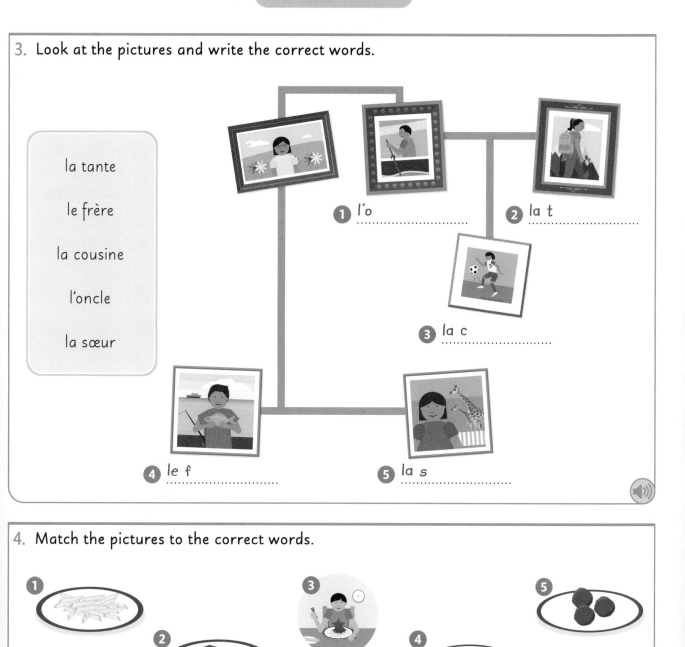

la tante

le frère

la cousine

l'oncle

la sœur

1 l'o ....................

2 la t ....................

3 la c ....................

4 le f ....................

5 la s ....................

4. Match the pictures to the correct words.

1

2

3

4

5

le dîner        les pâtes        les boulettes
de viande        la sauce        le pain

**Day 1**

Listen, repeat, and copy.

① jouer

② escalader

③ courir

④ sauter

⑤ sauter à la corde

Listen again and write the words.

j ..................................

e ..................................

c ..................................

s ..................................

s ..................................

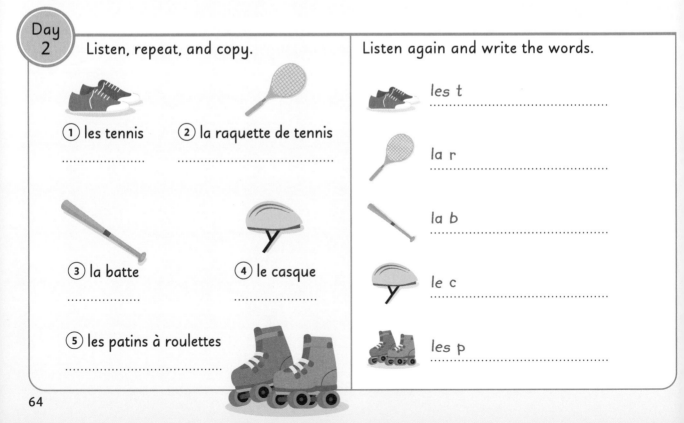

**Day 2**

Listen, repeat, and copy.

① les tennis

② la raquette de tennis

③ la batte

④ le casque

⑤ les patins à roulettes

Listen again and write the words.

les t ..................................

la r ..................................

la b ..................................

le c ..................................

les p ..................................

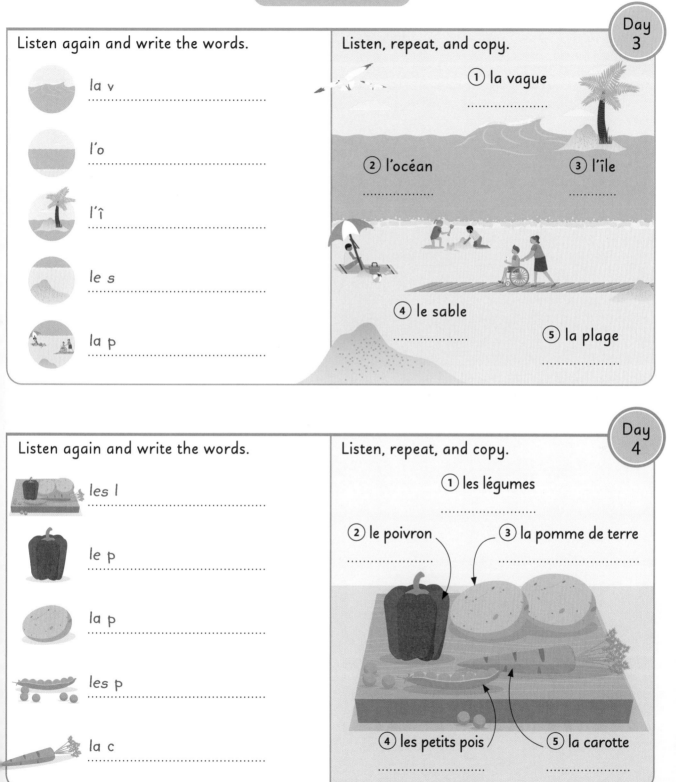

## Day 3

**Listen again and write the words.**

la v
.........................................

l'o
.........................................

l'î
.........................................

le s
.........................................

la p
.........................................

**Listen, repeat, and copy.**

① la vague
....................

② l'océan
....................

③ l'île
....................

④ le sable
....................

⑤ la plage
....................

## Day 4

**Listen again and write the words.**

les l
.........................................

le p
.........................................

la p
.........................................

les p
.........................................

la c
.........................................

**Listen, repeat, and copy.**

① les légumes
....................

② le poivron
....................

③ la pomme de terre
....................

④ les petits pois
....................

⑤ la carotte
....................

What can you remember from this week?

1. Look at the pictures and mark the correct words.

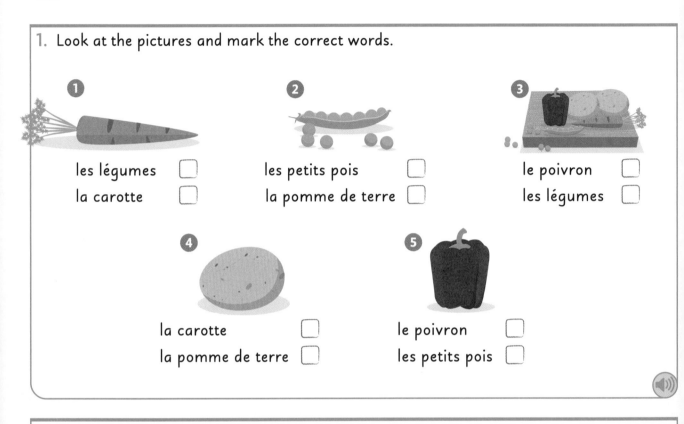

**①**
les légumes ☐
la carotte ☐

**②**
les petits pois ☐
la pomme de terre ☐

**③**
le poivron ☐
les légumes ☐

**④**
la carotte ☐
la pomme de terre ☐

**⑤**
le poivron ☐
les petits pois ☐

2. Look at the pictures and fill in the missing letters.

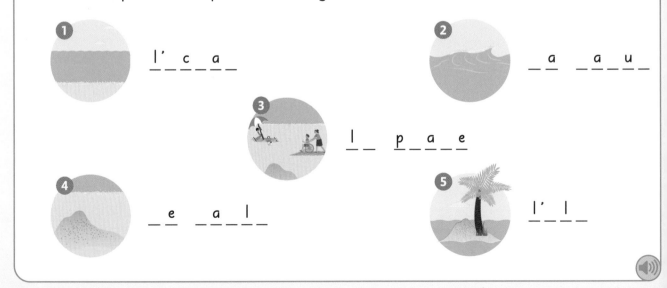

**①** l'_ c _ a _

**②** _ a _ _ a _ u

**③** l _ _ p _ a _ e

**④** _ e _ _ a _ l _

**⑤** l' _ l _

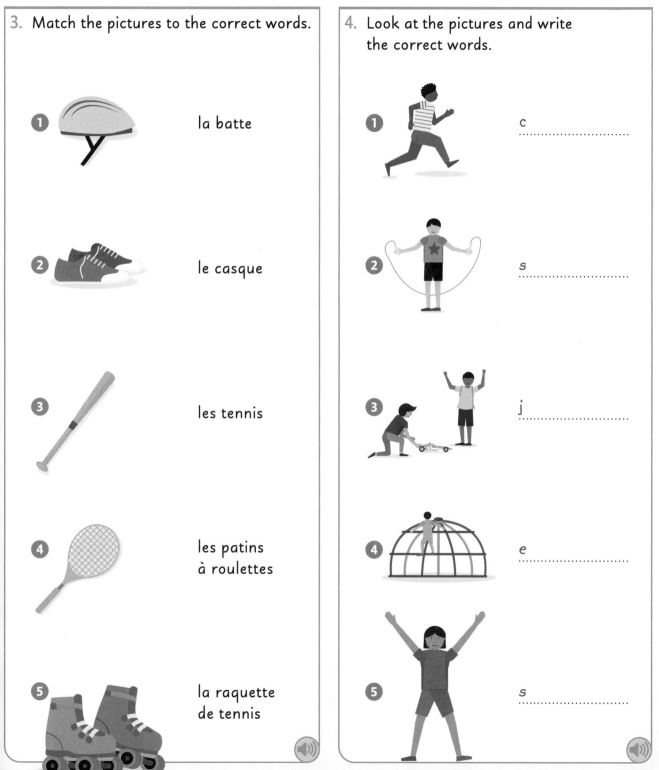

3. Match the pictures to the correct words.

1 la batte

2 le casque

3 les tennis

4 les patins à roulettes

5 la raquette de tennis

4. Look at the pictures and write the correct words.

1 c........................

2 s........................

3 j........................

4 e........................

5 s........................

### Day 1

Listen, repeat, and copy.

① l'horloge

.....................

② le téléphone

.....................

③ la lampe

.....................

④ le bureau

.....................

⑤ la chaise

.....................

Listen again and write the words.

l'h .....................

le t .....................

la l .....................

le b .....................

la c .....................

### Day 2

Listen, repeat, and copy.

① le chien

.....................

② le chiot

.....................

③ le chat

.....................

④ le chaton

.....................

⑤ la souris

.....................

Listen again and write the words.

le c .....................

le c .....................

le c .....................

le c .....................

la s .....................

Day 3

## Listen again and write the words.

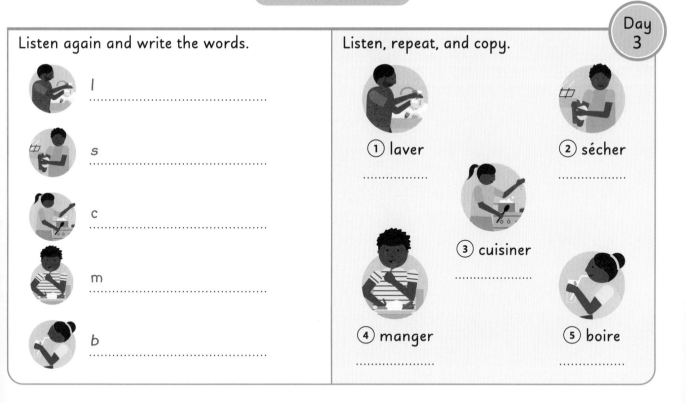

l ...............................................

s ...............................................

c ...............................................

m ...............................................

b ...............................................

## Listen, repeat, and copy.

① laver
...............

② sécher
...............

③ cuisiner
...............

④ manger
...............

⑤ boire
...............

Day 4

## Listen again and write the words.

la f ...............................................

le b ...............................................

le j ...............................................

les b ...............................................

l'i ...............................................

## Listen, repeat, and copy.

① la fête
...............

② le ballon
...............

③ le jeu
...............

④ les bonbons
...............

⑤ l'invitation

Day 5    What can you remember from this week?

1. Look at the pictures and mark the correct words.

① les bonbons ☐
le jeu ☐

② le ballon ☐
la fête ☐

③ la fête ☐
le jeu ☐

④ l'invitation ☐
les bonbons ☐

⑤ l'invitation ☐
le ballon ☐

2. Look at the pictures and write the letters in the correct order.

① c s i u i e n r
c _ _ _ _ _ _ _

② m n g r e a
m _ _ _ _ _

③ l r v a e
l _ _ _ _

④ s r h e c é
s _ _ _ _ _

⑤ b r o e i
b _ _ _ _

3. Look at the pictures and write the correct words.

le chien        la souris        le chat        le chiot        le chaton

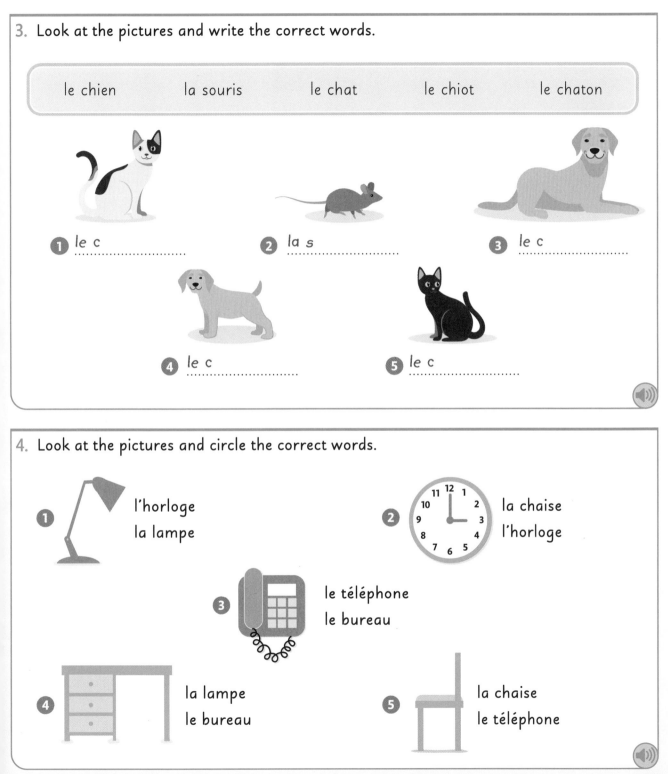

1 le c .....................

2 la s .....................

3 le c .....................

4 le c .....................

5 le c .....................

4. Look at the pictures and circle the correct words.

1 l'horloge
   la lampe

2 la chaise
   l'horloge

3 le téléphone
   le bureau

4 la lampe
   le bureau

5 la chaise
   le téléphone

## Day 1

Listen, repeat, and copy.

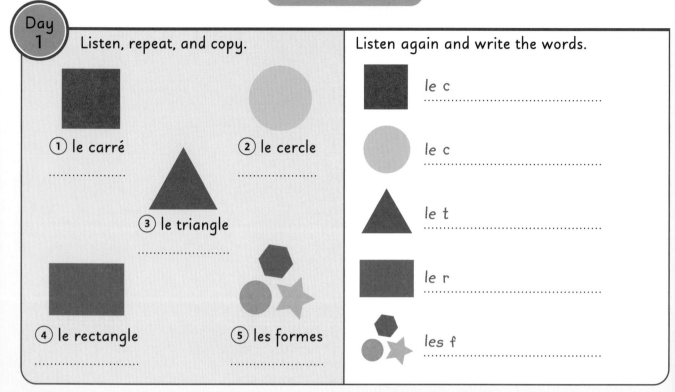

① le carré

② le cercle

③ le triangle

④ le rectangle

⑤ les formes

Listen again and write the words.

le c .............................

le c .............................

le t .............................

le r .............................

les f .............................

## Day 2

Listen, repeat, and copy.

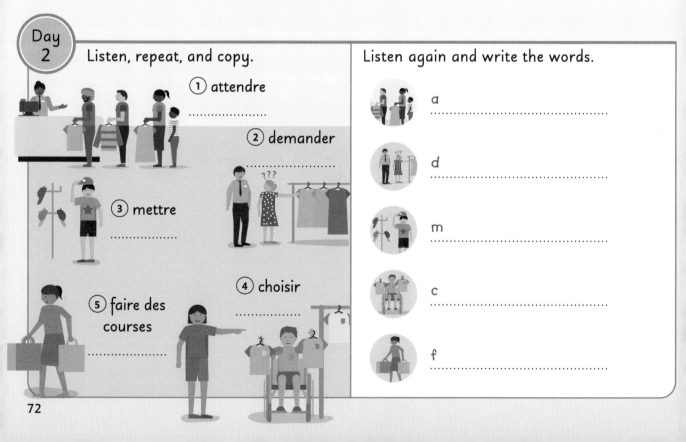

① attendre

② demander

③ mettre

④ choisir

⑤ faire des courses

Listen again and write the words.

a .............................

d .............................

m .............................

c .............................

f .............................

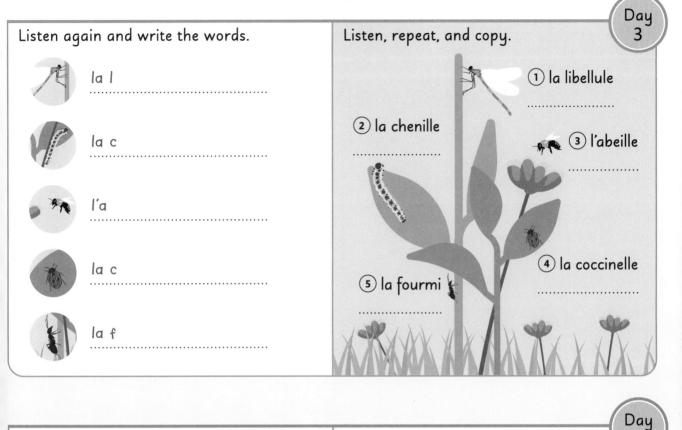

## Listen again and write the words.

la l .....................................

la c .....................................

l'a .....................................

la c .....................................

la f .....................................

## Listen, repeat, and copy.

① la libellule .....................................

② la chenille .....................................

③ l'abeille .....................................

④ la coccinelle .....................................

⑤ la fourmi .....................................

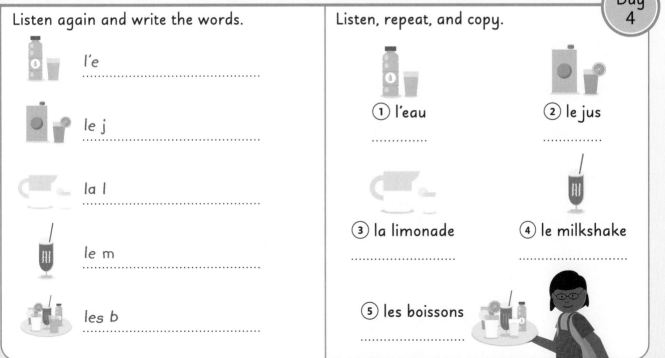

## Listen again and write the words.

l'e .....................................

le j .....................................

la l .....................................

le m .....................................

les b .....................................

## Listen, repeat, and copy.

① l'eau ..............

② le jus ..............

③ la limonade .....................................

④ le milkshake .....................................

⑤ les boissons .....................................

Day 5

What can you remember from this week?

1. Match the pictures to the correct words.

attendre

demander

faire des courses

choisir

mettre

2. Look at the pictures and mark the correct words.

1.
l'abeille ☐
la coccinelle ☐
la libellule ☐

2.
la chenille ☐
la fourmi ☐
l'abeille ☐

3.
la fourmi ☐
la libellule ☐
la coccinelle ☐

4.
la chenille ☐
l'abeille ☐
la libellule ☐

5.
la coccinelle ☐
la chenille ☐
la fourmi ☐

3. Look at the pictures and write the correct words.

l'eau     le jus     les boissons     le milkshake     la limonade

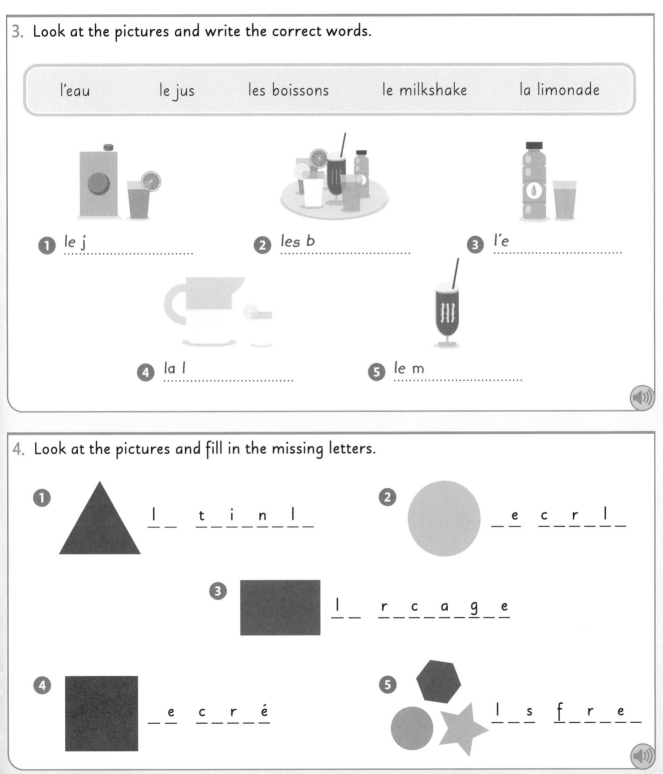

1 le j .......................................

2 les b ...................................

3 l'e ....................................

4 la l ...................................

5 le m ...................................

4. Look at the pictures and fill in the missing letters.

1 l _ t i n l

2 _ _ e c r l

3 l _ r c a g e

4 _ e c r é

5 l s f r e

### Day 1

Listen, repeat, and copy.

① voler

.................

② surfer

.................

③ naviguer

.................

④ nager

.................

⑤ pêcher

.................

Listen again and write the words.

v ..................................................

s ..................................................

n ..................................................

n ..................................................

p ..................................................

### Day 2

Listen, repeat, and copy.

① courts

.................

② longs

.................

③ raides

.................

④ bouclés

.................

 ⑤ les cheveux

.................

Listen again and write the words.

c ..................................................

l ..................................................

r ..................................................

b ..................................................

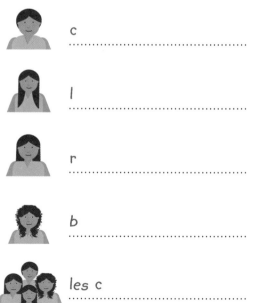 les c ..........................................

# Week 18

## Listen again and write the words.

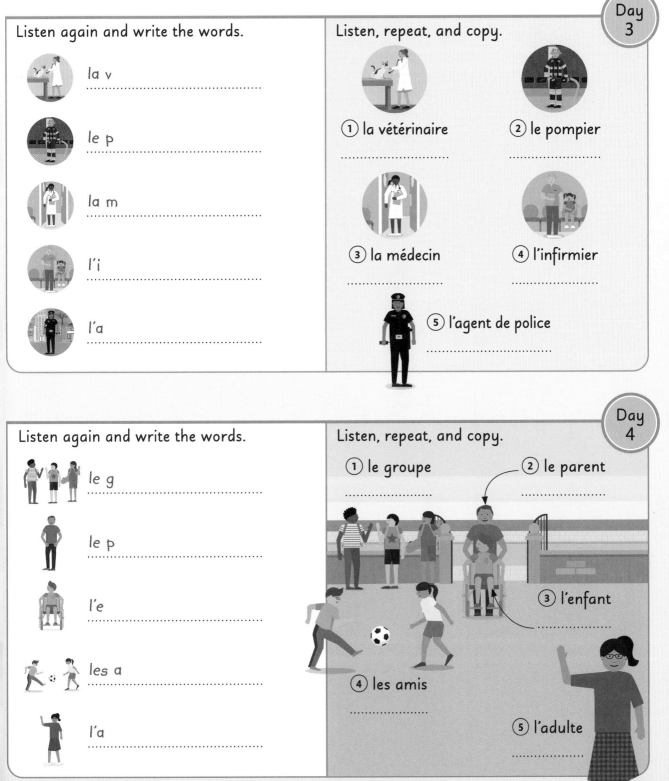

la v ...................................................

le p ...................................................

la m ...................................................

l'i ...................................................

l'a ...................................................

## Listen, repeat, and copy.

① la vétérinaire ...................................

② le pompier ...................................

③ la médecin ...................................

④ l'infirmier ...................................

⑤ l'agent de police ...................................

## Listen again and write the words.

le g ...................................................

le p ...................................................

l'e ...................................................

les a ...................................................

l'a ...................................................

## Listen, repeat, and copy.

① le groupe ...................................

② le parent ...................................

③ l'enfant ...................................

④ les amis ...................................

⑤ l'adulte ...................................

**Day 5**

## What can you remember from this week?

---

**1. Read the words and mark the correct pictures.**

**1** la vétérinaire

A ☐    B ☐

**2** le pompier

A ☐    B ☐

**3** la médecin

A ☐    B ☐

**4** l'agent de police

A ☐    B ☐

**5** l'infirmier

A ☐    B ☐

---

**2. Look at the picture and write the correct words.**

longs

bouclés

les cheveux

courts

raides

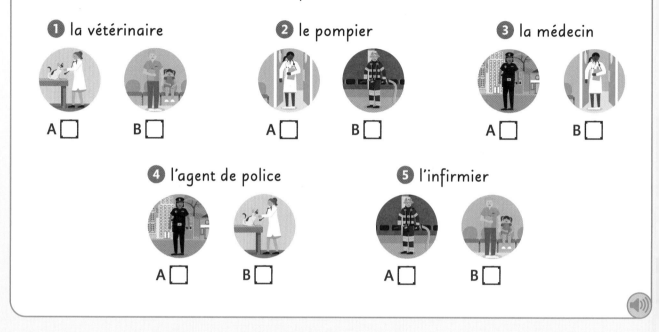

**1** les c ........................

**2** c ........................

**3** l ........................

**4** r ........................

**5** b ........................

3. Look at the pictures and write the letters in the correct order.

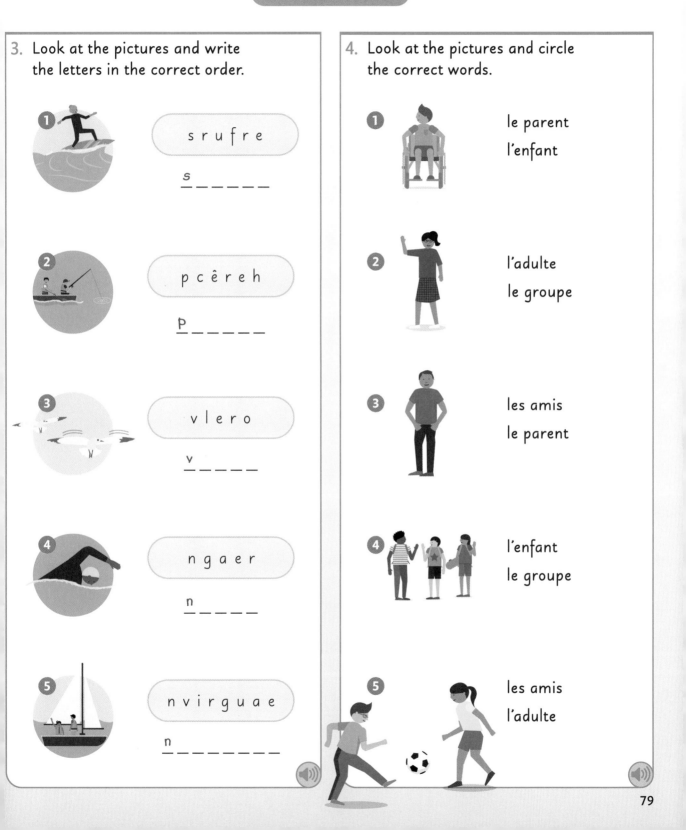

1. s r u f r e

s _ _ _ _ _

2. p c ê r e h

p _ _ _ _ _

3. v l e r o

v _ _ _ _

4. n g a e r

n _ _ _ _

5. n v i r g u a e

n _ _ _ _ _ _ _

4. Look at the pictures and circle the correct words.

1. le parent
l'enfant

2. l'adulte
le groupe

3. les amis
le parent

4. l'enfant
le groupe

5. les amis
l'adulte

**Day 1**

Listen, repeat, and copy.

① les lumières

② le coussin

③ la table

④ la chaise

⑤ la moquette

Listen again and write the words.

les l

le c

la t

la c

la m

**Day 2**

Listen, repeat, and copy.

① l'oiseau

② l'âne

③ le cochon

④ le fermier

⑤ l'étable

Listen again and write the words.

l'o

l'â

le c

le f

l'é

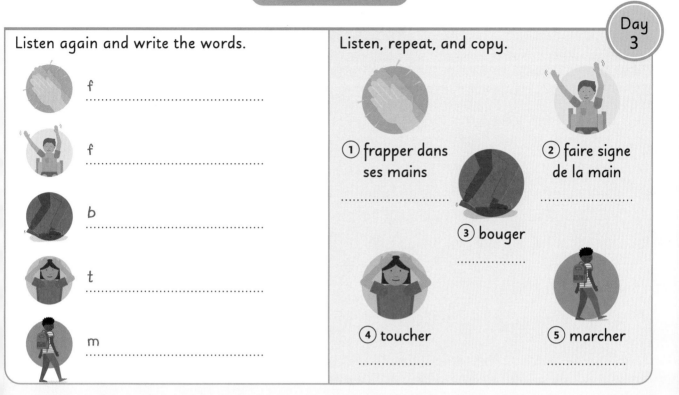

Day 3

**Listen again and write the words.**

f ...............................................

f ...............................................

b ...............................................

t ...............................................

m ...............................................

**Listen, repeat, and copy.**

① frapper dans ses mains
.........................

② faire signe de la main
.........................

③ bouger
.........................

④ toucher
.........................

⑤ marcher
.........................

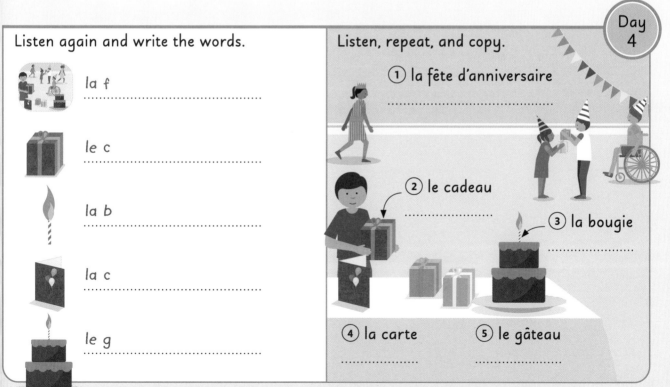

Day 4

**Listen again and write the words.**

la f ...............................................

le c ...............................................

la b ...............................................

la c ...............................................

le g ...............................................

**Listen, repeat, and copy.**

① la fête d'anniversaire
.........................................

② le cadeau
.........................

③ la bougie
.........................

④ la carte
.........................

⑤ le gâteau
.........................

81

**Day 5**

## What can you remember from this week?

1. Match the pictures to the correct words.

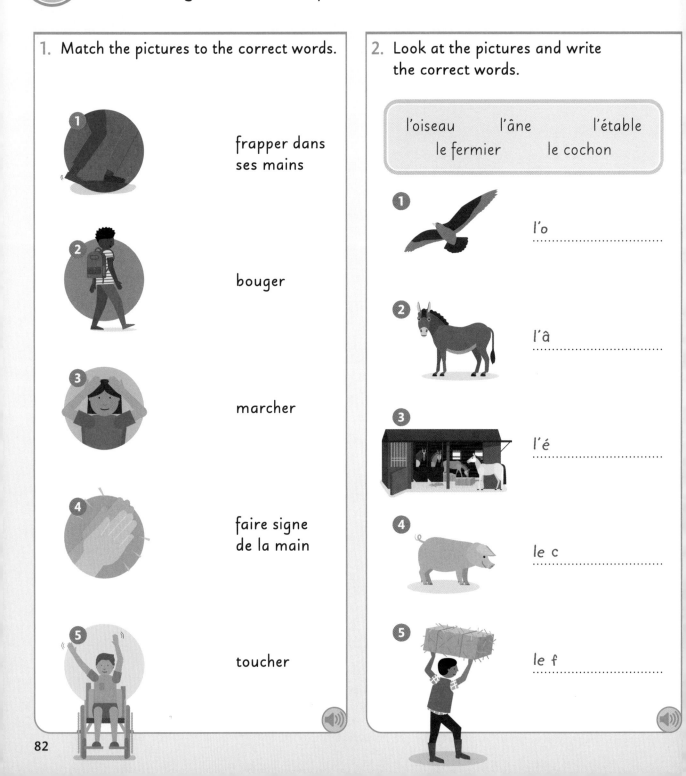

frapper dans ses mains

bouger

marcher

faire signe de la main

toucher

2. Look at the pictures and write the correct words.

l'oiseau    l'âne    l'étable
le fermier    le cochon

1. l'o .................................

2. l'â .................................

3. l'é .................................

4. le c .................................

5. le f .................................

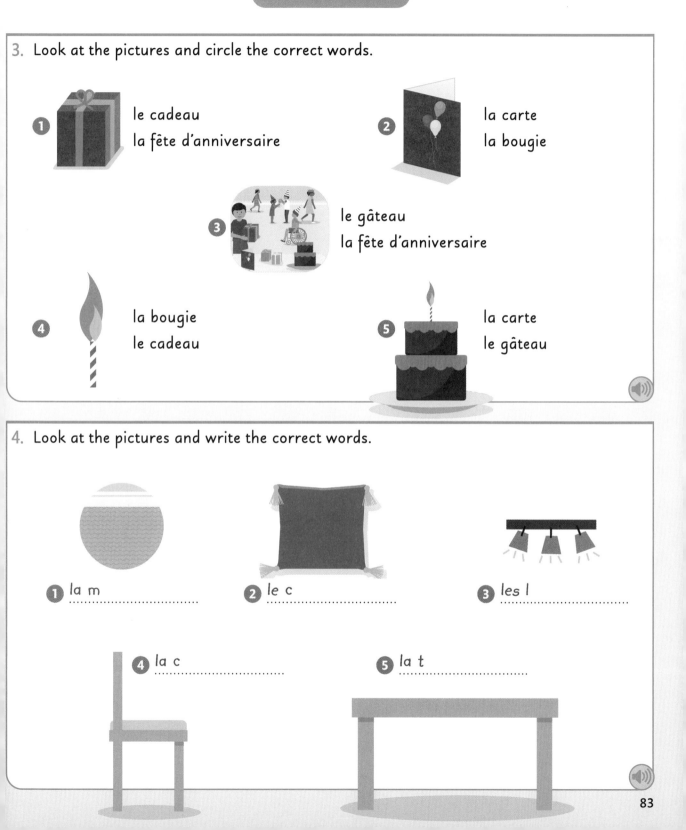

3. Look at the pictures and circle the correct words.

1. le cadeau
   la fête d'anniversaire

2. la carte
   la bougie

3. le gâteau
   la fête d'anniversaire

4. la bougie
   le cadeau

5. la carte
   le gâteau

4. Look at the pictures and write the correct words.

1. la m ...............................

2. le c ...............................

3. les l ...............................

4. la c ...............................

5. la t ...............................

## Day 1

**Listen, repeat, and copy.**

① skier

② faire du vélo

③ marquer

④ patiner

⑤ faire du skateboard

**Listen again and write the words.**

s .................................................

f .................................................

m .................................................

p .................................................

f .................................................

## Day 2

**Listen, repeat, and copy.**

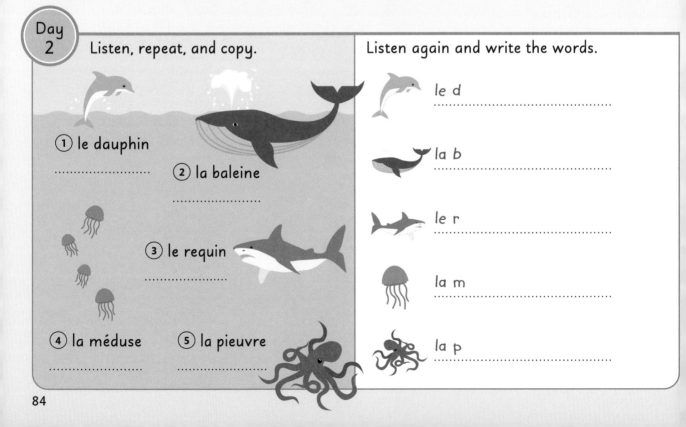

① le dauphin

② la baleine

③ le requin

④ la méduse

⑤ la pieuvre

**Listen again and write the words.**

le d .................................................

la b .................................................

le r .................................................

la m .................................................

la p .................................................

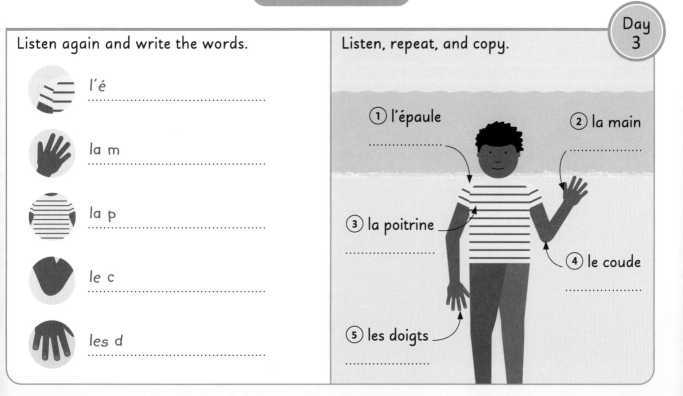

### Listen again and write the words.

l'é ..................................................

la m ..................................................

la p ..................................................

le c ..................................................

les d ..................................................

### Listen, repeat, and copy.

① l'épaule .....................

② la main .....................

③ la poitrine .....................

④ le coude .....................

⑤ les doigts .....................

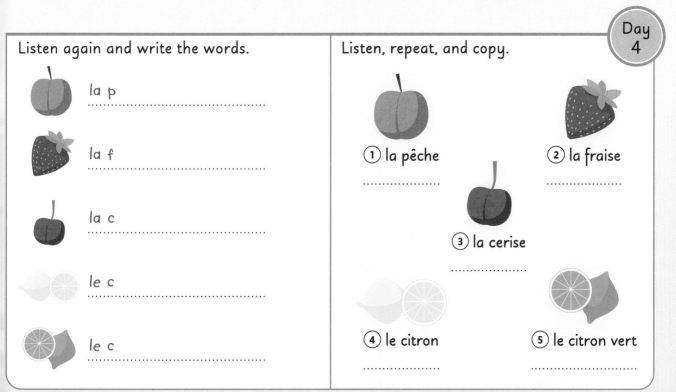

### Listen again and write the words.

la p ..................................................

la f ..................................................

la c ..................................................

le c ..................................................

le c ..................................................

### Listen, repeat, and copy.

① la pêche .....................

② la fraise .....................

③ la cerise .....................

④ le citron .....................

⑤ le citron vert .....................

Day 5 What can you remember from this week?

1. Read the words and mark the correct pictures.

① marquer
A ☐   B ☐

② patiner
A ☐   B ☐

③ skier
A ☐   B ☐

④ faire du vélo
A ☐   B ☐

⑤ faire du skateboard
A ☐   B ☐

2. Look at the pictures and fill in the missing letters.

① l _ _ d _ u _ h _ n

② _ a _ é u _ e

③ l _ p _ e _ v _ e

④ _ e _ e _ u _ n

⑤ l _ b _ l _ i _ e

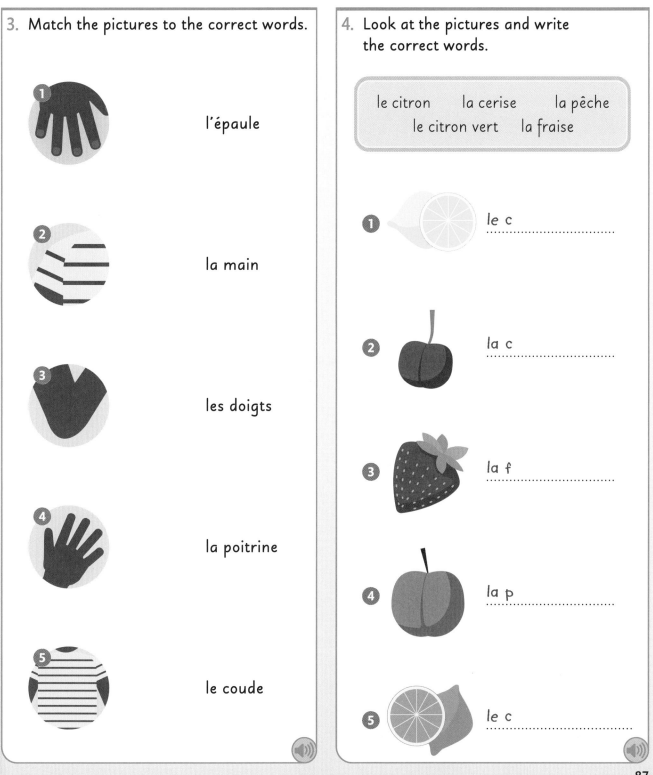

3. Match the pictures to the correct words.

1

l'épaule

2

la main

3

les doigts

4

la poitrine

5

le coude

4. Look at the pictures and write the correct words.

le citron    la cerise    la pêche
le citron vert    la fraise

1    le c .............................

2    la c .............................

3    la f .............................

4    la p .............................

5    le c .............................

### Day 1

**Listen, repeat, and copy.**

① la ville
..................

② le café
..................

③ le bureau de poste
..................

④ le magasin de jouets
..................

⑤ la librairie
..................

**Listen again and write the words.**

la v ..................

le c ..................

le b ..................

le m ..................

la l ..................

### Day 2

**Listen, repeat, and copy.**

① le cinéma
..................

② la star de cinéma
..................

③ le film
..................

④ le billet
..................

⑤ le siège
..................

**Listen again and write the words.**

le c ..................

la s ..................

le f ..................

le b ..................

le s ..................

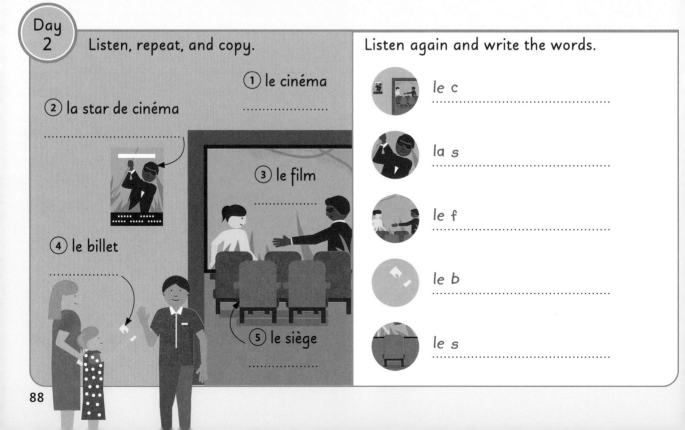

# Week 21

## Listen again and write the words.

la t ...............................................

l'e- ...............................................

le l ...............................................

le m ...............................................

les a ...............................................

## Listen, repeat, and copy.

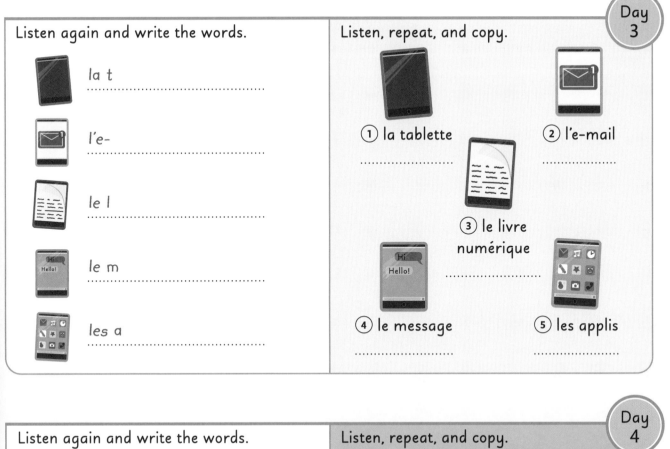

① la tablette ...............................

② l'e-mail ...............................

③ le livre numérique ...............................

④ le message ...............................

⑤ les applis ...............................

## Listen again and write the words.

la b ...............................................

la b ...............................................

le t ...............................................

le b ...............................................

le v ...............................................

## Listen, repeat, and copy.

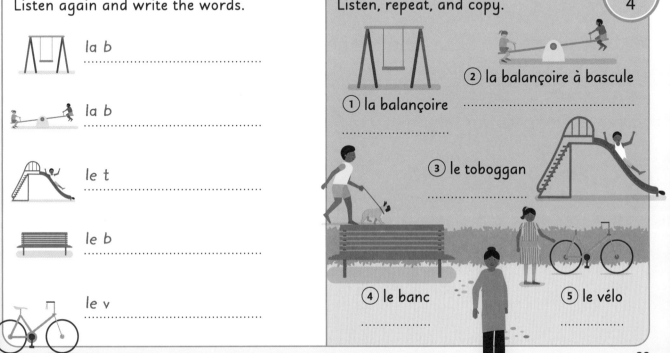

① la balançoire ...............................

② la balançoire à bascule

③ le toboggan ...............................

④ le banc ...............................

⑤ le vélo ...............................

Day 5

What can you remember from this week?

1. Look at the pictures and write the correct words.

① la t ......................................

② le l ......................................

③ le m ......................................

④ les a ......................................

⑤ l'e- ......................................

2. Match the pictures to the correct words.

① le bureau de poste

② le café

③ la librairie

④ la ville

⑤ le magasin de jouets

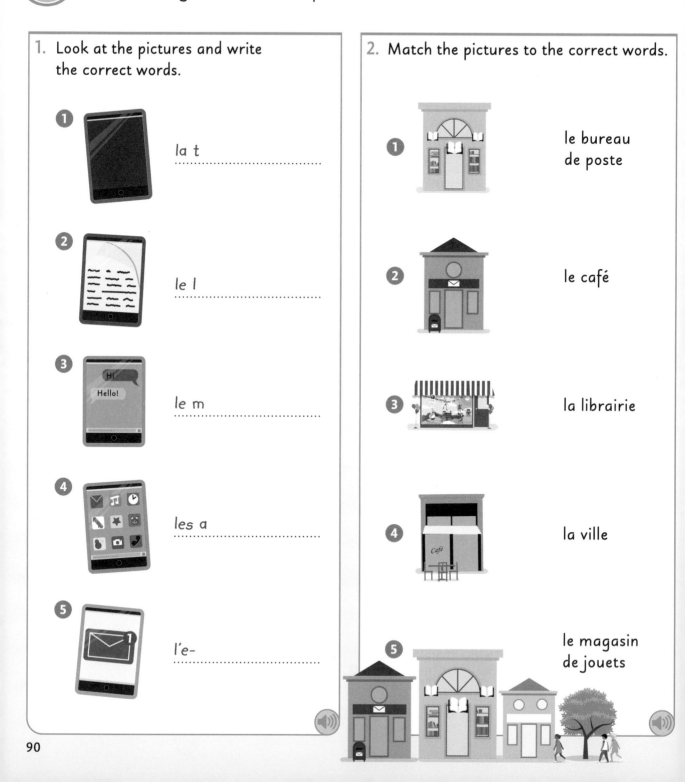

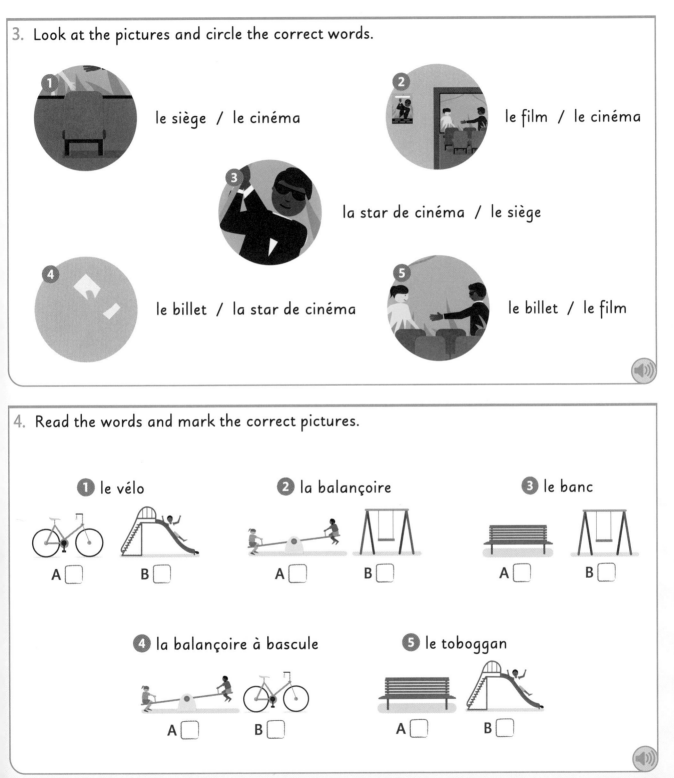

3. Look at the pictures and circle the correct words.

1. le siège / le cinéma

2. le film / le cinéma

3. la star de cinéma / le siège

4. le billet / la star de cinéma

5. le billet / le film

4. Read the words and mark the correct pictures.

1. le vélo
A ☐   B ☐

2. la balançoire
A ☐   B ☐

3. le banc
A ☐   B ☐

4. la balançoire à bascule
A ☐   B ☐

5. le toboggan
A ☐   B ☐

## Day 1

Listen, repeat, and copy.

① la date

② la question

.....................    .....................

12 mai

Qu'est-ce que c'est?

Qu'est-ce que c'est?

C'est un chien.

✓ un chat    ④ exact
.................

✗ un kat

③ la phrase    ⑤ l'erreur

.....................    .....................

Listen again and write the words.

12 mai    la d
.............................

Qu'est-ce que c-est?    la q
.............................

C'est un chien.    la p
.............................

✓ un chat    e
.............................

✗ un kat    l'e
.............................

## Day 2

Listen, repeat, and copy.

① l'entrée    ② en haut

.................    .................

③ en bas

.................

④ le sous-sol

.................

⑤ l'escalier

.................

Listen again and write the words.

l'e
.............................

e
.............................

e
.............................

le s
.............................

l'e
.............................

# Week 22

## Listen again and write the words.

n ..............................

s ..............................

f ..............................

r ..............................

t ..............................

## Listen, repeat, and copy.

(1) nettoyer

..............................

(2) se détendre

..............................

(3) faire ses devoirs

..............................

(4) ranger

..............................

(5) travailler

..............................

## Listen again and write the words.

la p ..............................

la n ..............................

les l ..............................

la s ..............................

le m ..............................

## Listen, repeat, and copy.

(1) la piscine

..............................

(2) la natation

..............................

(3) les lunettes de natation

..............................

(4) la serviette

..............................

(5) le maillot de bain

..............................

Day 5

What can you remember from this week?

1. Look at the picture and write the correct words.

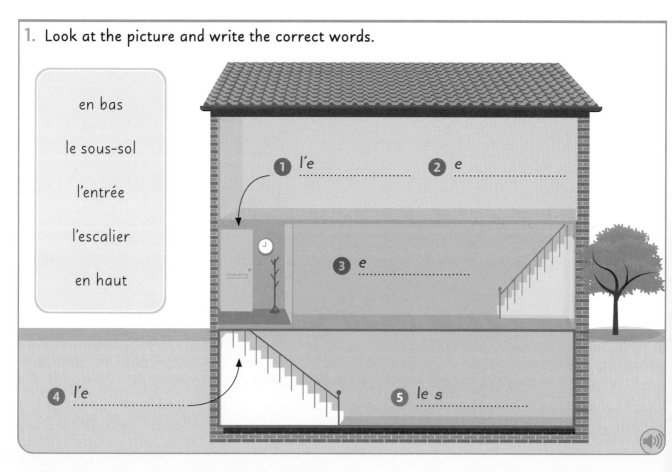

en bas

le sous-sol

l'entrée

l'escalier

en haut

① l'e _____

② e _____

③ e _____

④ l'e _____

⑤ le s _____

2. Match the pictures to the correct words.

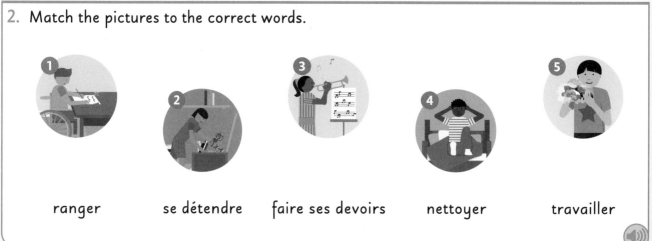

ranger          se détendre     faire ses devoirs     nettoyer     travailler

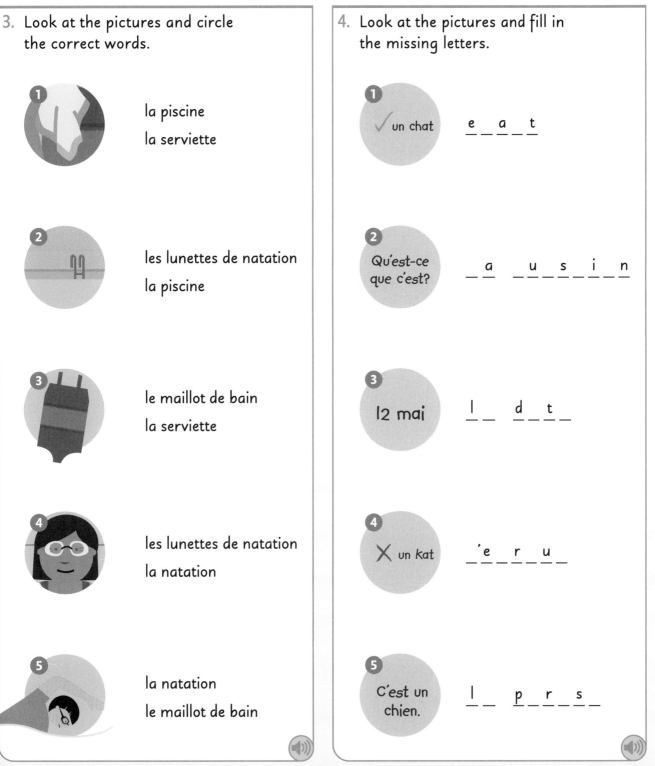

3. Look at the pictures and circle the correct words.

1. la piscine
   la serviette

2. les lunettes de natation
   la piscine

3. le maillot de bain
   la serviette

4. les lunettes de natation
   la natation

5. la natation
   le maillot de bain

4. Look at the pictures and fill in the missing letters.

1. ✓ un chat
   _e_ _ _a_ _ t

2. Qu'est-ce que c'est?
   _ _a_ _ _u_ _s_ _i_ _ n

3. 12 mai
   l_ _ _ _d_ _t_ _

4. ✗ un kat
   _'e_ _ _r_ _u_ _

5. C'est un chien.
   l_ _ _p_ _r_ _s_ _

## Day 1

Listen, repeat, and copy.

Listen again and write the words.

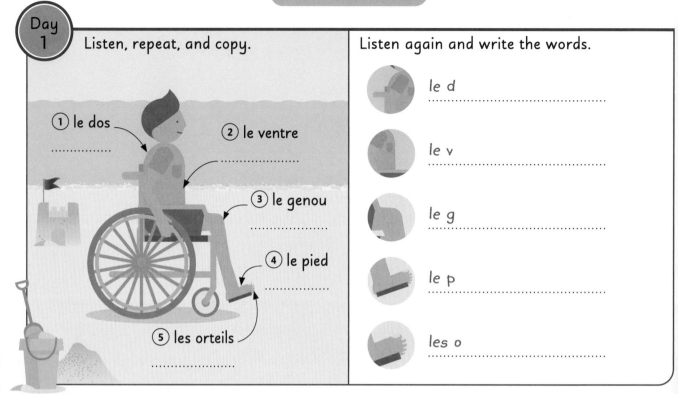

① le dos

...............

② le ventre

...............

③ le genou

...............

④ le pied

...............

⑤ les orteils

...............

le d

.................................

le v

.................................

le g

.................................

le p

.................................

les o

.................................

## Day 2

Listen, repeat, and copy.

Listen again and write the words.

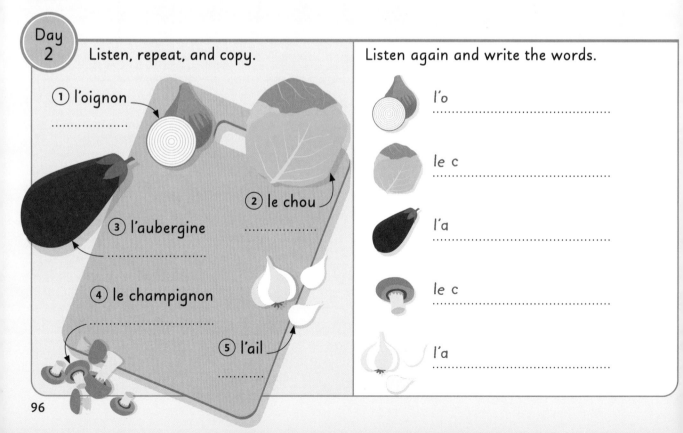

① l'oignon

...............

② le chou

...............

③ l'aubergine

...............

④ le champignon

...............

⑤ l'ail

...............

l'o

.................................

le c

.................................

l'a

.................................

le c

.................................

l'a

.................................

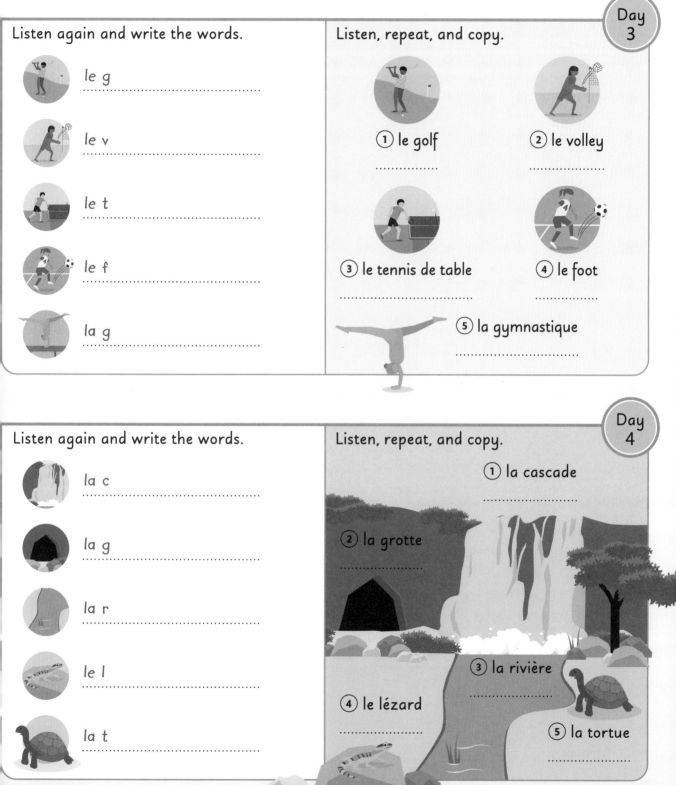

**Listen again and write the words.**

le g ............................................

le v ............................................

le t ............................................

le f ............................................

la g ............................................

**Listen, repeat, and copy.**

① le golf ...................

② le volley ...................

③ le tennis de table ...................

④ le foot ...................

⑤ la gymnastique ...................

**Listen again and write the words.**

la c ............................................

la g ............................................

la r ............................................

le l ............................................

la t ............................................

**Listen, repeat, and copy.**

① la cascade ...................

② la grotte ...................

③ la rivière ...................

④ le lézard ...................

⑤ la tortue ...................

Day 5

What can you remember from this week?

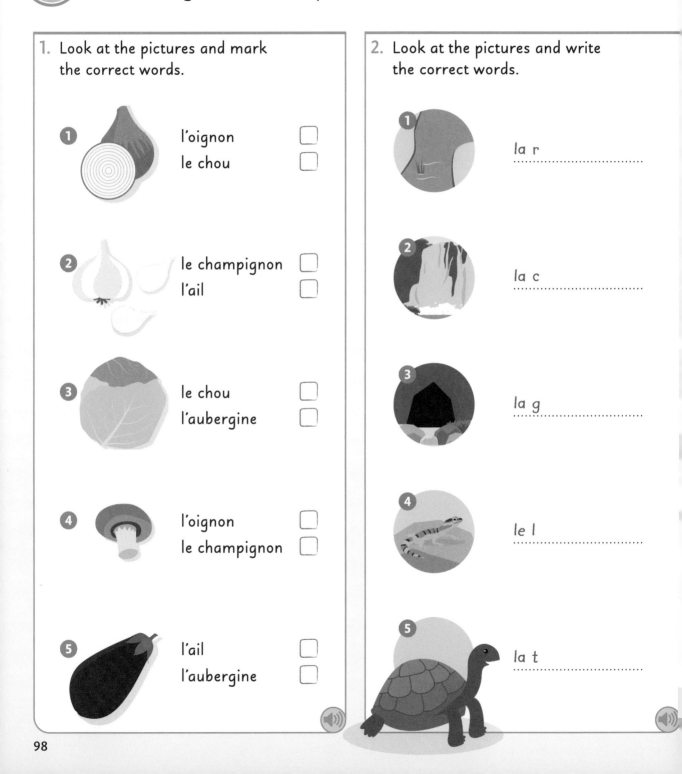

1. Look at the pictures and mark the correct words.

1. l'oignon ☐
   le chou ☐

2. le champignon ☐
   l'ail ☐

3. le chou ☐
   l'aubergine ☐

4. l'oignon ☐
   le champignon ☐

5. l'ail ☐
   l'aubergine ☐

2. Look at the pictures and write the correct words.

1. la r ...................

2. la c ...................

3. la g ...................

4. le l ...................

5. la t ...................

3. Look at the pictures and circle the correct words.

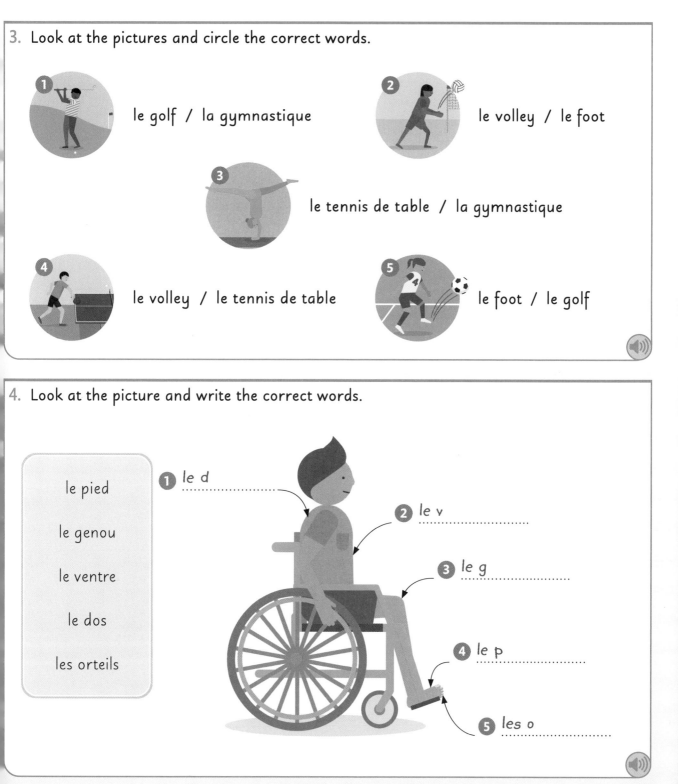

1  le golf / la gymnastique

2  le volley / le foot

3  le tennis de table / la gymnastique

4  le volley / le tennis de table

5  le foot / le golf

4. Look at the picture and write the correct words.

le pied

le genou

le ventre

le dos

les orteils

1 le d .......................

2 le v .......................

3 le g .......................

4 le p .......................

5 les o .......................

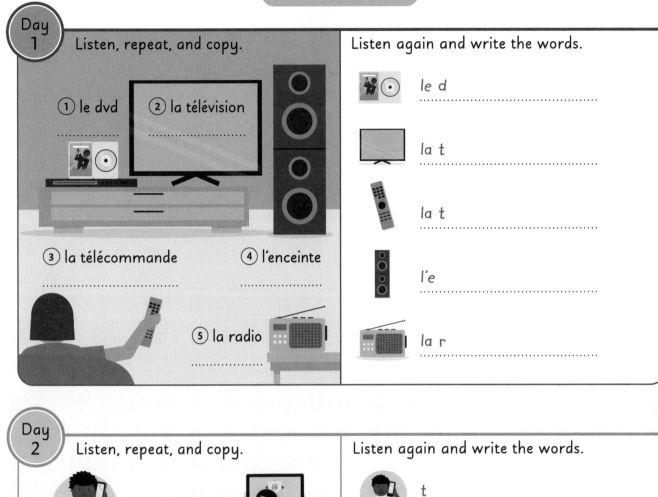

**Day 1**

Listen, repeat, and copy.

① le dvd
② la télévision
③ la télécommande
④ l'enceinte
⑤ la radio

Listen again and write the words.

le d ........................

la t ........................

la t ........................

l'e ........................

la r ........................

**Day 2**

Listen, repeat, and copy.

① téléphoner
② envoyer un e-mail
③ poster
④ parler
⑤ crier

Listen again and write the words.

t ........................

e ........................

p ........................

p ........................

c ........................

Day 3

## Listen again and write the words.

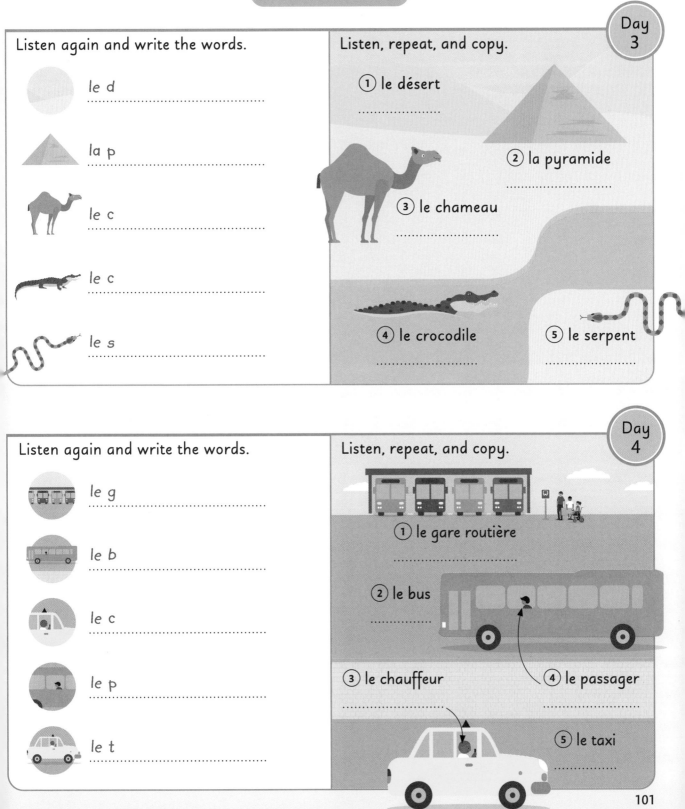

le d ....................

la p ....................

le c ....................

le c ....................

le s ....................

## Listen, repeat, and copy.

① le désert
....................

② la pyramide
....................

③ le chameau
....................

④ le crocodile
....................

⑤ le serpent
....................

Day 4

## Listen again and write the words.

le g ....................

le b ....................

le c ....................

le p ....................

le t ....................

## Listen, repeat, and copy.

① le gare routière
....................

② le bus
....................

③ le chauffeur
....................

④ le passager
....................

⑤ le taxi
....................

Day 5

What can you remember from this week?

1. Read the words and mark the correct pictures.

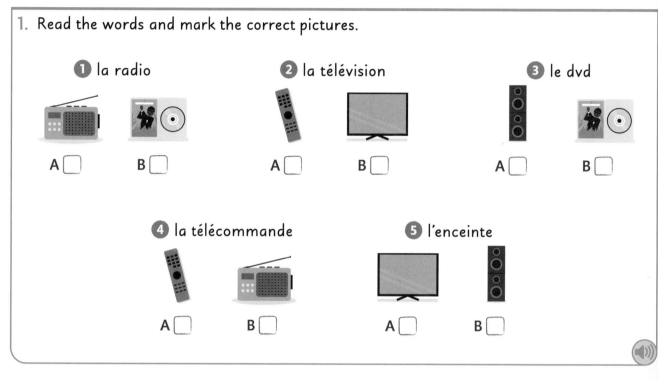

1 la radio

A ☐    B ☐

2 la télévision

A ☐    B ☐

3 le dvd

A ☐    B ☐

4 la télécommande

A ☐    B ☐

5 l'enceinte

A ☐    B ☐

2. Look at the pictures and write the correct words.

1 le c ......................

2 la p ......................

3 le d ......................

4 le s ......................

5 le c ......................

3. Match the pictures to the correct words.

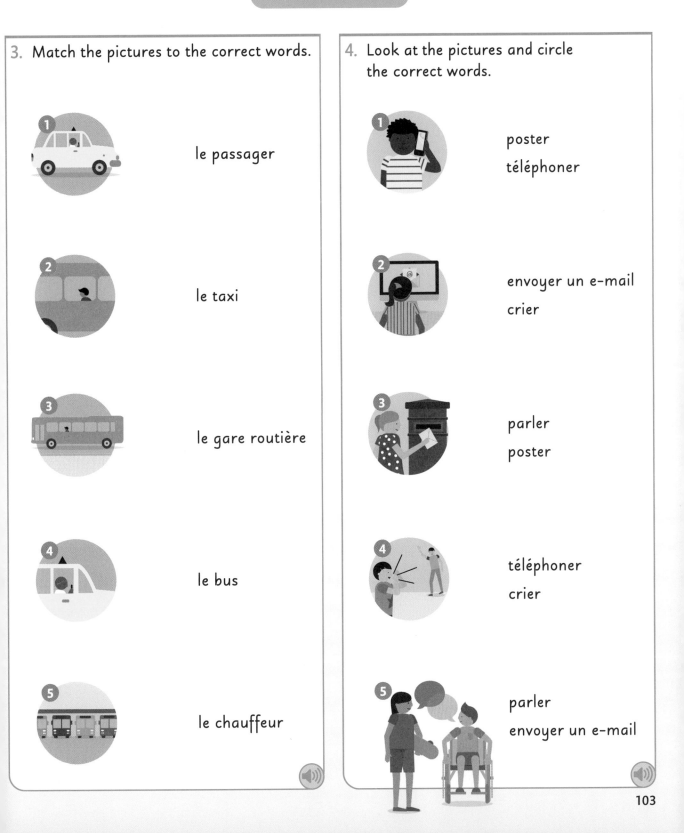

1.      le passager

2.      le taxi

3.      le gare routière

4.      le bus

5.      le chauffeur

4. Look at the pictures and circle the correct words.

1.      poster / téléphoner

2.      envoyer un e-mail / crier

3.      parler / poster

4.      téléphoner / crier

5.      parler / envoyer un e-mail

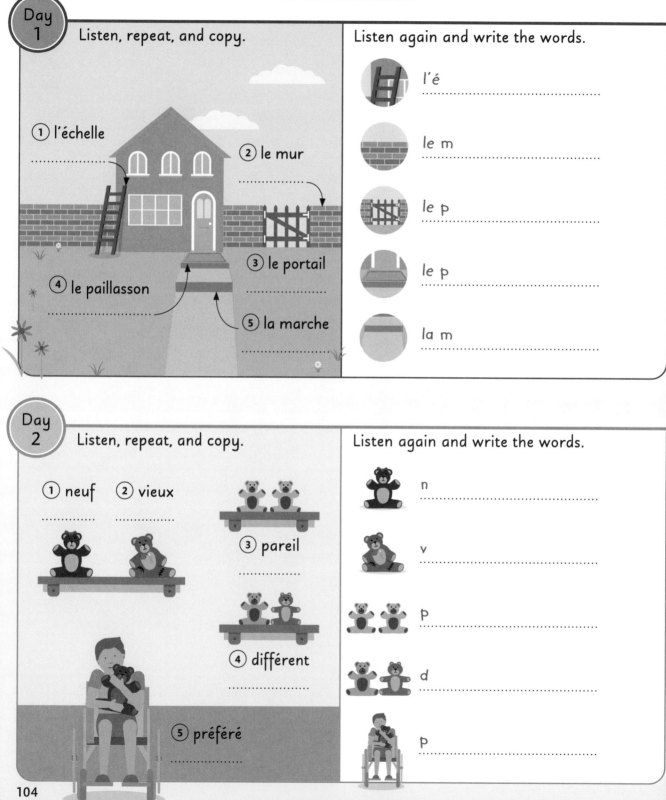

**Day 1**

Listen, repeat, and copy.

① l'échelle
② le mur
③ le portail
④ le paillasson
⑤ la marche

Listen again and write the words.

l'é ......................
le m ......................
le p ......................
le p ......................
la m ......................

**Day 2**

Listen, repeat, and copy.

① neuf
② vieux
③ pareil
④ différent
⑤ préféré

Listen again and write the words.

n ......................
v ......................
p ......................
d ......................
p ......................

104

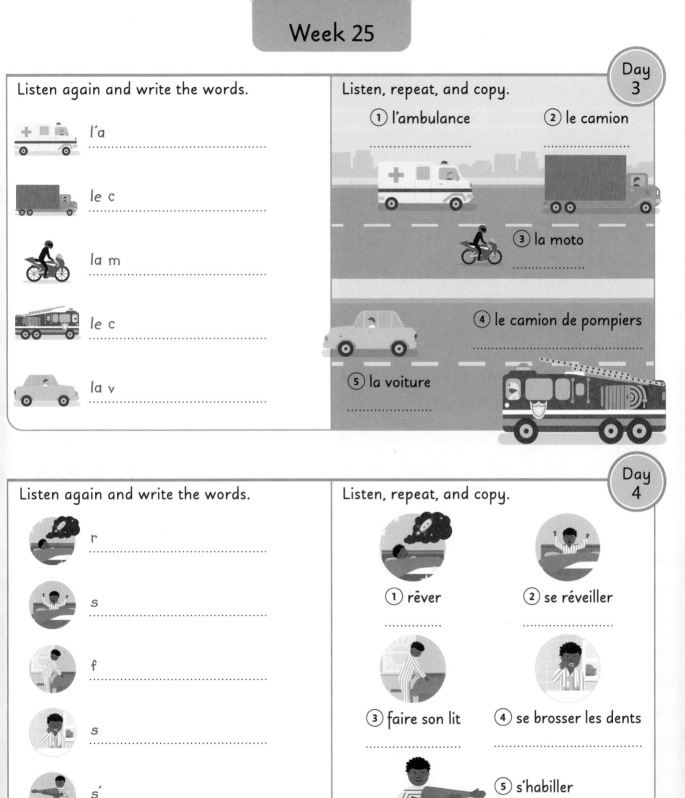

**Day 3**

## Listen again and write the words.

l'a ....................

le c ....................

la m ....................

le c ....................

la v ....................

## Listen, repeat, and copy.

① l'ambulance ....................

② le camion ....................

③ la moto ....................

④ le camion de pompiers ....................

⑤ la voiture ....................

**Day 4**

## Listen again and write the words.

r ....................

s ....................

f ....................

s ....................

s' ....................

## Listen, repeat, and copy.

① rêver ....................

② se réveiller ....................

③ faire son lit ....................

④ se brosser les dents ....................

⑤ s'habiller ....................

Day 5

## What can you remember from this week?

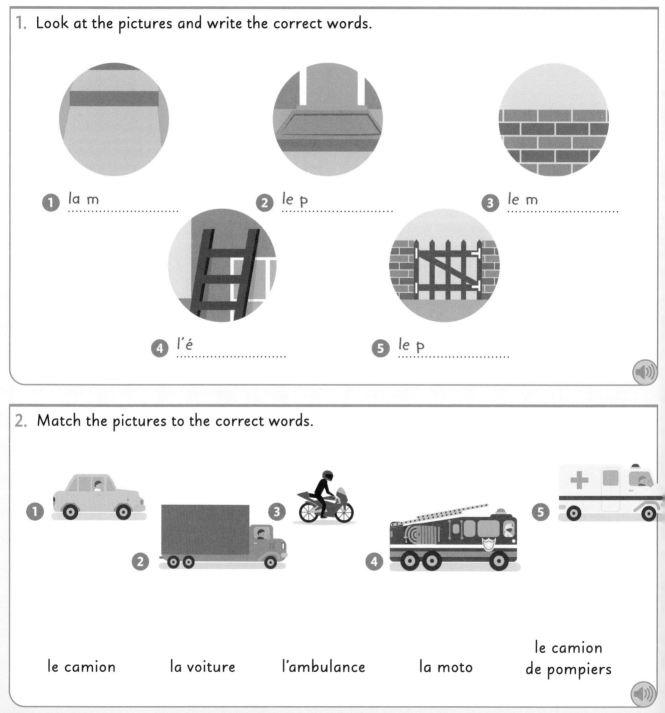

1. Look at the pictures and write the correct words.

1 la m ........................

2 le p ........................

3 le m ........................

4 l'é ........................

5 le p ........................

2. Match the pictures to the correct words.

1

2

3

4

5

le camion       la voiture       l'ambulance       la moto       le camion
de pompiers

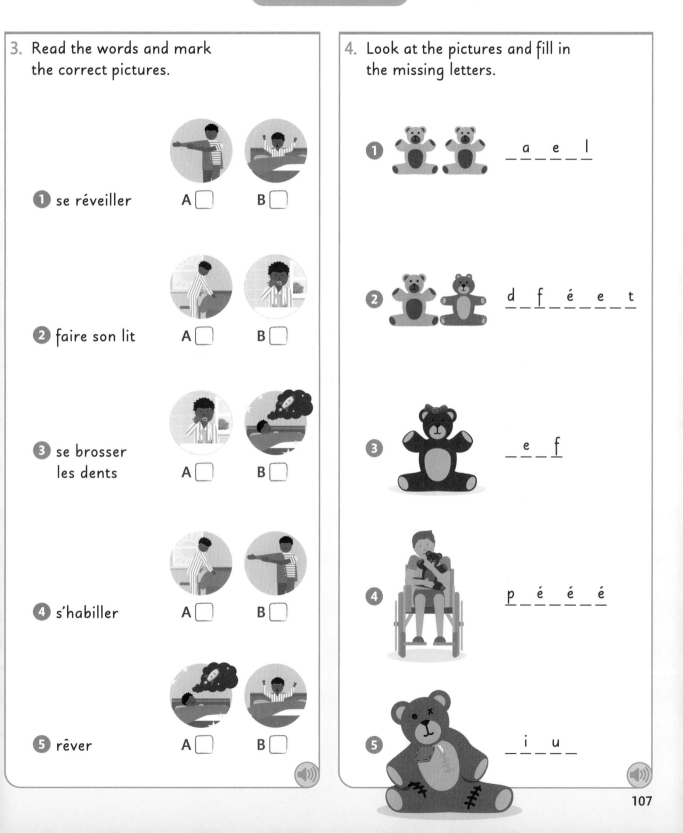

3. Read the words and mark the correct pictures.

1 se réveiller     A ☐     B ☐

2 faire son lit     A ☐     B ☐

3 se brosser les dents     A ☐     B ☐

4 s'habiller     A ☐     B ☐

5 rêver     A ☐     B ☐

4. Look at the pictures and fill in the missing letters.

1  _ a _ e _ l

2  d _ f _ é _ e _ t

3  _ e _ f

4  p _ é _ é _ é

5  _ i _ u _

**Day 1**

Listen, repeat, and copy.

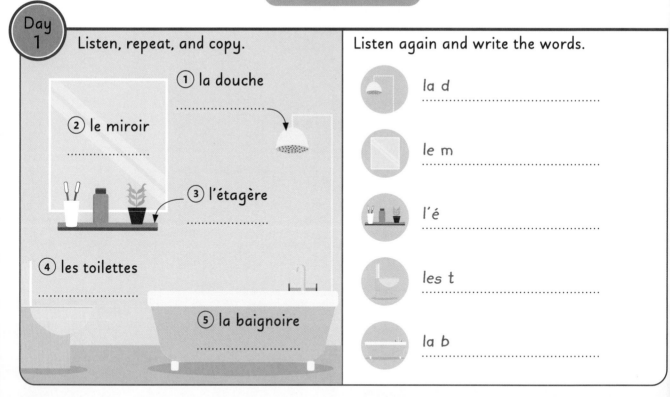

① la douche

② le miroir

③ l'étagère

④ les toilettes

⑤ la baignoire

Listen again and write the words.

la d ..........................

le m ..........................

l'é ..........................

les t ..........................

la b ..........................

**Day 2**

Listen, repeat, and copy.

① le gorille

② le panda

③ le rhinocéros

④ le perroquet

⑤ le kangourou

Listen again and write the words.

le g ..........................

le p ..........................

le r ..........................

le p ..........................

le k ..........................

# Week 26

**Listen again and write the words.**

t ......................................

s ......................................

p ......................................

a ......................................

r ......................................

**Listen, repeat, and copy.**

① tomber  ......................

② se faire mal  ......................

③ pleurer  ......................

④ aider  ......................

⑤ raconter  ......................

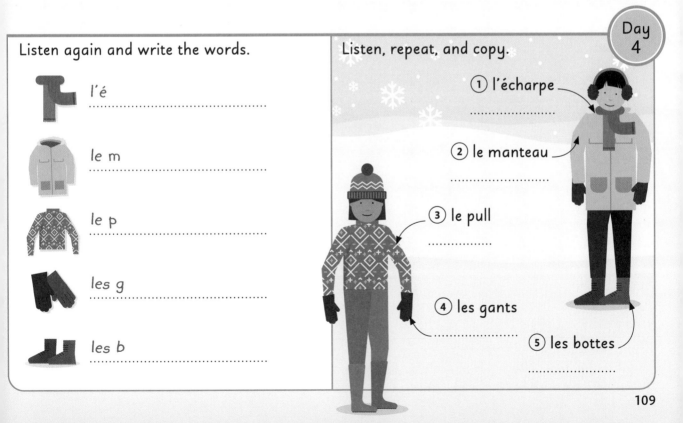

**Listen again and write the words.**

l'é ......................................

le m ......................................

le p ......................................

les g ......................................

les b ......................................

**Listen, repeat, and copy.**

① l'écharpe  ......................

② le manteau  ......................

③ le pull  ......................

④ les gants  ......................

⑤ les bottes  ......................

Day 5

What can you remember from this week?

1. Look at the pictures and write the correct words.

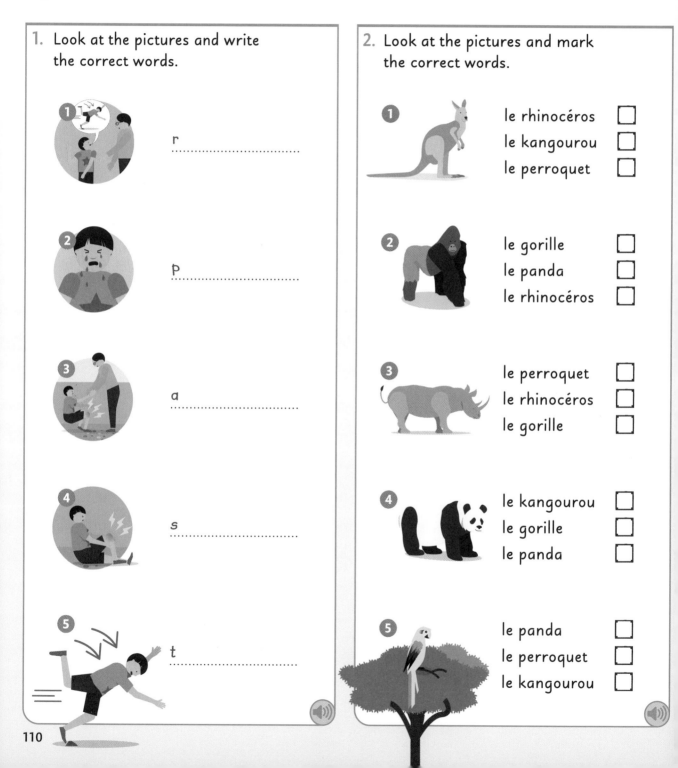

1. r ................................

2. p ................................

3. a ................................

4. s ................................

5. t ................................

2. Look at the pictures and mark the correct words.

1. le rhinocéros ☐
   le kangourou ☐
   le perroquet ☐

2. le gorille ☐
   le panda ☐
   le rhinocéros ☐

3. le perroquet ☐
   le rhinocéros ☐
   le gorille ☐

4. le kangourou ☐
   le gorille ☐
   le panda ☐

5. le panda ☐
   le perroquet ☐
   le kangourou ☐

3. Look at the pictures and write the correct words.

| le manteau | les bottes | les gants | l'écharpe | le pull |

1 les b ........................

2 le p ........................

3 l'é ........................

4 le m ........................

5 les g ........................

4. Look at the pictures and circle the correct words.

1
la douche
la baignoire

2
les toilettes
l'étagère

3
la baignoire
le miroir

4
le miroir
l'étagère

5
la douche
les toilettes

## Day 1

Listen, repeat, and copy.

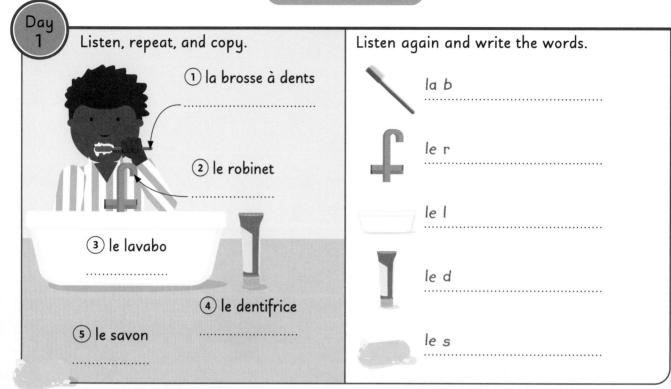

① la brosse à dents

......................

② le robinet

......................

③ le lavabo

......................

④ le dentifrice

......................

⑤ le savon

......................

Listen again and write the words.

la b ......................

le r ......................

le l ......................

le d ......................

le s ......................

## Day 2

Listen, repeat, and copy.

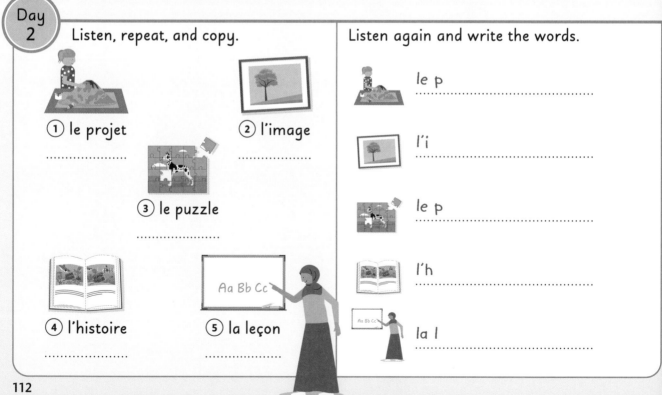

① le projet

......................

② l'image

......................

③ le puzzle

......................

④ l'histoire

......................

⑤ la leçon

......................

Listen again and write the words.

le p ......................

l'i ......................

le p ......................

l'h ......................

la l ......................

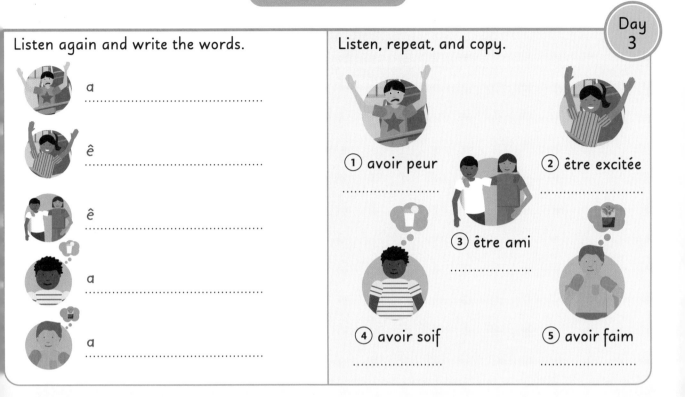

## Listen again and write the words.

a ....................................

ê ....................................

ê ....................................

a ....................................

a ....................................

## Listen, repeat, and copy.

1 avoir peur ....................................

2 être excitée ....................................

3 être ami ....................................

4 avoir soif ....................................

5 avoir faim ....................................

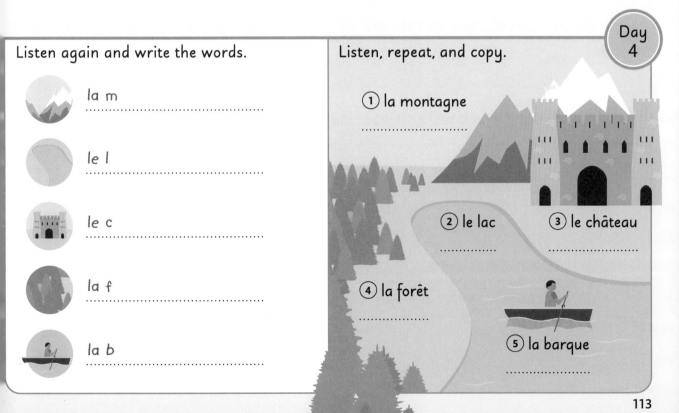

## Listen again and write the words.

la m ....................................

le l ....................................

le c ....................................

la f ....................................

la b ....................................

## Listen, repeat, and copy.

1 la montagne ....................................

2 le lac ....................................

3 le château ....................................

4 la forêt ....................................

5 la barque ....................................

Day 5 — What can you remember from this week?

**1.** Look at the pictures and write the letters in the correct order.

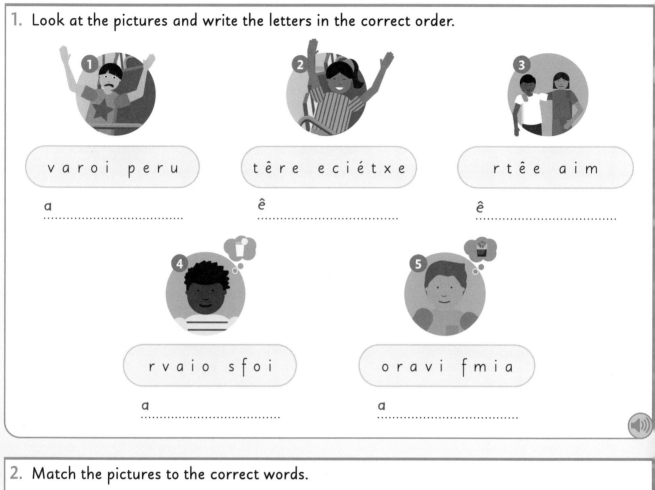

1. v a r o i   p e r u

a ..................................................

2. t ê r e   e c i é t x e

ê ..................................................

3. r t ê e   a i m

ê ..................................................

4. r v a i o   s f o i

a ..................................................

5. o r a v i   f m i a

a ..................................................

**2.** Match the pictures to the correct words.

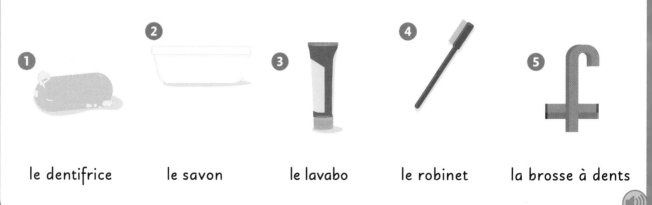

le dentifrice    le savon    le lavabo    le robinet    la brosse à dents

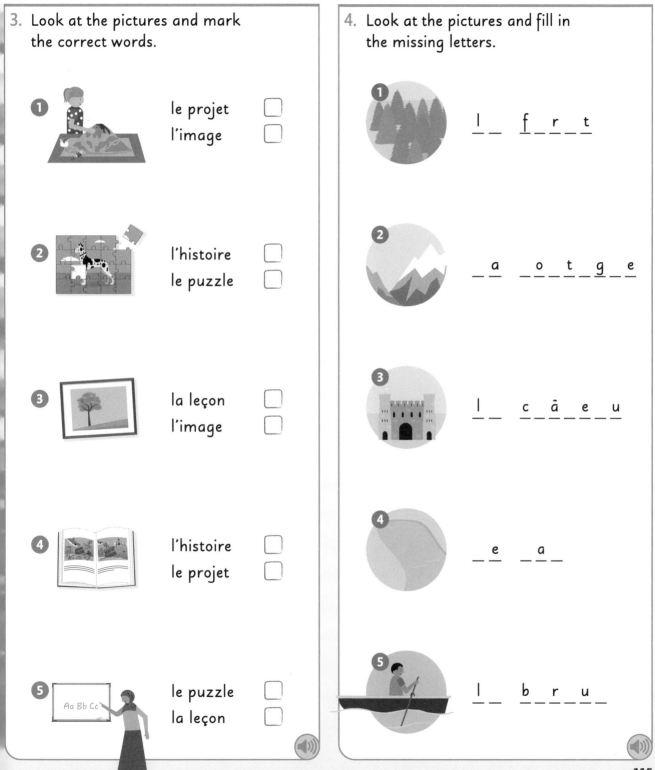

3. Look at the pictures and mark the correct words.

1. le projet ☐
   l'image ☐

2. l'histoire ☐
   le puzzle ☐

3. la leçon ☐
   l'image ☐

4. l'histoire ☐
   le projet ☐

5. le puzzle ☐
   la leçon ☐

4. Look at the pictures and fill in the missing letters.

1. l _ _ f _ r _ t

2. _ a _ _ o _ t _ g _ e

3. l _ _ c _ â _ e _ u

4. _ e _ _ a _ _

5. l _ _ b _ r _ u _

**Day 1**

Listen, repeat, and copy.

① l'ordinateur
...................

② l'écran
...................

③ l'imprimante
...................

④ le clavier
...................

⑤ la souris
...................

Listen again and write the words.

l'o
...................

l'é
...................

l'i
...................

le c
...................

la s
...................

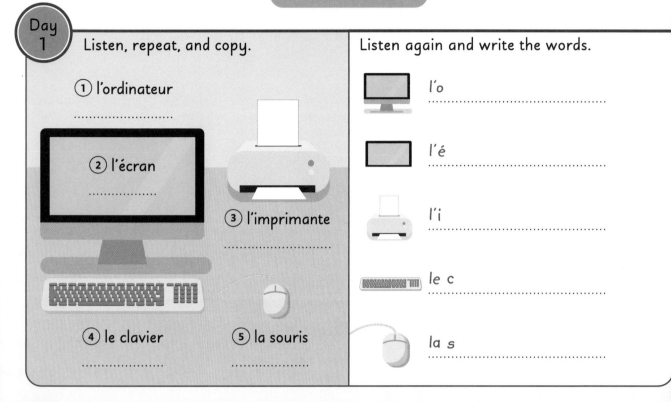

**Day 2**

Listen, repeat, and copy.

① à l'intérieur
...................

② à l'extérieur
...................

③ entre
...................

④ par-dessus
...................

⑤ sous
...................

Listen again and write the words.

à
...................

à
...................

e
...................

p
...................

s
...................

**Day 3**

Listen again and write the words.

la m
.....................................

b
.....................................

n
.....................................

e
.....................................

v
.....................................

Listen, repeat, and copy.

① la météo
.....................

② brumeux
.....................

③ nuageux
.....................

④ ensoleillé
.....................

⑤ venteux
.....................

**Day 4**

Listen again and write the words.

la f
.....................................

le c
.....................................

le m
.....................................

la g
.....................................

le c
.....................................

Listen, repeat, and copy.

① la fête foraine
.........................

② le cirque
.....................

③ le manège
.....................

④ la glace
.....................

⑤ le clown
.....................

Day
5

What can you remember from this week?

1. Read the words and mark
   the correct pictures.

❶ à l'intérieur          A ☐          B ☐

❷ à l'extérieur          A ☐          B ☐

❸ entre                 A ☐          B ☐

❹ par-dessus            A ☐          B ☐

❺ sous                  A ☐          B ☐

2. Look at the pictures and write
   the correct words.

1    b ................................

2    e ................................

3    la m ................................

4    v ................................

5    n ................................

3. Look at the pictures and circle the correct words.

1 l'ordinateur
la souris

2 l'imprimante
l'écran

3 l'imprimante
l'ordinateur

4 l'écran
le clavier

5 le clavier
la souris

4. Look at the pictures and write the correct words.

la glace    le cirque    la fête foraine    le clown    le manège

1 le c ...........

2 le m ...........

3 la g ...........

4 la f ...........

5 le c ...........

# Week 29

## Day 1

Listen, repeat, and copy.

① la soupe

② la tourte

③ le riz

④ les haricots

⑤ la viande

Listen again and write the words.

la s ..............

la t ..............

le r ..............

les h ..............

la v ..............

## Day 2

Listen, repeat, and copy.

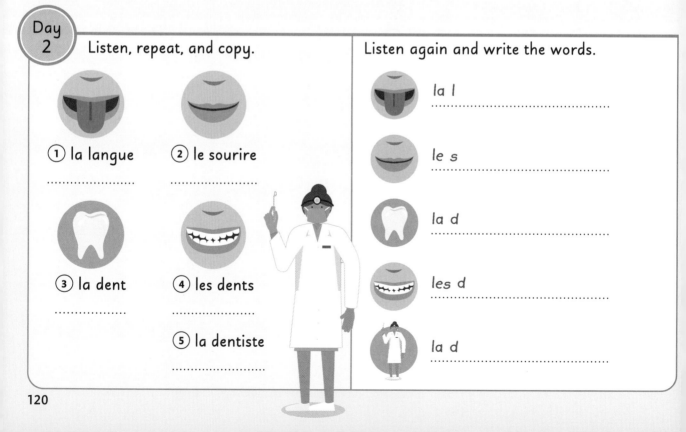

① la langue

② le sourire

③ la dent

④ les dents

⑤ la dentiste

Listen again and write the words.

la l ..............

le s ..............

la d ..............

les d ..............

la d ..............

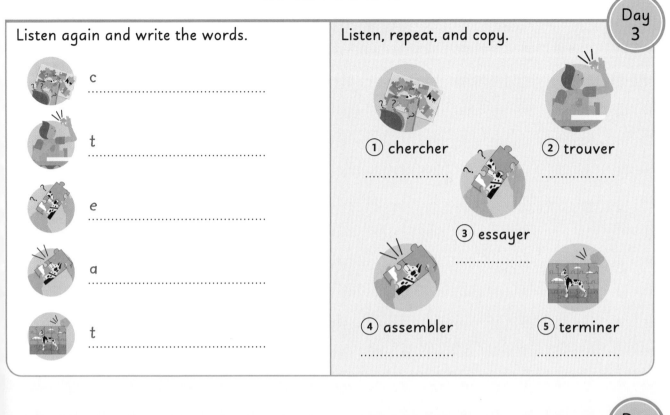

**Day 3**

## Listen again and write the words.

c .................................

t .................................

e .................................

a .................................

t .................................

## Listen, repeat, and copy.

① chercher
.......................

② trouver
.......................

③ essayer
.......................

④ assembler
.......................

⑤ terminer
.......................

**Day 4**

## Listen again and write the words.

la p .................................

le g .................................

la c .................................

le p .................................

le f .................................

## Listen, repeat, and copy.

① la pêche
.......................

② le gilet de sauvetage
.......................

③ la canne à pêche
.......................

④ le poisson
.......................

⑤ le filet
.......................

121

Day 5

## What can you remember from this week?

1. Look at the pictures and fill in the missing letters.

1. c e c e _ _ _ _ _ _

2. _ r u e _ _ _ _ _ _

3. a s m l r _ _ _ _ _ _

4. _ e m n r _ _ _ _ _ _

5. e s y r _ _ _ _ _ _

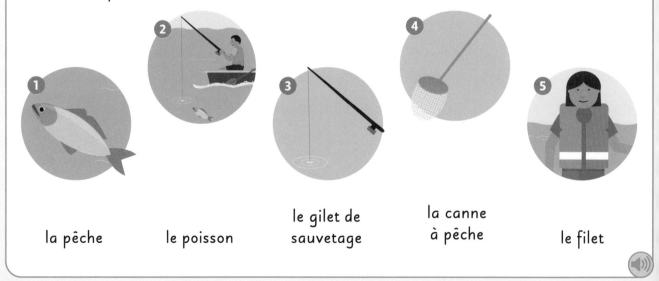

2. Match the pictures to the correct words.

la pêche

le poisson

le gilet de
sauvetage

la canne
à pêche

le filet

3. Look at the pictures and write the correct words.

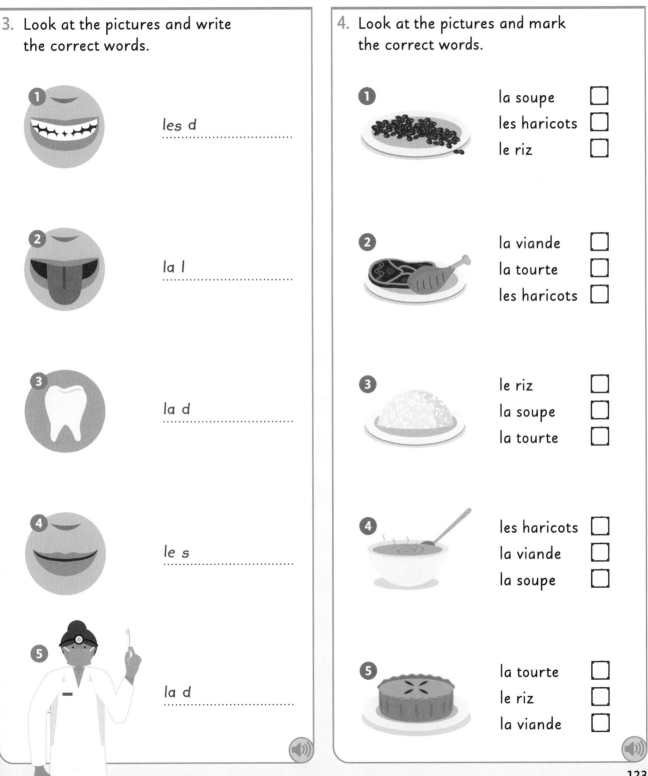

1   les d .........................

2   la l .........................

3   la d .........................

4   le s .........................

5   la d .........................

4. Look at the pictures and mark the correct words.

1   la soupe ☐
   les haricots ☐
   le riz ☐

2   la viande ☐
   la tourte ☐
   les haricots ☐

3   le riz ☐
   la soupe ☐
   la tourte ☐

4   les haricots ☐
   la viande ☐
   la soupe ☐

5   la tourte ☐
   le riz ☐
   la viande ☐

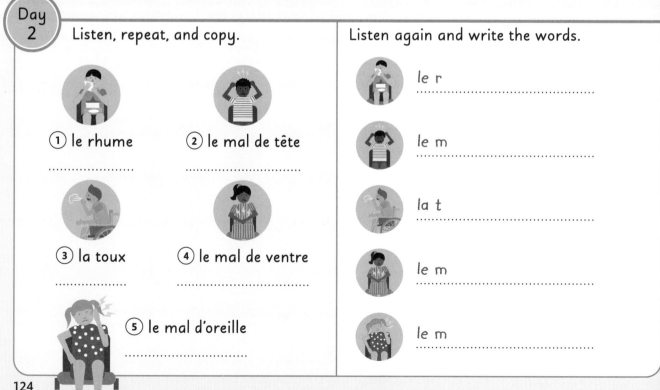

## Day 1

### Listen, repeat, and copy.

1 le plafond

2 la porte

3 la fenêtre

4 la clé

5 le sol

### Listen again and write the words.

le p

la p

la f

la c

le s

## Day 2

### Listen, repeat, and copy.

1 le rhume

2 le mal de tête

3 la toux

4 le mal de ventre

5 le mal d'oreille

### Listen again and write the words.

le r

le m

la t

le m

le m

# Week 30

## Listen again and write the words.

la l .........................................

le t .........................................

l'e .........................................

le n .........................................

l'a .........................................

## Listen, repeat, and copy.

① la lettre .........................................

② le timbre .........................................

③ l'enveloppe .........................................

④ le nom .........................................

Sofia

10 rue de l'Église
Paris
75018

⑤ l'adresse .........................................

## Listen again and write the words.

la c .........................................

les c .........................................

le v .........................................

le b .........................................

le m .........................................

## Listen, repeat, and copy.

① la campagne .........................................

② les collines .........................................

③ le village .........................................

④ le bois .........................................

⑤ le marché .........................................

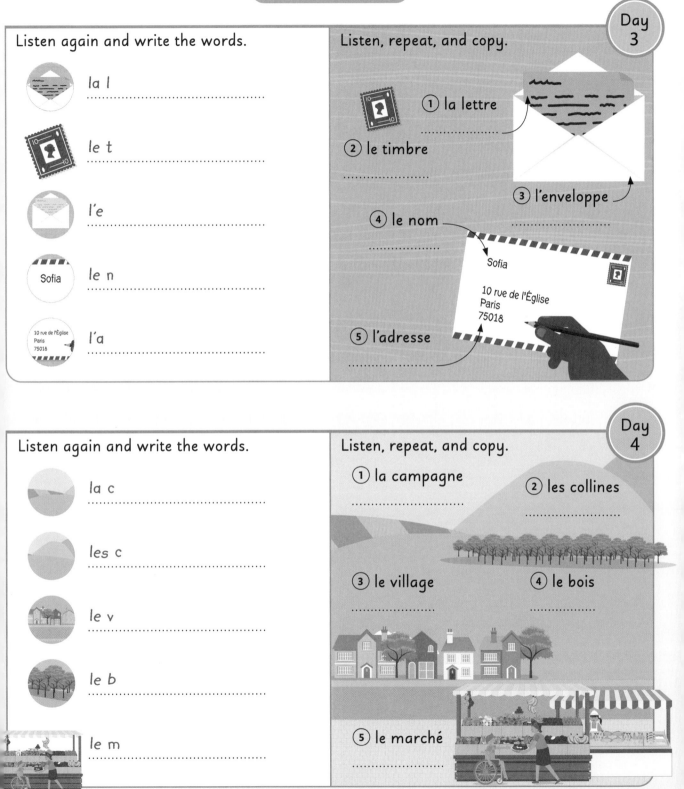

Day 5

What can you remember from this week?

1. Look at the pictures and write the correct words.

les collines    le village    le bois
la campagne    le marché

1. le v .................................

2. les c .................................

3. la c .................................

4. le b .................................

5. le m .................................

2. Look at the pictures and mark the correct words.

1.
la lettre ☐
le timbre ☐

2.
10 rue de l'Église
Paris
75018

le nom ☐
l'adresse ☐

3.
l'enveloppe ☐
la lettre ☐

4.
l'adresse ☐
le timbre ☐

5.
Sofia
l'enveloppe ☐
le nom ☐

3. Read the words and mark the correct pictures.

1 le rhume

A ☐     B ☐

2 le mal de tête

A ☐     B ☐

3 la toux

A ☐     B ☐

4 le mal d'oreille

A ☐     B ☐

5 le mal de ventre

A ☐     B ☐

4. Look at the pictures and write the correct words.

1 le p ........................................

2 la f ........................................

3 la p ........................................

4 le s ........................................

5 la c ........................................

**Day 1**

Listen, repeat, and copy.

① le site web

② le chargeur

③ l'ordinateur portable

④ les écouteurs

⑤ le portable

Listen again and write the words.

le s ....................

le c ....................

l'o ....................

les é ....................

le p ....................

**Day 2**

Listen, repeat, and copy.

① la cuisinière

② le four

③ la poubelle

④ le placard

⑤ le réfrigérateur

Listen again and write the words.

la c ....................

le f ....................

la p ....................

le p ....................

le r ....................

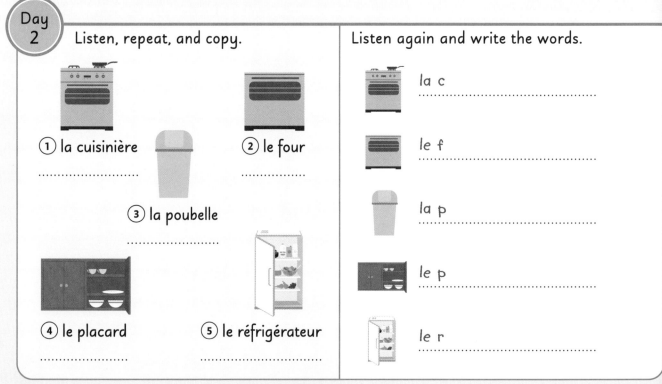

**Listen again and write the words.**

le s ......................

le s ......................

la s ......................

la b ......................

le b ......................

**Listen, repeat, and copy.**

① le stade ......................

② le supermarché ......................

③ la salle de sport ......................

④ la bibliothèque ......................

⑤ le bureau ......................

**Listen again and write the words.**

le c ......................

le n ......................

la t ......................

la p ......................

les i ......................

**Listen, repeat, and copy.**

① le ciel ......................

② le nuage ......................

③ la terre ......................

④ la pierre ......................

⑤ les insectes ......................

Day 5

What can you remember from this week?

1. Read the words and mark the correct pictures.

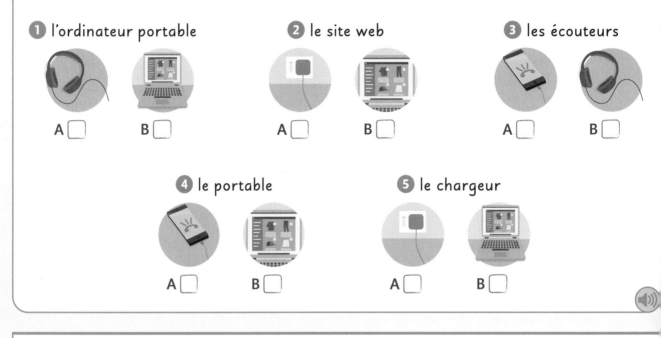

① l'ordinateur portable

A ☐   B ☐

② le site web

A ☐   B ☐

③ les écouteurs

A ☐   B ☐

④ le portable

A ☐   B ☐

⑤ le chargeur

A ☐   B ☐

2. Look at the pictures and write the correct words.

① le b ....................

② la b ....................

③ le s ....................

④ la s ....................

⑤ le s ....................

**3.** Look at the pictures and circle the correct words.

1. la cuisinière
   le placard

2. la poubelle
   la cuisinière

3. le four
   la poubelle

4. le réfrigérateur
   le placard

5. le four
   le réfrigérateur

**4.** Look at the pictures and fill in the missing letters.

1. l _ _ p _ e _ r _

2. _ e _ _ i _ l

3. l _ _ n _ a _ e

4. _ _ a _ _ e _ r _

5. _ _ l _ s _ _ n _ e _ t _ s

# Week 32

## Day 1

Listen, repeat, and copy.

① le flocon de neige

.............................

② le bonhomme de neige

.............................

③ la boule de neige

.............................

④ la neige

.................

⑤ la glace

.................

### Listen again and write the words.

le f ............................................

le b ............................................

la b ............................................

la n ............................................

la g ............................................

## Day 2

Listen, repeat, and copy.

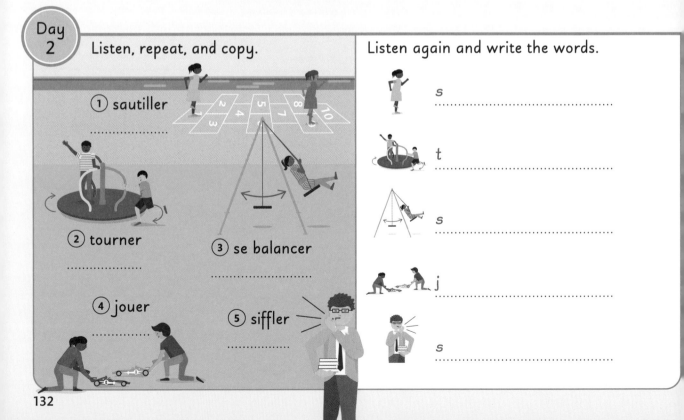

① sautiller

.................

② tourner

.................

③ se balancer

.................

④ jouer

.................

⑤ siffler

.................

### Listen again and write the words.

s ............................................

t ............................................

s ............................................

j ............................................

s ............................................

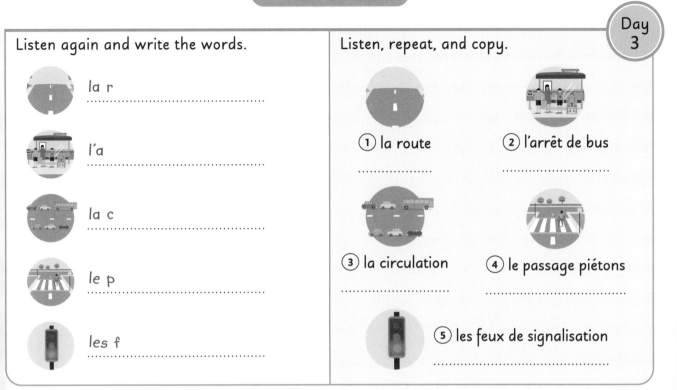

**Listen again and write the words.**

la r .....................................

l'a .....................................

la c .....................................

le p .....................................

les f .....................................

**Listen, repeat, and copy.**

① la route .....................................

② l'arrêt de bus .....................................

③ la circulation .....................................

④ le passage piétons .....................................

⑤ les feux de signalisation .....................................

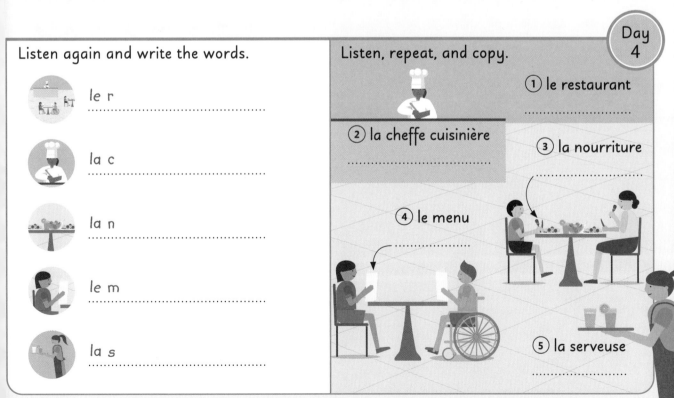

**Listen again and write the words.**

le r .....................................

la c .....................................

la n .....................................

le m .....................................

la s .....................................

**Listen, repeat, and copy.**

① le restaurant .....................................

② la cheffe cuisinière .....................................

③ la nourriture .....................................

④ le menu .....................................

⑤ la serveuse .....................................

What can you remember from this week?

1. Read the words and mark the correct pictures.

① le bonhomme
   de neige          A ☐      B ☐

② la neige          A ☐      B ☐

③ le flocon
   de neige          A ☐      B ☐

④ la boule
   de neige          A ☐      B ☐

⑤ la glace          A ☐      B ☐

2. Look at the pictures and write the correct words.

① le m ...............................

② le r ...............................

③ la c ...............................

④ la n ...............................

⑤ la s ...............................

3. Look at the pictures and write the letters in the correct order.

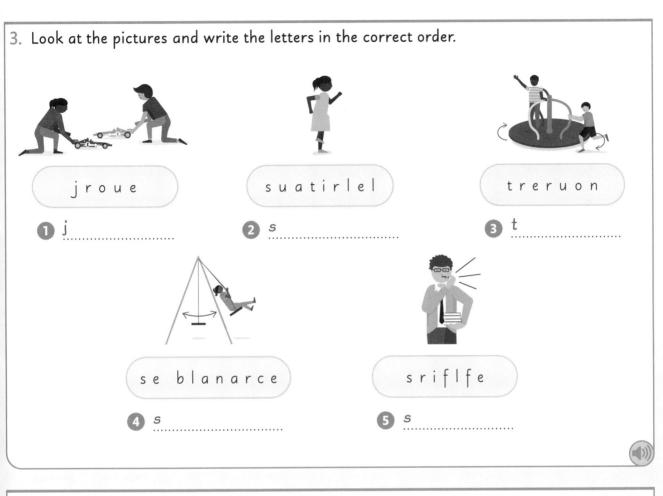

j r o u e

**1** j .................................

s u a t i r l e l

**2** s .................................

t r e r u o n

**3** t .................................

s e  b l a n a r c e

**4** s .................................

s r i f l f e

**5** s .................................

4. Match the pictures to the correct words.

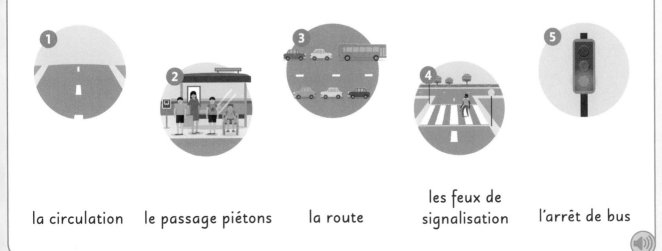

la circulation    le passage piétons    la route    les feux de signalisation    l'arrêt de bus

## Day 1

**Listen, repeat, and copy.**

① la tasse
..............

② l'assiette
..............

③ le bol
..............

④ le verre
..............

⑤ la bouteille
..............

**Listen again and write the words.**

la t ..............

l'a ..............

le b ..............

le v ..............

la b ..............

## Day 2

**Listen, repeat, and copy.**

① la ville
..............

② le gratte-ciel
..............

③ le musée
..............

④ l'université
..............

⑤ le zoo
..............

**Listen again and write the words.**

la v ..............

le g ..............

le m ..............

l'u ..............

le z ..............

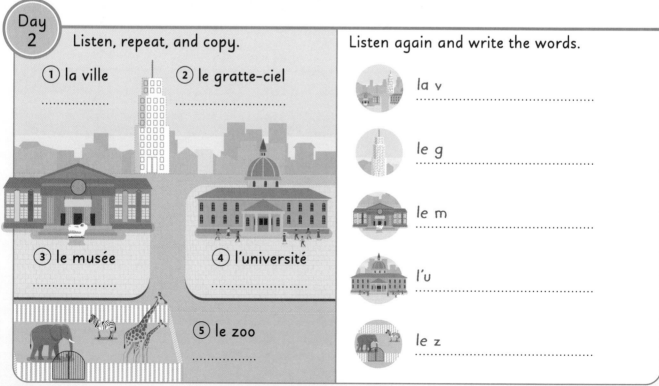

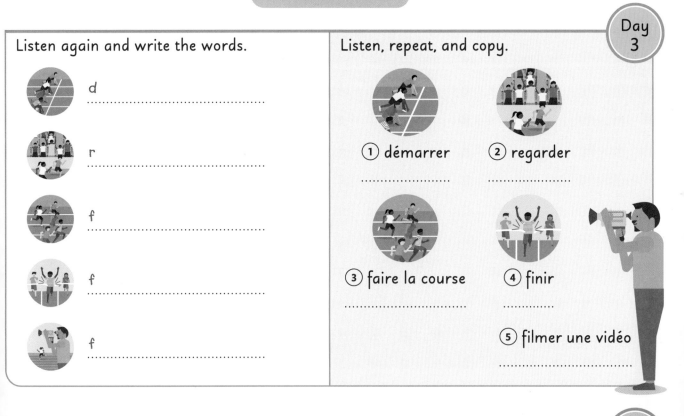

**Listen again and write the words.**

d ........................

r ........................

f ........................

f ........................

f ........................

**Listen, repeat, and copy.**

① démarrer ........................

② regarder ........................

③ faire la course ........................

④ finir ........................

⑤ filmer une vidéo ........................

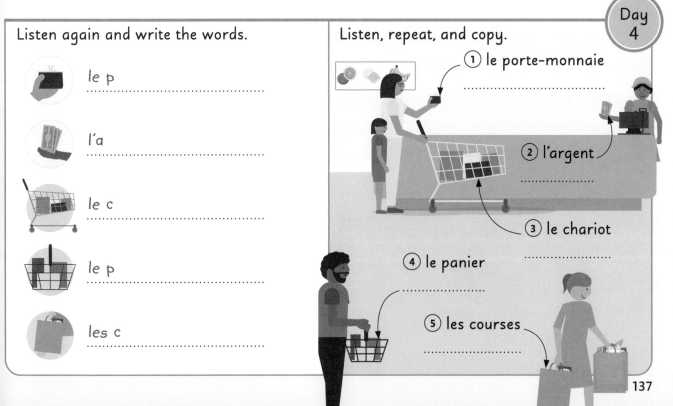

**Listen again and write the words.**

le p ........................

l'a ........................

le c ........................

le p ........................

les c ........................

**Listen, repeat, and copy.**

① le porte-monnaie ........................

② l'argent ........................

③ le chariot ........................

④ le panier ........................

⑤ les courses ........................

**Day 5**

## What can you remember from this week?

1. Look at the pictures and fill in the missing letters.

1 l'  s  i  t  e
_ _ _ _ _ _ _ _

2 _ a _ o _ t _ i _ l _
_ _ _ _ _ _ _ _ _ _

3 _ e _ e r
_ _ _ _ _ _ _ _

4 l _ b _ l
_ _ _ _ _

5 _ a _ a s
_ _ _ _ _ _ _

2. Read the words and mark the correct pictures.

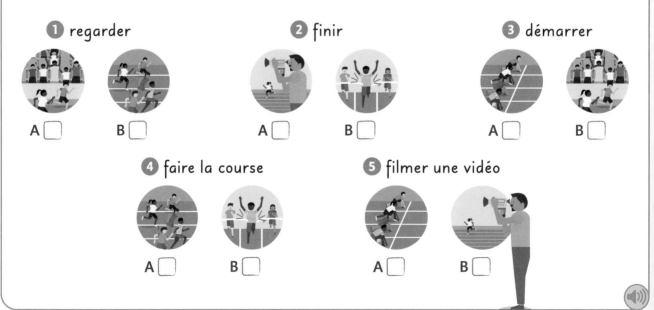

1 regarder   A ☐   B ☐

2 finir   A ☐   B ☐

3 démarrer   A ☐   B ☐

4 faire la course   A ☐   B ☐

5 filmer une vidéo   A ☐   B ☐

3. Look at the pictures and circle the correct words.

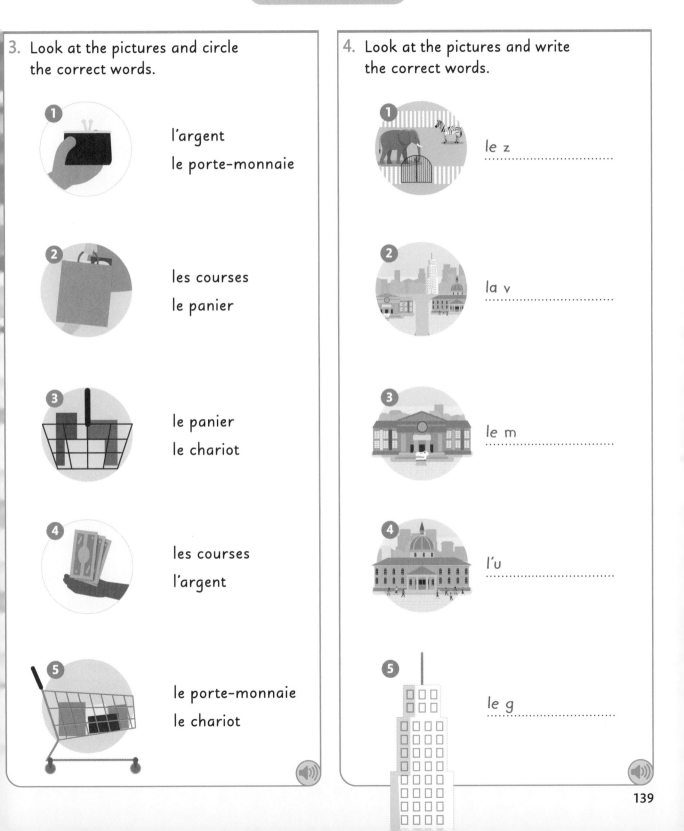

1. l'argent
   le porte-monnaie

2. les courses
   le panier

3. le panier
   le chariot

4. les courses
   l'argent

5. le porte-monnaie
   le chariot

4. Look at the pictures and write the correct words.

1. le z .................................

2. la v .................................

3. le m .................................

4. l'u .................................

5. le g .................................

139

# Week 34

## Day 1

Listen, repeat, and copy.

① le pique-nique

② le chemin

③ la couverture

④ le pont

⑤ le ruisseau

Listen again and write the words.

le p ......................

le c ......................

la c ......................

le p ......................

le r ......................

## Day 2

Listen, repeat, and copy.

① l'excursion

② la vue

③ la photo

④ la carte postale

⑤ l'appareil photo

Listen again and write the words.

l'e ......................

la v ......................

la p ......................

la c ......................

l'a ......................

# Week 34

## Listen again and write the words.

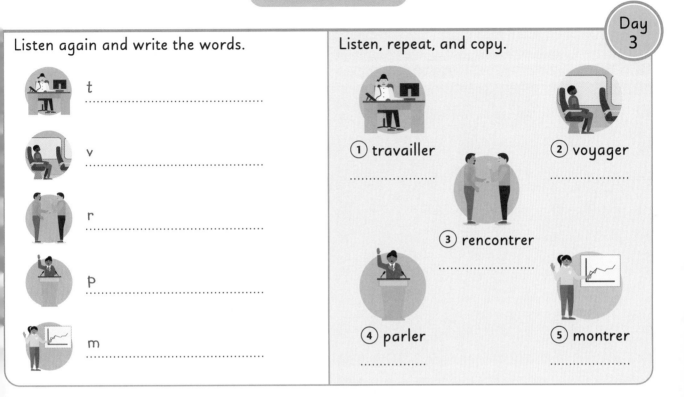

t .................................

v .................................

r .................................

p .................................

m .................................

## Listen, repeat, and copy.

① travailler
.................................

② voyager
.................................

③ rencontrer
.................................

④ parler
.................................

⑤ montrer
.................................

## Listen again and write the words.

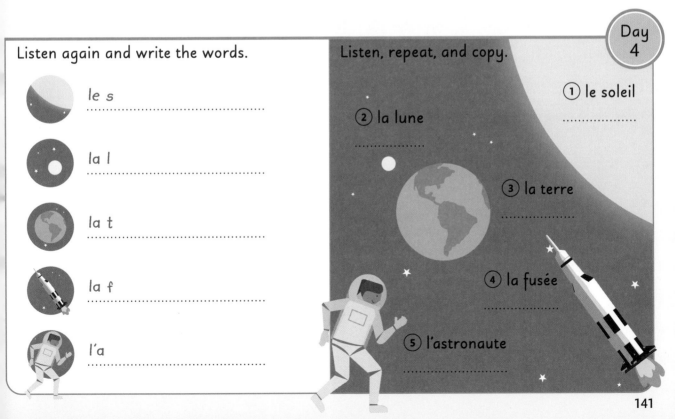

le s .................................

la l .................................

la t .................................

la f .................................

l'a .................................

## Listen, repeat, and copy.

① le soleil
.................................

② la lune
.................................

③ la terre
.................................

④ la fusée
.................................

⑤ l'astronaute
.................................

Day 5

What can you remember from this week?

1. Look at the pictures and write the letters in the correct order.

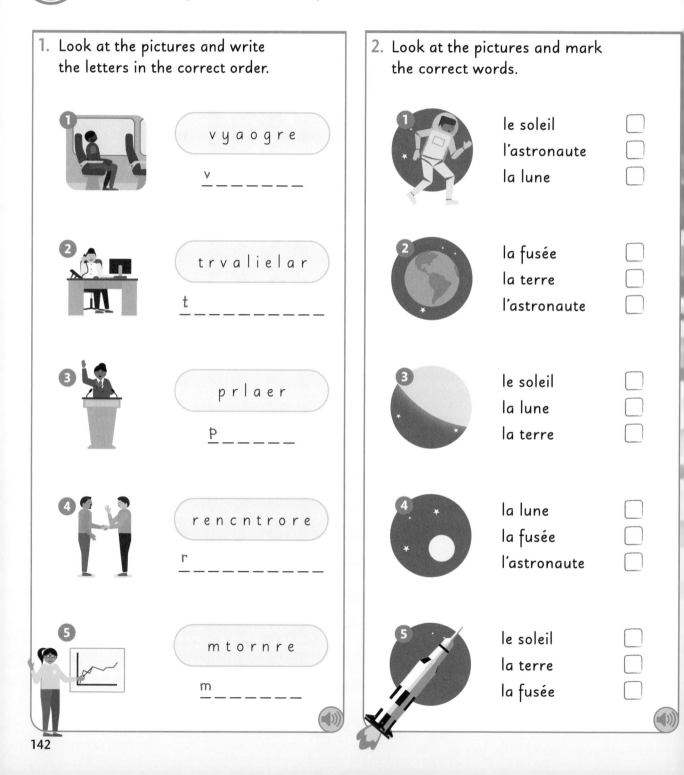

1  v y a o g r e

v _ _ _ _ _ _ _

2  t r v a l i e l a r

t _ _ _ _ _ _ _ _ _

3  p r l a e r

p _ _ _ _ _ _

4  r e n c n t r o r e

r _ _ _ _ _ _ _ _ _

5  m t o r n r e

m _ _ _ _ _ _ _

2. Look at the pictures and mark the correct words.

1  le soleil ☐
l'astronaute ☐
la lune ☐

2  la fusée ☐
la terre ☐
l'astronaute ☐

3  le soleil ☐
la lune ☐
la terre ☐

4  la lune ☐
la fusée ☐
l'astronaute ☐

5  le soleil ☐
la terre ☐
la fusée ☐

3. Look at the pictures and write the correct words.

> le chemin    le pont    le pique-nique    le ruisseau    la couverture

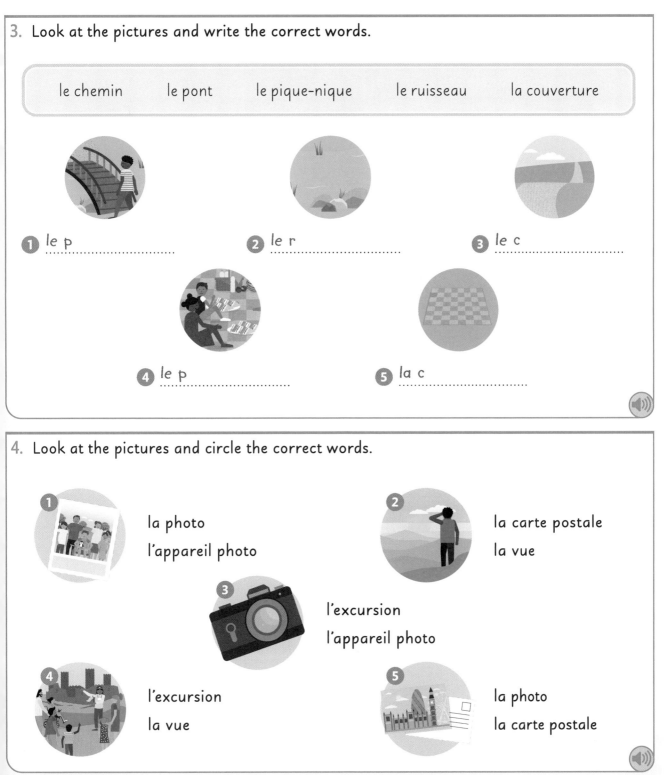

**1** le p .............................

**2** le r .............................

**3** le c .............................

**4** le p .............................

**5** la c .............................

4. Look at the pictures and circle the correct words.

**1**
la photo
l'appareil photo

**2**
la carte postale
la vue

**3**
l'excursion
l'appareil photo

**4**
l'excursion
la vue

**5**
la photo
la carte postale

**Day 1**

### Listen, repeat, and copy.

① en haut

② au milieu

③ en bas

④ petite

⑤ grand

### Listen again and write the words.

en h ............................

au m ............................

en b ............................

p ............................

g ............................

**Day 2**

### Listen, repeat, and copy.

① l'hôpital

② l'usine

③ le centre sportif

④ la banque

⑤ la caserne de pompiers

### Listen again and write the words.

l'h ............................

l'u ............................

le c ............................

la b ............................

la c ............................

# Week 35

## Listen again and write the words.

m ...........................

s ...........................

c ...........................

t ...........................

f ...........................

## Listen, repeat, and copy.

① mouillée ..................

② sèche ..................

③ chaud ..................

④ très chaud .................. ⑤ froid ..................

## Listen again and write the words.

e ...........................

c ...........................

c ...........................

é ...........................

l ...........................

## Listen, repeat, and copy.

① emprunter ..................

② chuchoter ..................

③ chercher ..................

④ étudier .................. ⑤ lire ..................

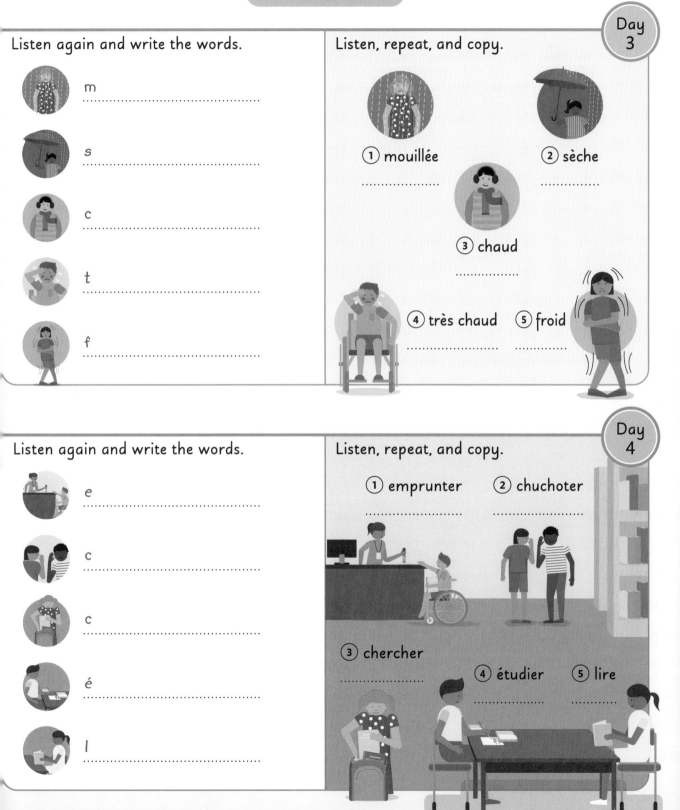

Day 5

## What can you remember from this week?

1. Read the words and mark the correct pictures.

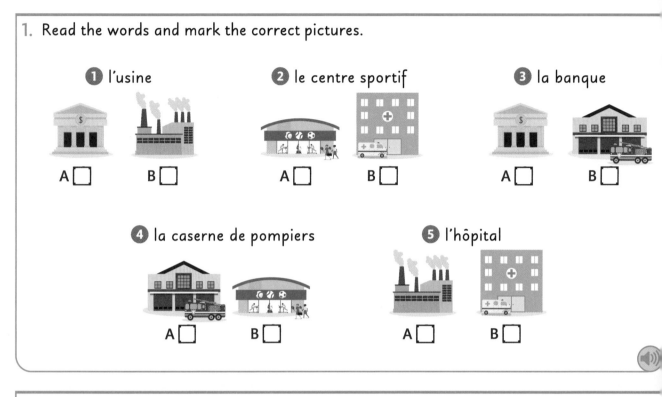

**1** l'usine

A ☐   B ☐

**2** le centre sportif

A ☐   B ☐

**3** la banque

A ☐   B ☐

**4** la caserne de pompiers

A ☐   B ☐

**5** l'hôpital

A ☐   B ☐

2. Look at the pictures and fill in the missing letters.

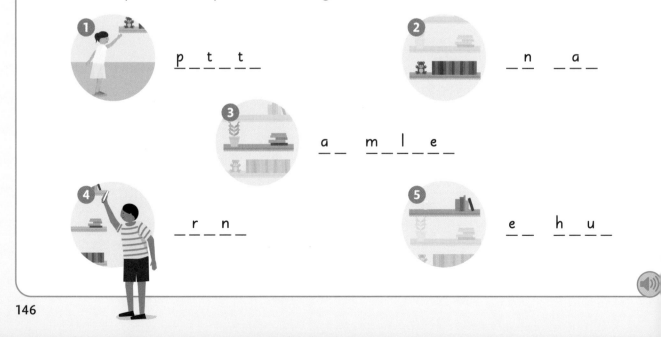

**1** p _ t _ t _

**2** _ n _ _ a _

**3** a _ m _ l _ e _

**4** _ r _ n _

**5** e _ h _ u _

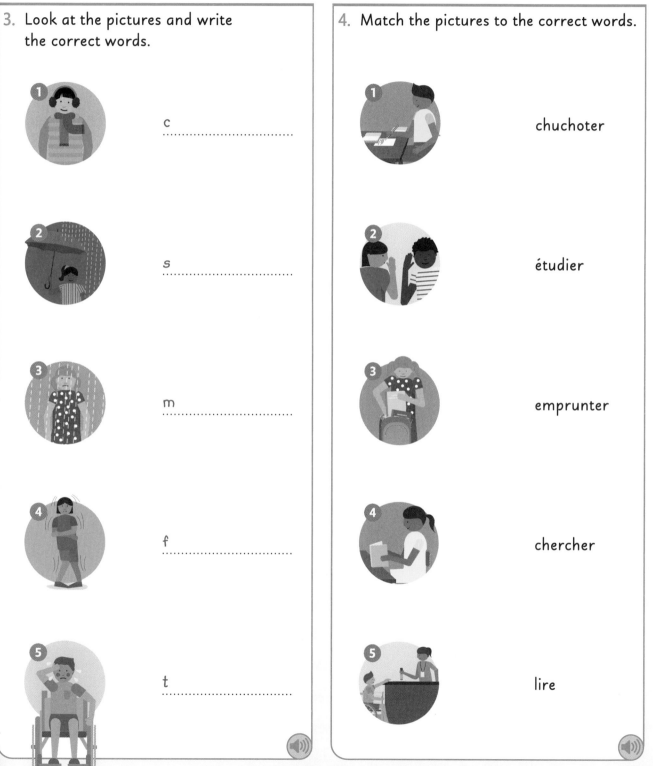

3. Look at the pictures and write the correct words.

1   c ........................................

2   s ........................................

3   m ........................................

4   f ........................................

5   t ........................................

4. Match the pictures to the correct words.

1       chuchoter

2       étudier

3       emprunter

4       chercher

5       lire

## Day 1

Listen, repeat, and copy.

① le thé

..................

② le lait

..................

③ le sucre

..................

④ le café

..................

⑤ le biscuit

..................

Listen again and write the words.

le t

..........................................

le l

..........................................

le s

..........................................

le c

..........................................

le b

..........................................

## Day 2

Listen, repeat, and copy.

① décoller

..................

② atterrir

..................

③ descendre

..................

④ monter

..................

⑤ se dépêcher

..................

Listen again and write the words.

d

..........................................

a

..........................................

d

..........................................

m

..........................................

s

..........................................

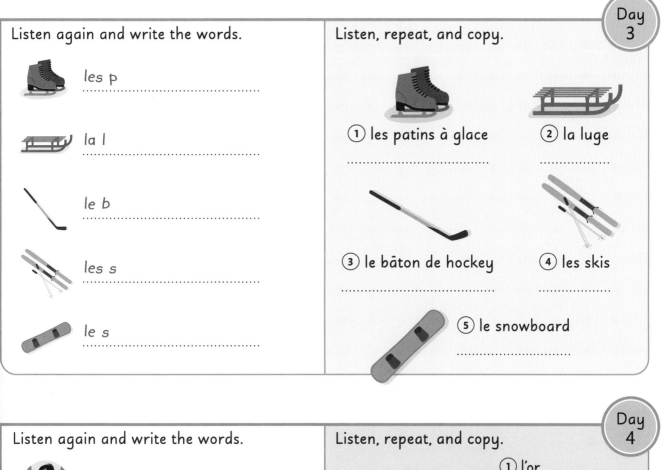

**Listen again and write the words.**

les p ...............................

la l ...............................

le b ...............................

les s ...............................

le s ...............................

**Listen, repeat, and copy.**

① les patins à glace ...............................

② la luge ...............................

③ le bâton de hockey ...............................

④ les skis ...............................

⑤ le snowboard ...............................

**Listen again and write the words.**

l'o ...............................

l'a ...............................

le b ...............................

la c ...............................

le g ...............................

**Listen, repeat, and copy.**

① l'or ...............................

② l'argent ...............................

③ le bronze ...............................

④ la course ...............................

⑤ le gagnant ...............................

Day 5

What can you remember from this week?

1. Look at the pictures and write the correct words.

le lait   le thé   le café
le sucre   le biscuit

1 le t .....................................

2 le b .....................................

3 le c .....................................

4 le l .....................................

5 le s .....................................

2. Look at the pictures and circle the correct words.

1 la course / l'or

2 le gagnant / l'argent

3 l'argent / l'or

4 le gagnant / le bronze

5 le bronze / la course

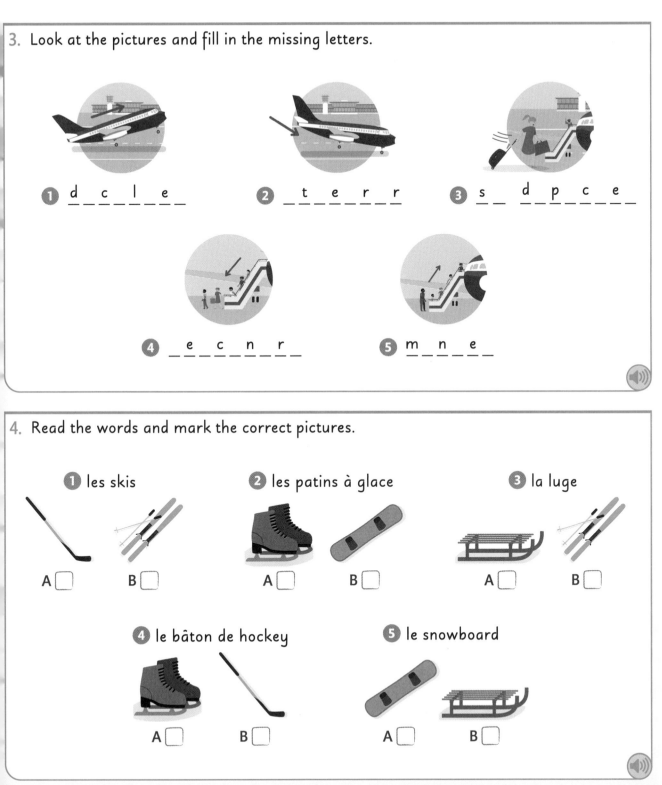

3. Look at the pictures and fill in the missing letters.

1 d _ c _ l _ e _

2 _ t _ e _ r _ r _

3 s _ _ _ d _ p _ c _ e _

4 _ e _ c _ n _ r _

5 m _ n _ e _

4. Read the words and mark the correct pictures.

1 les skis

A ☐    B ☐

2 les patins à glace

A ☐    B ☐

3 la luge

A ☐    B ☐

4 le bâton de hockey

A ☐    B ☐

5 le snowboard

A ☐    B ☐

## Day 1

Listen, repeat, and copy.

① l'herbe

② le cygne

③ le canard

④ l'étang

⑤ la grenouille

Listen again and write the words.

l'h
..................................

le c
..................................

le c
..................................

l'é
..................................

la g
..................................

## Day 2

Listen, repeat, and copy.

① préparer

② commander

③ payer

④ aimer

⑤ ne pas aimer

Listen again and write the words.

p
..................................

c
..................................

p
..................................

a
..................................

n
..................................

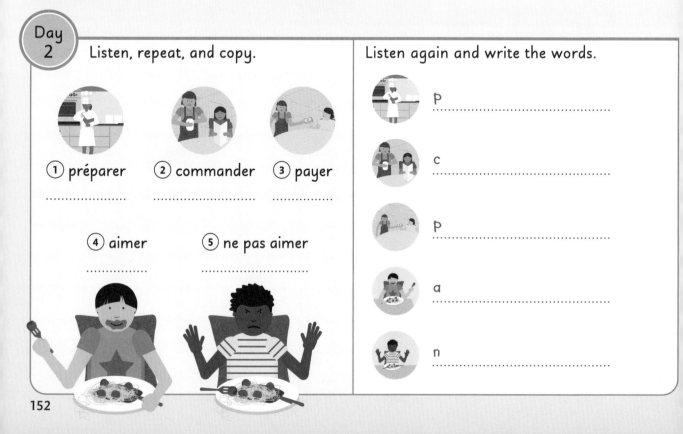

### Listen again and write the words.

l'o

le m

le p

le p

le r

### Listen, repeat, and copy.

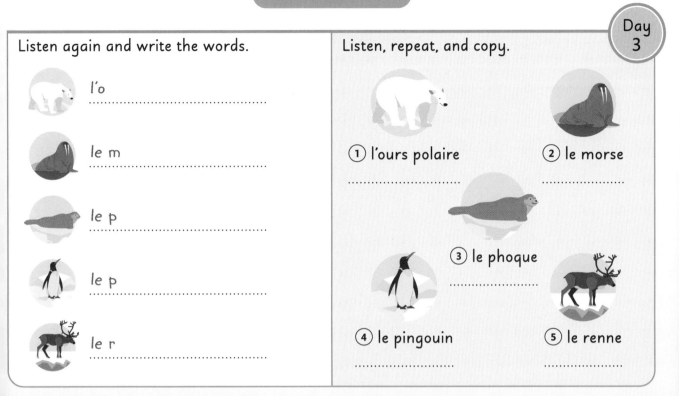

① l'ours polaire

② le morse

③ le phoque

④ le pingouin

⑤ le renne

### Listen again and write the words.

le p

les b

les l

le p

la b

### Listen, repeat, and copy.

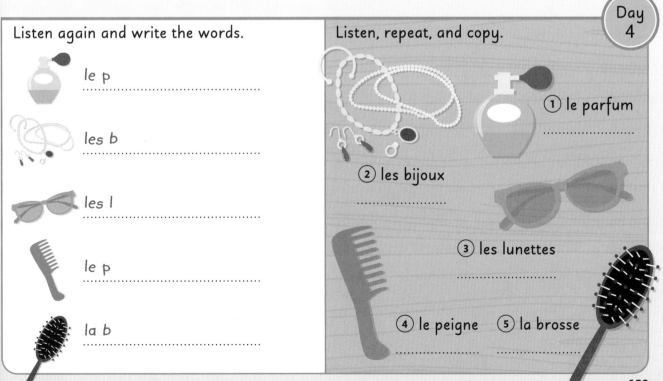

① le parfum

② les bijoux

③ les lunettes

④ le peigne   ⑤ la brosse

Day
5

What can you remember from this week?

1. Look at the pictures and write the correct words.

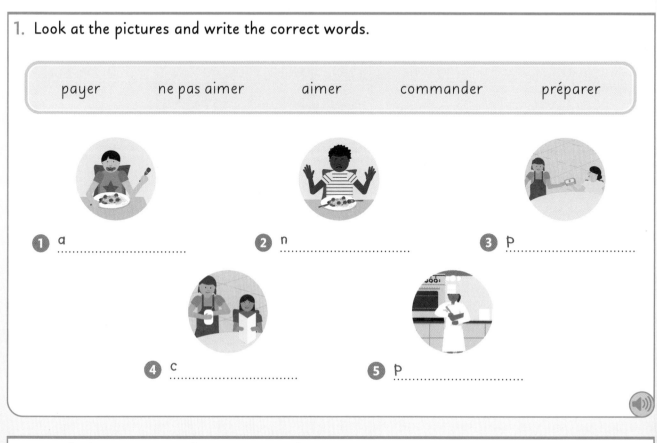

payer          ne pas aimer          aimer          commander          préparer

1 a ..............................

2 n ..............................

3 p ..............................

4 c ..............................

5 p ..............................

2. Match the pictures to the correct words.

la brosse          le peigne          les bijoux          les lunettes          le parfum

3. Look at the pictures and mark the correct words.

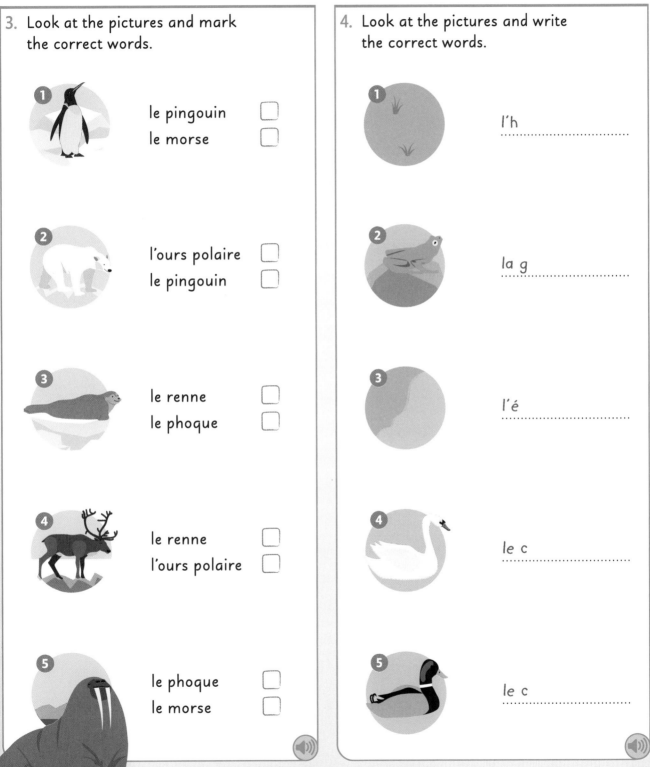

1. le pingouin ☐
   le morse ☐

2. l'ours polaire ☐
   le pingouin ☐

3. le renne ☐
   le phoque ☐

4. le renne ☐
   l'ours polaire ☐

5. le phoque ☐
   le morse ☐

4. Look at the pictures and write the correct words.

1. l'h .....................................

2. la g .....................................

3. l'é .....................................

4. le c .....................................

5. le c .....................................

**Day 1**

Listen, repeat, and copy.

① la salade

......................

② la tomate   ③ le fromage

......................

④ les olives

......................

⑤ la laitue

......................

Listen again and write the words.

la s ......................

la t ......................

le f ......................

les o ......................

la l ......................

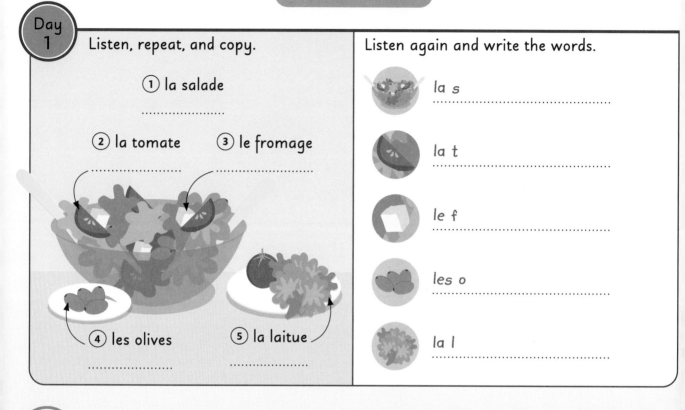

**Day 2**

Listen, repeat, and copy.

① bruns

......................

② blonds

......................

③ noirs

......................

④ gris

......................

⑤ roux

......................

Listen again and write the words.

b ......................

b ......................

n ......................

g ......................

r ......................

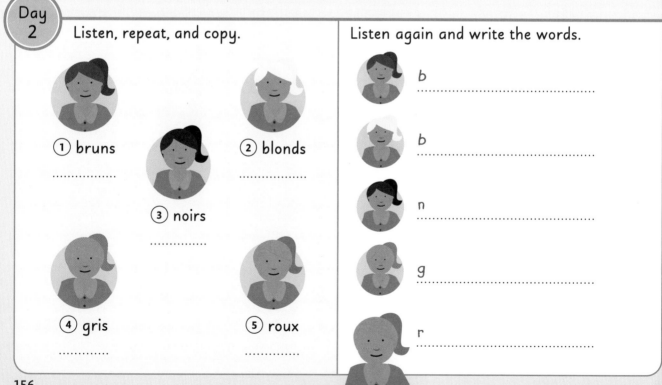

# Week 38

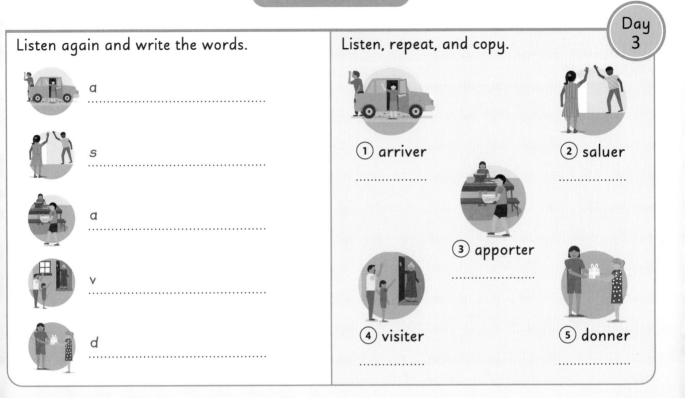

**Listen again and write the words.**

a ...................

s ...................

a ...................

v ...................

d ...................

**Listen, repeat, and copy.**

① arriver    ② saluer

...............    ...............

③ apporter

...............

④ visiter    ⑤ donner

...............    ...............

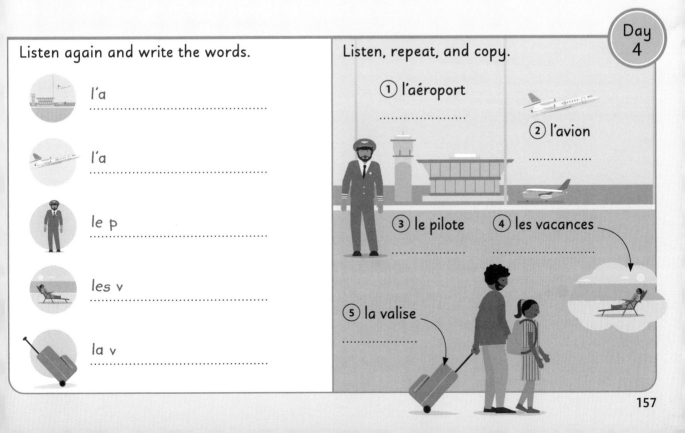

**Listen again and write the words.**

l'a ...................

l'a ...................

le p ...................

les v ...................

la v ...................

**Listen, repeat, and copy.**

① l'aéroport

...............

② l'avion

...............

③ le pilote    ④ les vacances

...............    ...............

⑤ la valise

...............

Day 5

What can you remember from this week?

1. Look at the pictures and mark the correct words.

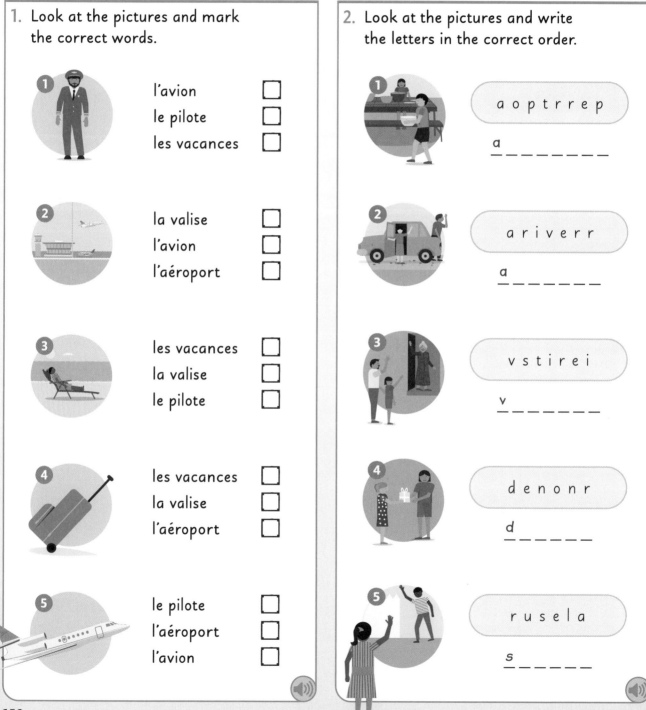

1.
- l'avion ☐
- le pilote ☐
- les vacances ☐

2.
- la valise ☐
- l'avion ☐
- l'aéroport ☐

3.
- les vacances ☐
- la valise ☐
- le pilote ☐

4.
- les vacances ☐
- la valise ☐
- l'aéroport ☐

5.
- le pilote ☐
- l'aéroport ☐
- l'avion ☐

2. Look at the pictures and write the letters in the correct order.

1. a o p t r r e p

a _ _ _ _ _ _ _

2. a r i v e r r

a _ _ _ _ _ _

3. v s t i r e i

v _ _ _ _ _ _

4. d e n o n r

d _ _ _ _ _

5. r u s e l a

s _ _ _ _ _

3. Look at the pictures and write the correct words.

| gris | blonds | noirs | roux | bruns |

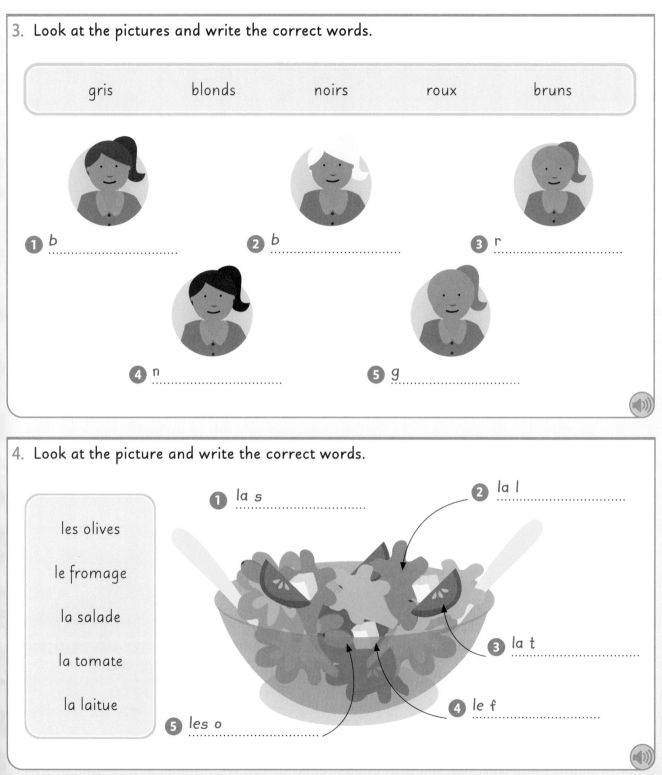

1 b ............................................

2 b ............................................

3 r ............................................

4 n ............................................

5 g ............................................

4. Look at the picture and write the correct words.

les olives

le fromage

la salade

la tomate

la laitue

1 la s ............................................

2 la l ............................................

3 la t ............................................

4 le f ............................................

5 les o ............................................

### Day 1

Listen, repeat, and copy.

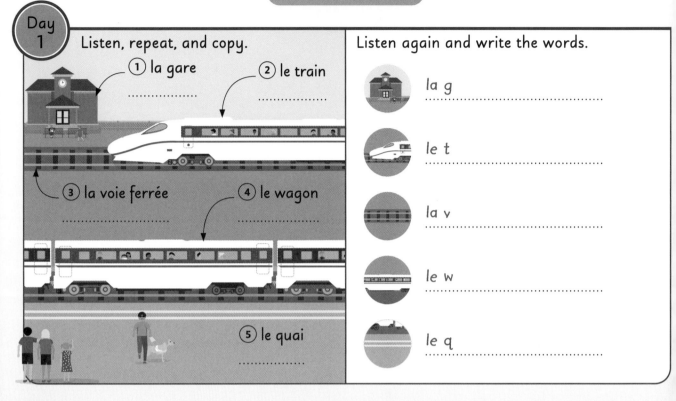

① la gare
...................

② le train
...................

③ la voie ferrée
...................

④ le wagon
...................

⑤ le quai
...................

Listen again and write the words.

la g .......................................

le t .......................................

la v .......................................

le w .......................................

le q .......................................

### Day 2

Listen, repeat, and copy.

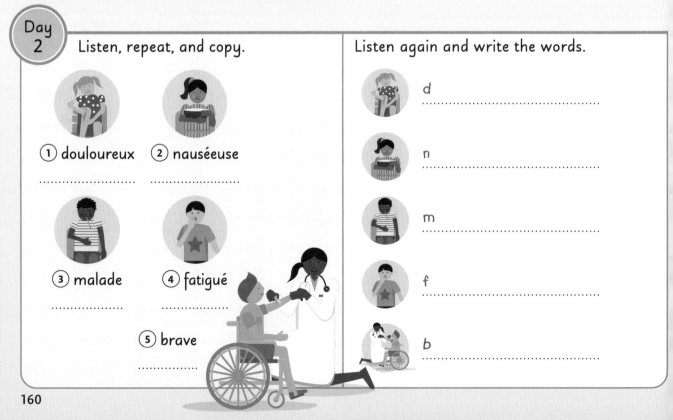

① douloureux
........................

② nauséeuse
........................

③ malade
...............

④ fatigué
................

⑤ brave
...............

Listen again and write the words.

d .......................................

n .......................................

m .......................................

f .......................................

b .......................................

Listen again and write the words.

le m .................................

le s .................................

le t .................................

le j .................................

l'é .................................

Listen, repeat, and copy.

① le match .................

② le score .................

③ le tir ..............

④ le joueur .................

⑤ l'équipe .................

Listen again and write the words.

le p .................................

la m .................................

l'a .................................

le c .................................

l'e .................................

Listen, repeat, and copy.

① le papillon .................

② la mouche .................

③ l'araignée .................

④ le coléoptère .................

⑤ l'escargot .................

Day 5

What can you remember from this week?

1. Look at the pictures and circle the correct words.

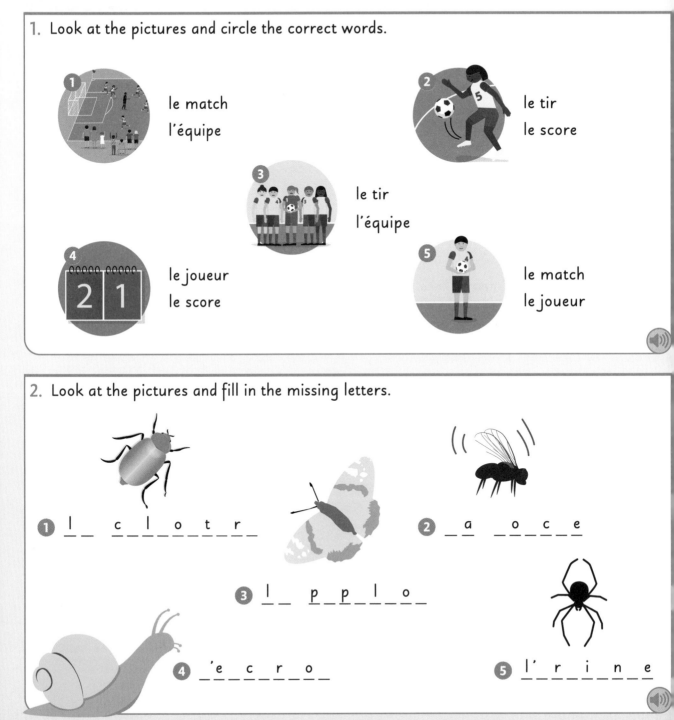

1. le match
   l'équipe

2. le tir
   le score

3. le tir
   l'équipe

4. le joueur
   le score

5. le match
   le joueur

2. Look at the pictures and fill in the missing letters.

1. l _ c _ l o t r _

2. _ a _ o c _ e

3. l _ p p _ l o _

4. _ ' e c r o _

5. l ' r i n e

## 3. Look at the pictures and write the letters in the correct order.

1. b r v a e

b _ _ _ _ _

2. n u e a s é s e u

n _ _ _ _ _ _ _ _

3. d r u o l o u e x u

d _ _ _ _ _ _ _ _ _

4. f t g a u é i

f _ _ _ _ _ _

5. m l a d a e

m _ _ _ _ _

## 4. Read the words and mark the correct pictures.

1. le train     A ☐     B ☐

2. la gare     A ☐     B ☐

3. le quai     A ☐     B ☐

4. la voie ferrée     A ☐     B ☐

5. le wagon     A ☐     B ☐

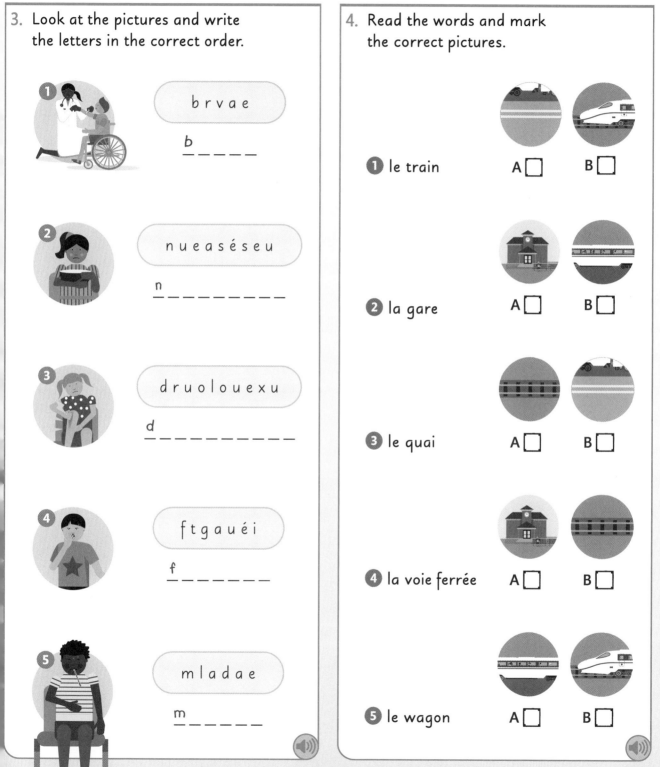

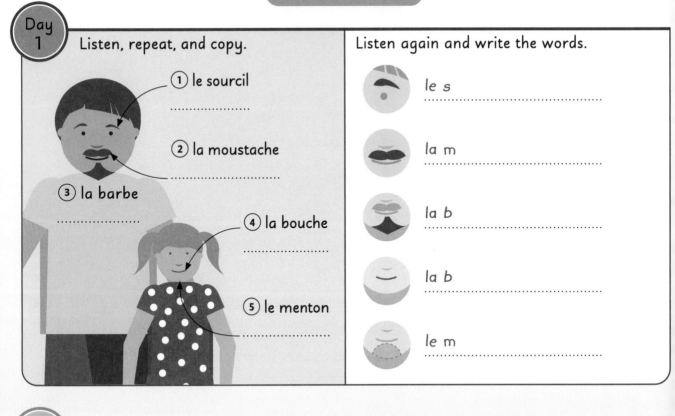

**Day 1**

Listen, repeat, and copy.

① le sourcil

..................

② la moustache

..................

③ la barbe

..................

④ la bouche

..................

⑤ le menton

..................

Listen again and write the words.

le s ..................

la m ..................

la b ..................

la b ..................

le m ..................

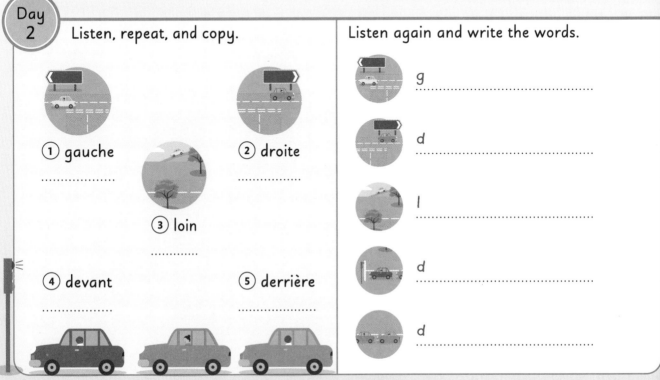

**Day 2**

Listen, repeat, and copy.

① gauche

..................

② droite

..................

③ loin

..................

④ devant

..................

⑤ derrière

..................

Listen again and write the words.

g ..................

d ..................

l ..................

d ..................

d ..................

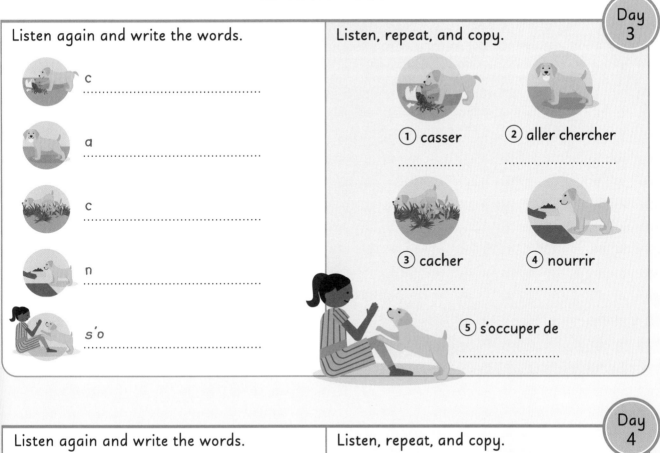

**Day 3**

Listen again and write the words.

c
.................................

a
.................................

c
.................................

n
.................................

s'o
.................................

Listen, repeat, and copy.

① casser
..................

② aller chercher
..........................

③ cacher
..................

④ nourrir
..................

⑤ s'occuper de
.........................

**Day 4**

Listen again and write the words.

c
.................................

s
.................................

r
.................................

e
.................................

f
.................................

Listen, repeat, and copy.

① clair
...............

② sombre
...................

③ réveillé
.................

④ endormi
..................

⑤ fort
...............

## What can you remember from this week?

1. Look at the pictures and write the letters in the correct order.

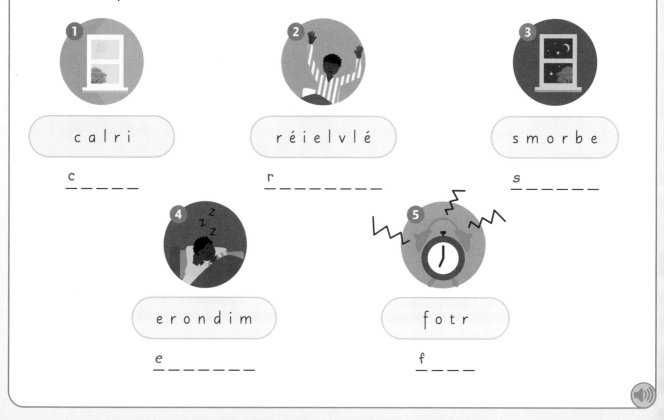

**1** c a l r i

c _ _ _ _ _

**2** r é i e l v l é

r _ _ _ _ _ _ _ _

**3** s m o r b e

s _ _ _ _ _

**4** e r o n d i m

e _ _ _ _ _ _ _

**5** f o t r

f _ _ _ _

2. Match the pictures to the correct words.

aller chercher          cacher          s'occuper de          nourrir          casser

3. Look at the pictures and mark the correct words.

1. loin ☐
droite ☐

2. derrière ☐
gauche ☐

3. loin ☐
derrière ☐

4. devant ☐
droite ☐

5. devant ☐
gauche ☐

4. Look at the pictures and write the correct words.

le sourcil    la bouche    le menton
la moustache    la barbe

1 la b ........................

2 le m ........................

3 le s ........................

4 la m ........................

5 la b ........................

# Week 41

## Day 1

Listen, repeat, and copy.

① couper

......................

② faire pousser

......................

③ arroser

......................

④ planter

......................

⑤ cueillir

......................

Listen again and write the words.

c ...............................

f ...............................

a ...............................

p ...............................

c ...............................

## Day 2

Listen, repeat, and copy.

① la musique

......................

② le groupe

......................

③ le musicien

......................

④ la pop star

......................

⑤ le festival

......................

Listen again and write the words.

la m ...........................

le g ...........................

le m ...........................

la p ...........................

le f ...........................

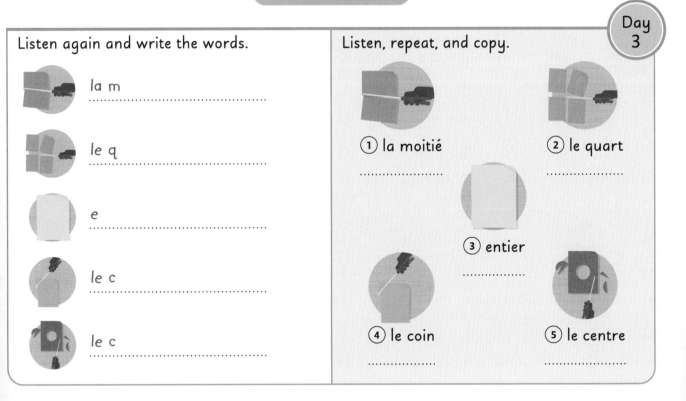

**Day 3**

### Listen again and write the words.

la m ..............................

le q ..............................

e ..............................

le c ..............................

le c ..............................

### Listen, repeat, and copy.

① la moitié ..............................

② le quart ..............................

③ entier ..............................

④ le coin ..............................

⑤ le centre ..............................

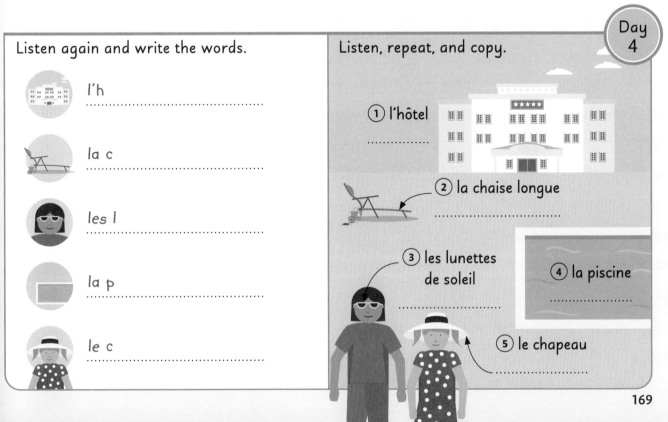

**Day 4**

### Listen again and write the words.

l'h ..............................

la c ..............................

les l ..............................

la p ..............................

le c ..............................

### Listen, repeat, and copy.

① l'hôtel ..............................

② la chaise longue ..............................

③ les lunettes de soleil ..............................

④ la piscine ..............................

⑤ le chapeau ..............................

**Day 5**

# What can you remember from this week?

**1.** Look at the pictures and write the correct words.

le centre    entier    la moitié
le coin    le quart

1. e ...........................................

2. le c ...........................................

3. la m ...........................................

4. le c ...........................................

5. le q ...........................................

**2.** Look at the pictures and circle the correct words.

1. les lunettes de soleil
   la piscine

2. le chapeau
   la chaise longue

3. l'hôtel
   la piscine

4. la chaise longue
   l'hôtel

5. le chapeau
   les lunettes de soleil

3. Read the words and mark the correct pictures.

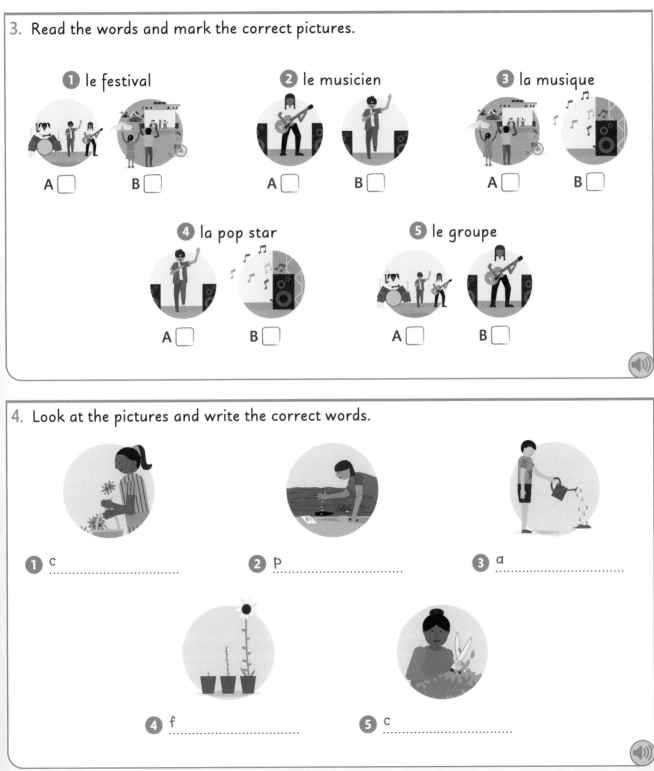

1 le festival
A ☐   B ☐

2 le musicien
A ☐   B ☐

3 la musique
A ☐   B ☐

4 la pop star
A ☐   B ☐

5 le groupe
A ☐   B ☐

4. Look at the pictures and write the correct words.

1 c ............................

2 p ............................

3 a ............................

4 f ............................

5 c ............................

## Day 1

Listen, repeat, and copy.

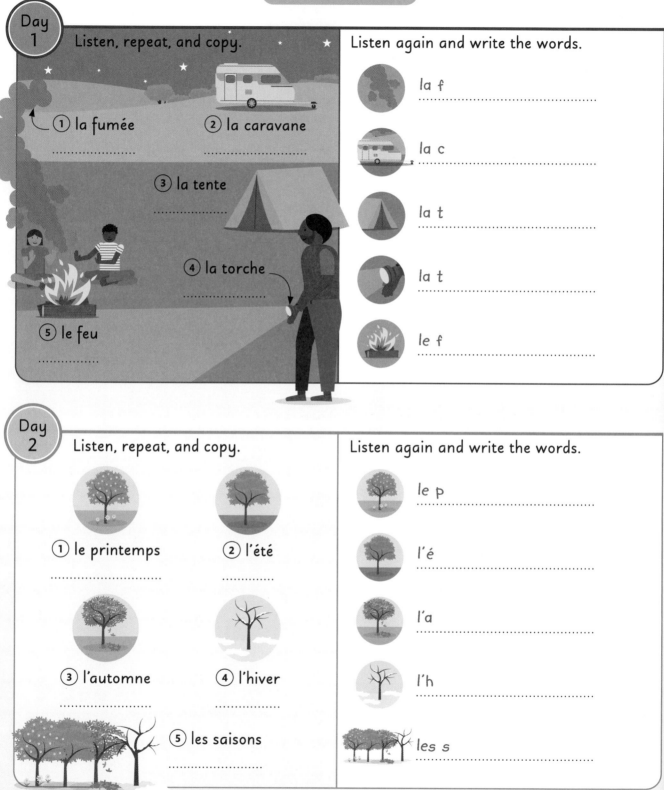

① la fumée ..................

② la caravane ..................

③ la tente ..................

④ la torche ..................

⑤ le feu ..................

Listen again and write the words.

la f ..................

la c ..................

la t ..................

la t ..................

le f ..................

## Day 2

Listen, repeat, and copy.

① le printemps ..................

② l'été ..................

③ l'automne ..................

④ l'hiver ..................

⑤ les saisons ..................

Listen again and write the words.

le p ..................

l'é ..................

l'a ..................

l'h ..................

les s ..................

# Week 42

## Listen again and write the words.

`12:01` l'h
..................................

`12:00` l'h
..................................

`12:01` la m
..................................

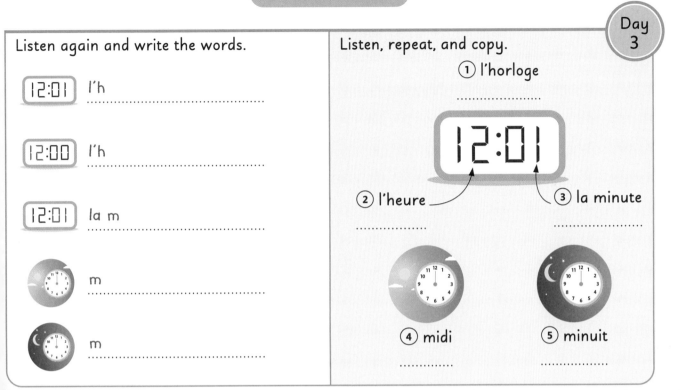 m
..................................

m
..................................

## Listen, repeat, and copy.

① l'horloge
..................................

② l'heure
..................................

③ la minute
..................................

④ midi
..................................

⑤ minuit
..................................

## Listen again and write the words.

l'i
..................................

la m
..................................

la b
..................................

la c
..................................

les o
..................................

## Listen, repeat, and copy.

① l'ingénieure
..................................

② la machine
..................................

③ la boîte à outils
..................................

④ la colle
..................................

⑤ les outils
..................................

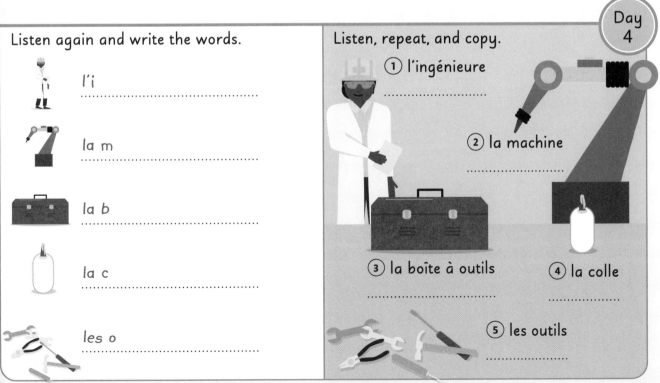

Day 5

## What can you remember from this week?

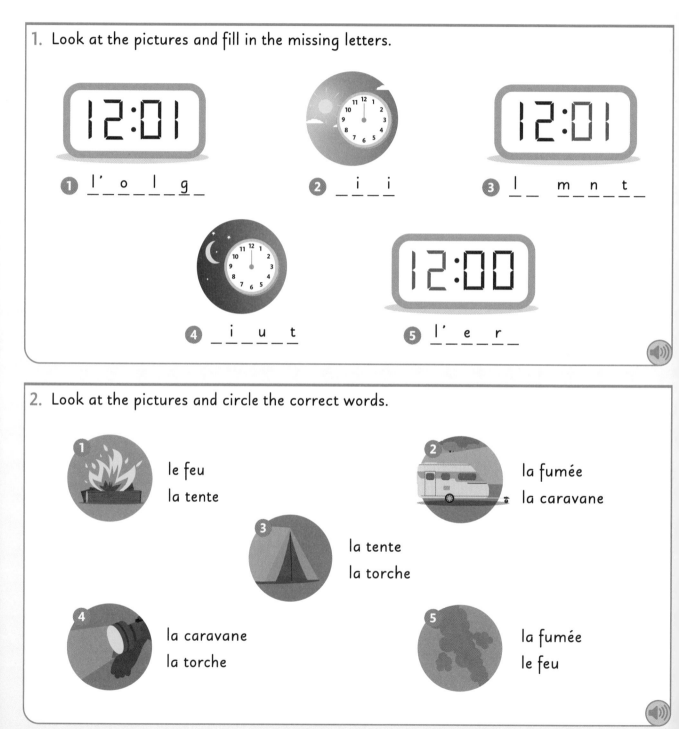

1. Look at the pictures and fill in the missing letters.

① l'_ _ o _ l _ g _

② _ i _ i

③ l _ _ m _ n _ t _

④ _ i _ u _ t

⑤ l' _ e _ r _

2. Look at the pictures and circle the correct words.

1. le feu
   la tente

2. la fumée
   la caravane

3. la tente
   la torche

4. la caravane
   la torche

5. la fumée
   le feu

3. Look at the pictures and write the correct words.

**1** l'é .........................................

**2** l'h .........................................

**3** l'a .........................................

**4** le p .........................................

**5** les s .........................................

4. Look at the pictures and mark the correct words.

**1** la colle ☐
la machine ☐

**2** les outils ☐
l'ingénieure ☐

**3** la boîte à outils ☐
la colle ☐

**4** l'ingénieure ☐
les outils ☐

**5** la machine ☐
la boîte à outils ☐

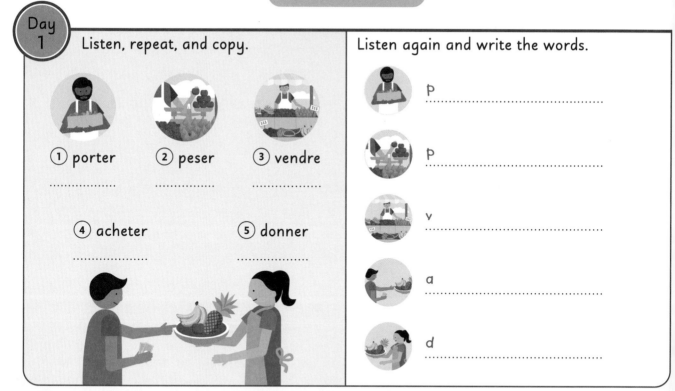

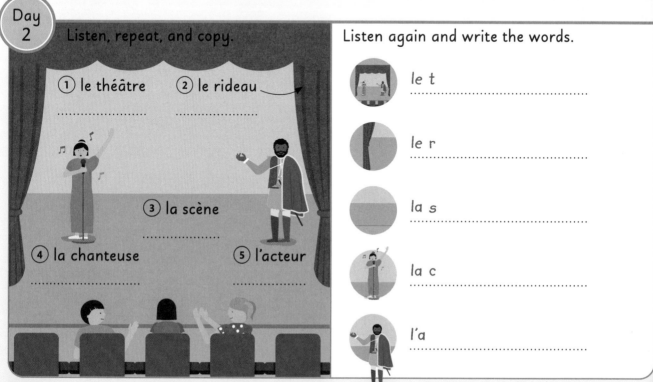

## Day 1

Listen, repeat, and copy.

① porter

② peser

③ vendre

④ acheter

⑤ donner

Listen again and write the words.

p .................................

p .................................

v .................................

a .................................

d .................................

## Day 2

Listen, repeat, and copy.

① le théâtre    ② le rideau

③ la scène

④ la chanteuse    ⑤ l'acteur

Listen again and write the words.

le t .................................

le r .................................

la s .................................

la c .................................

l'a .................................

# Week 43

## Listen again and write the words.

le d .....................

le b .....................

la p .....................

le c .....................

le s .....................

## Listen, repeat, and copy.

① le drapeau
.....................

② le ballon de plage
.....................

③ la pelle
.....................

④ le château de sable
.....................

⑤ le seau
.....................

## Listen again and write the words.

la s .....................

le w .....................

le m .....................

l'a .....................

l'a .....................

## Listen, repeat, and copy.

① la semaine
.....................

② le week-end
.....................

③ le mois
.....................

④ l'année
.....................

⑤ l'agenda
.....................

Day 5    What can you remember from this week?

1. Look at the pictures and write the letters in the correct order.

p e s r e

p _ _ _ _ _

a h c t e e r

a _ _ _ _ _ _

d n r n o e

d _ _ _ _ _

v n e r e d

v _ _ _ _ _

p t r o r e

p _ _ _ _ _

2. Look at the pictures and circle the correct words.

1   le théâtre
    l'acteur

2   le rideau
    la chanteuse

3   l'acteur
    la scène

4   la chanteuse
    la scène

5   le rideau
    le théâtre

3. Match the pictures to the correct words.

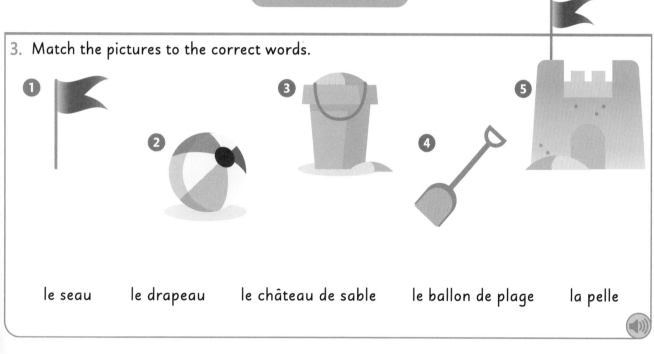

le seau     le drapeau     le château de sable     le ballon de plage     la pelle

4. Look at the pictures and write the correct words.

la semaine     le mois     le week-end     l'année     l'agenda

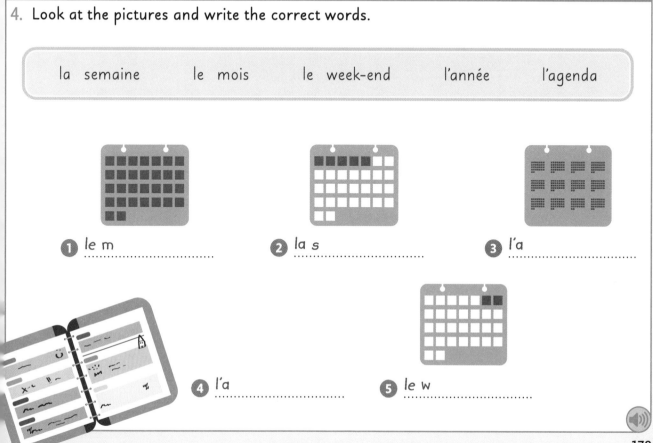

1 le m .........................................

2 la s .........................................

3 l'a .........................................

4 l'a .........................................

5 le w .........................................

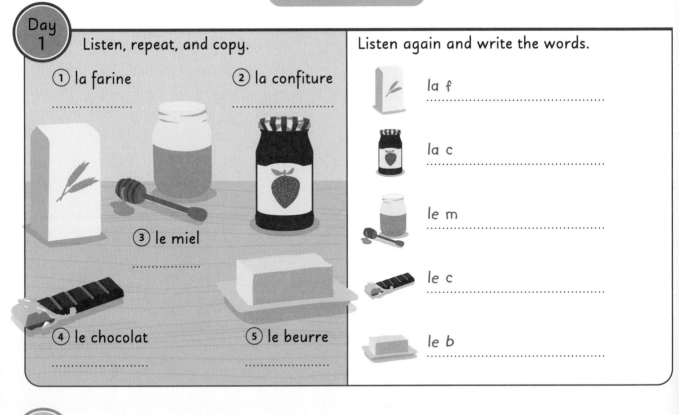

**Day 1**

Listen, repeat, and copy.

① la farine

② la confiture

③ le miel

④ le chocolat

⑤ le beurre

Listen again and write the words.

la f

la c

le m

le c

le b

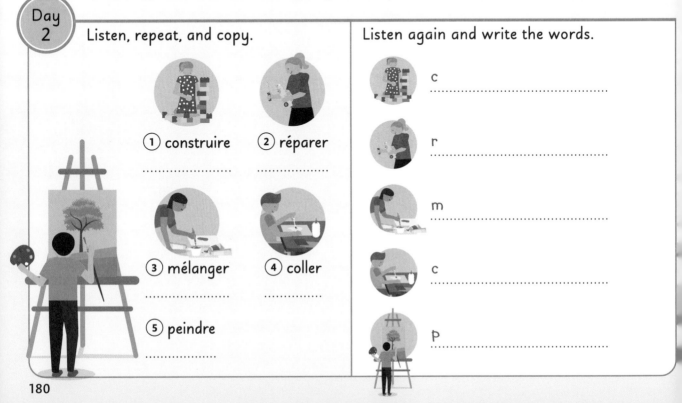

**Day 2**

Listen, repeat, and copy.

① construire

② réparer

③ mélanger

④ coller

⑤ peindre

Listen again and write the words.

c

r

m

c

p

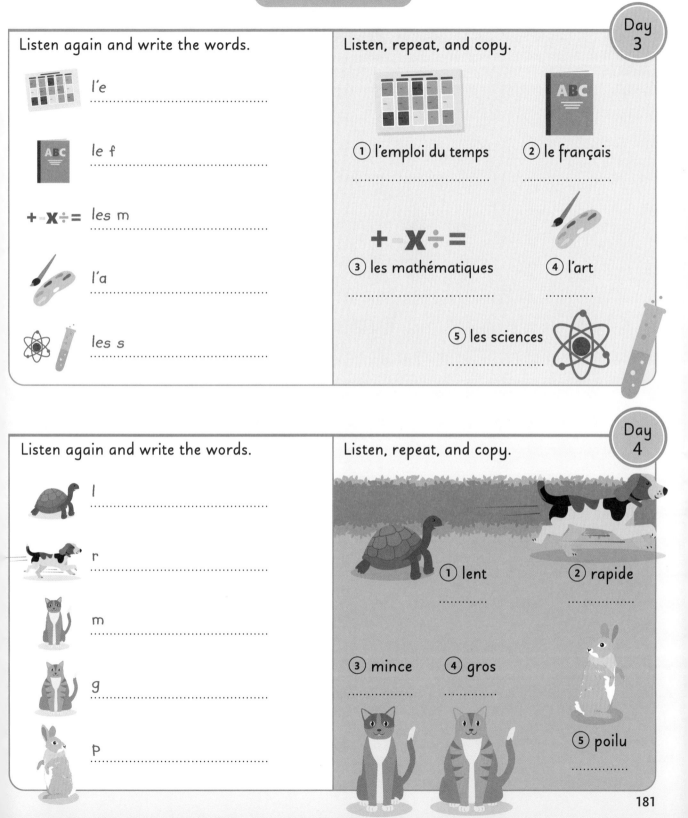

**Listen again and write the words.**

l'e ................................................

le f ................................................

les m ................................................

l'a ................................................

les s ................................................

**Listen, repeat, and copy.**

① l'emploi du temps ................................................

② le français ................................................

③ les mathématiques ................................................

④ l'art ................................................

⑤ les sciences ................................................

**Listen again and write the words.**

l ................................................

r ................................................

m ................................................

g ................................................

p ................................................

**Listen, repeat, and copy.**

① lent ................................................

② rapide ................................................

③ mince ................................................

④ gros ................................................

⑤ poilu ................................................

Day 5

What can you remember from this week?

1. Look at the pictures and circle the correct words.

1 le français
l'art

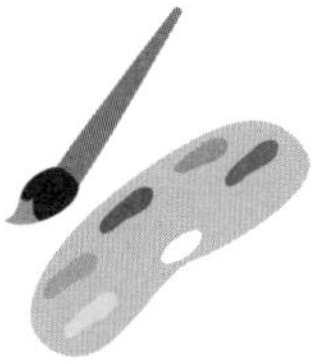

2 **+ - X ÷ =** les mathématiques
les sciences

3 l'emploi du temps
les sciences

4 **ABC** le français
les mathématiques

5 l'art
l'emploi du temps

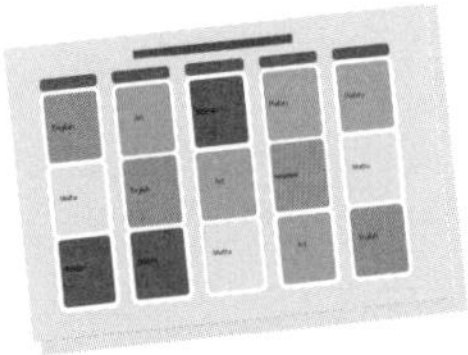

2. Look at the pictures and fill in the missing letters.

1 c _ n _ t _ u _ r _

2 _ e _ n _ r _

3 m _ l _ n _ e _

4 _ é _ a _ e _

5 c _ l _ e _

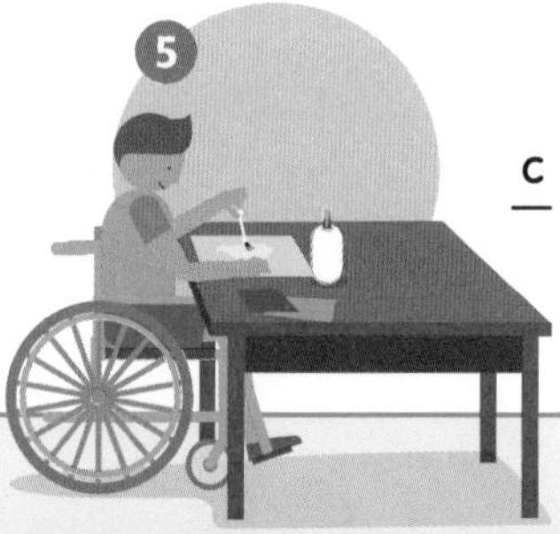

3. Look at the pictures and mark the correct words.

1.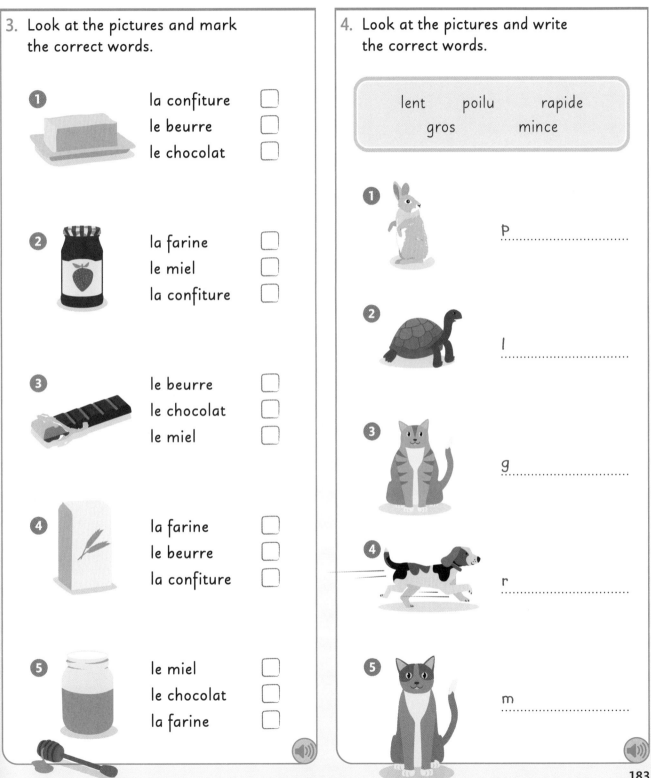
   - la confiture ☐
   - le beurre ☐
   - le chocolat ☐

2.
   - la farine ☐
   - le miel ☐
   - la confiture ☐

3.
   - le beurre ☐
   - le chocolat ☐
   - le miel ☐

4.
   - la farine ☐
   - le beurre ☐
   - la confiture ☐

5.
   - le miel ☐
   - le chocolat ☐
   - la farine ☐

4. Look at the pictures and write the correct words.

lent    poilu    rapide
gros       mince

1. p.................................

2. l.................................

3. g.................................

4. r.................................

5. m.................................

**Day 1**

Listen, repeat, and copy.

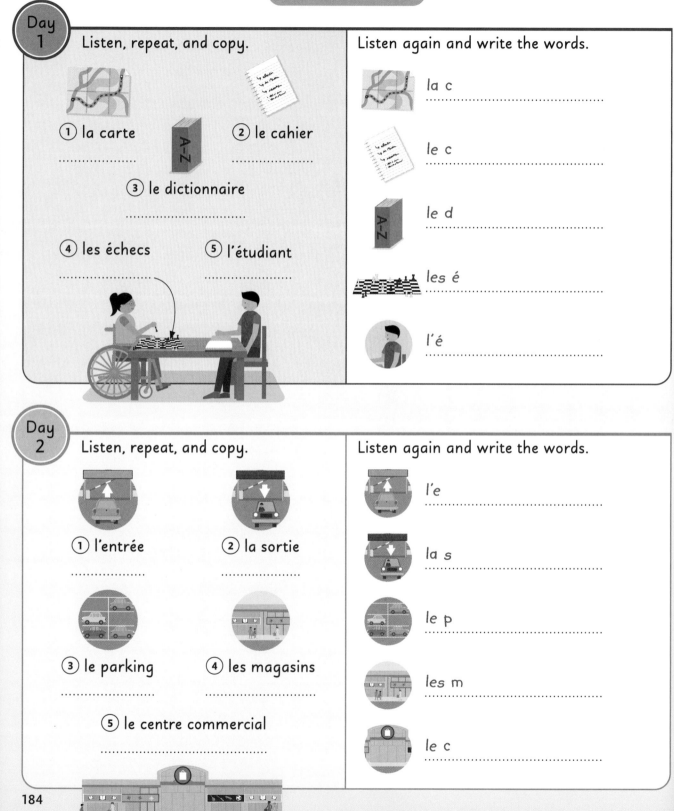

① la carte

② le cahier

③ le dictionnaire

④ les échecs

⑤ l'étudiant

Listen again and write the words.

la c ...................

le c ...................

le d ...................

les é ...................

l'é ...................

**Day 2**

Listen, repeat, and copy.

① l'entrée

② la sortie

③ le parking

④ les magasins

⑤ le centre commercial

Listen again and write the words.

l'e ...................

la s ...................

le p ...................

les m ...................

le c ...................

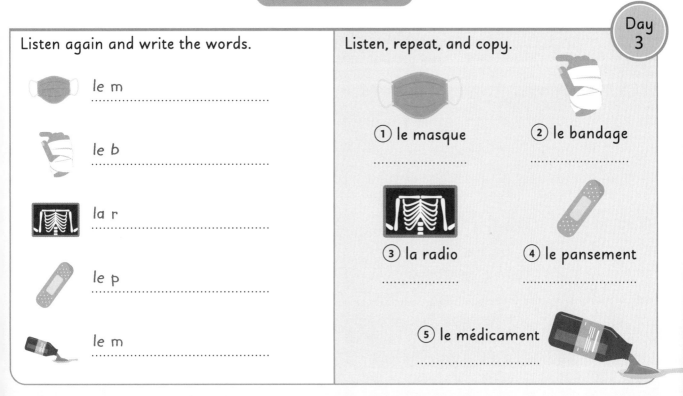

**Day 3**

Listen again and write the words.

le m ....................

le b ....................

la r ....................

le p ....................

le m ....................

Listen, repeat, and copy.

① le masque ....................

② le bandage ....................

③ la radio ....................

④ le pansement ....................

⑤ le médicament ....................

**Day 4**

Listen again and write the words.

c ....................

r ....................

b ....................

f ....................

d ....................

Listen, repeat, and copy.

① camper ....................

② rire ....................

③ bavarder ....................

④ faire du feu ....................

⑤ dormir ....................

**Day 5**

## What can you remember from this week?

**1.** Look at the pictures and circle the correct words.

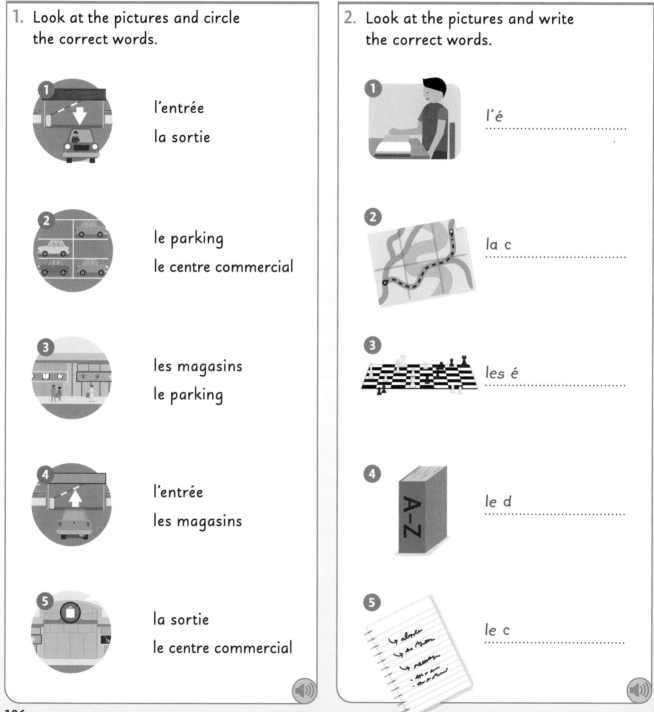

1. l'entrée
   la sortie

2. le parking
   le centre commercial

3. les magasins
   le parking

4. l'entrée
   les magasins

5. la sortie
   le centre commercial

**2.** Look at the pictures and write the correct words.

1. l' é ...................

2. la c ...................

3. les é ...................

4. le d ...................

5. le c ...................

3. Look at the pictures and mark the correct words.

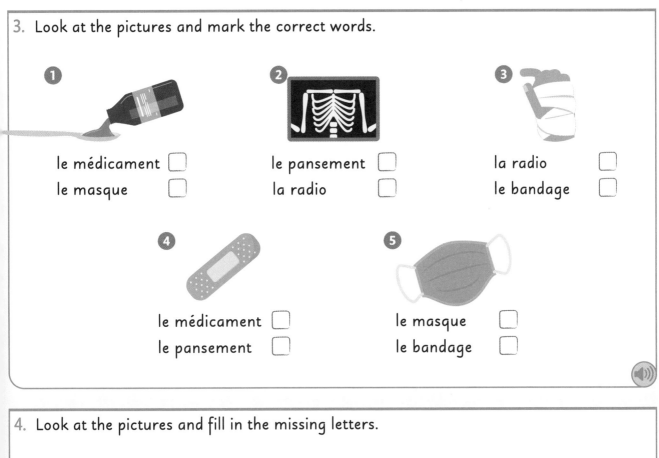

**1**

le médicament ☐
le masque ☐

**2**

le pansement ☐
la radio ☐

**3**

la radio ☐
le bandage ☐

**4**

le médicament ☐
le pansement ☐

**5**

le masque ☐
le bandage ☐

4. Look at the pictures and fill in the missing letters.

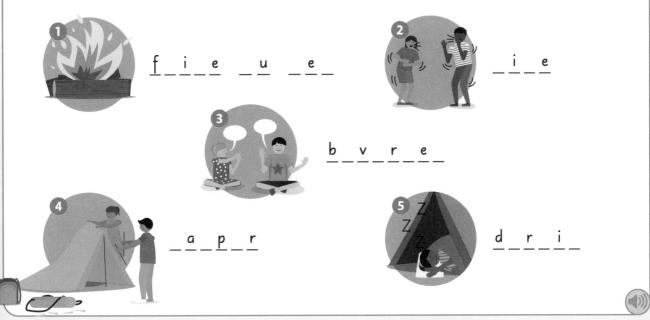

**1** f _ i _ e _ _ u _ _ e _

**2** _ _ i _ e

**3** b _ v _ r _ e _

**4** _ _ a _ p _ r

**5** d _ r _ i _

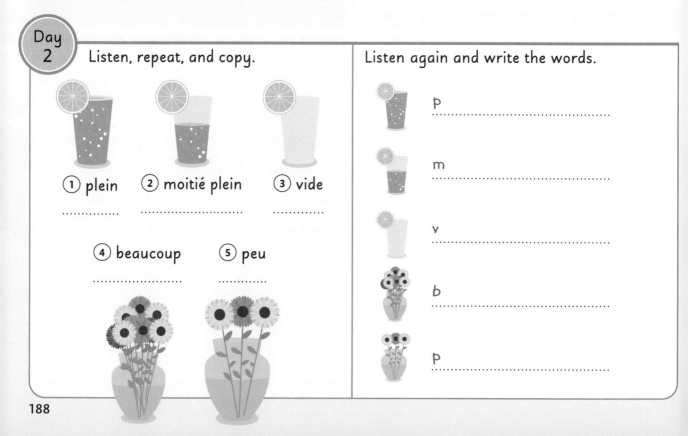

# Week 46

## Day 1

Listen, repeat, and copy.

① le hibou
..................

② l'écureuil
..................

③ le cerf
..................

④ le loup
..................

⑤ le renard
..................

Listen again and write the words.

le h
..................

l'é
..................

le c
..................

le l
..................

le r
..................

## Day 2

Listen, repeat, and copy.

① plein
..................

② moitié plein
..................

③ vide
..................

④ beaucoup
..................

⑤ peu
..................

Listen again and write the words.

p
..................

m
..................

v
..................

b
..................

p
..................

# Week 46

## Listen again and write the words.

le c
.....................

les a
.....................

l'é
.....................

les r
.....................

le c
.....................

## Listen, repeat, and copy.

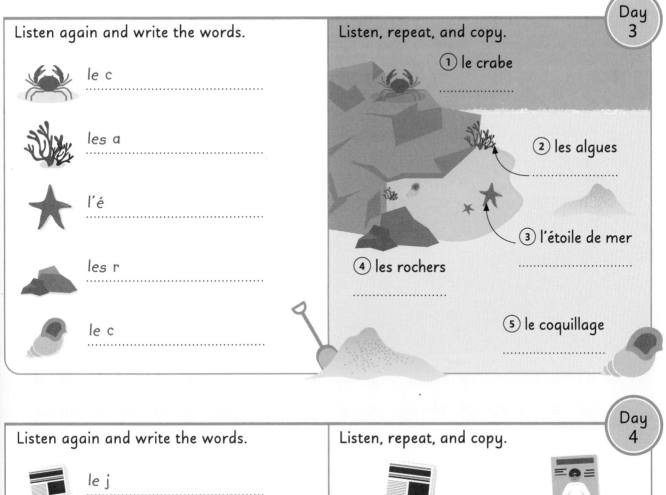

① le crabe
.....................

② les algues
.....................

③ l'étoile de mer
.....................

④ les rochers
.....................

⑤ le coquillage
.....................

## Listen again and write the words.

le j
.....................

le m
.....................

la b
.....................

le l
.....................

le d
.....................

## Listen, repeat, and copy.

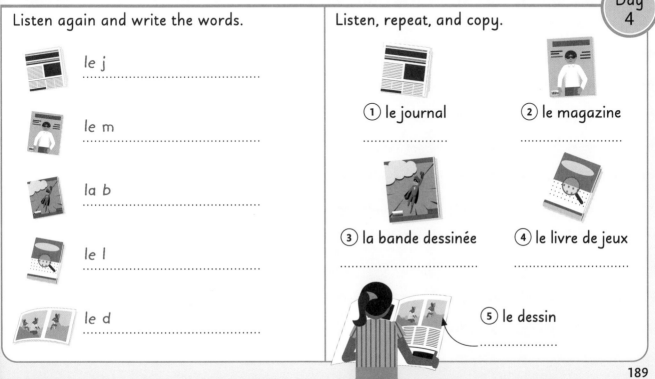

① le journal
.....................

② le magazine
.....................

③ la bande dessinée
.....................

④ le livre de jeux
.....................

⑤ le dessin
.....................

Day 5

What can you remember from this week?

1. Look at the pictures and write the correct words.

| le hibou | le loup | l'écureuil | le cerf | le renard |

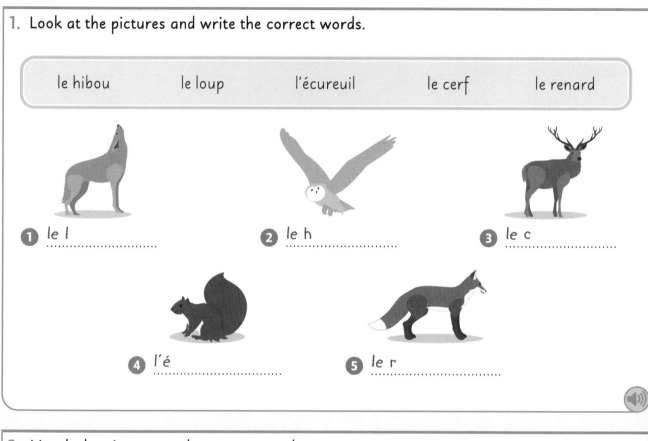

1 le l ................................

2 le h ................................

3 le c ................................

4 l'é ................................

5 le r ................................

2. Match the pictures to the correct words.

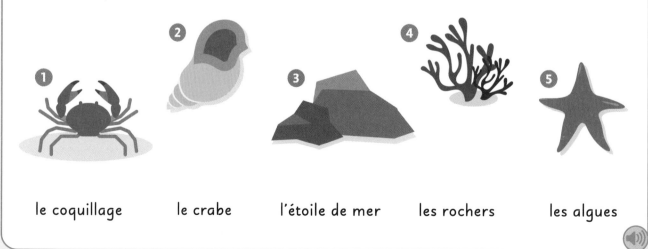

le coquillage    le crabe    l'étoile de mer    les rochers    les algues

3. Look at the pictures and write the correct words.

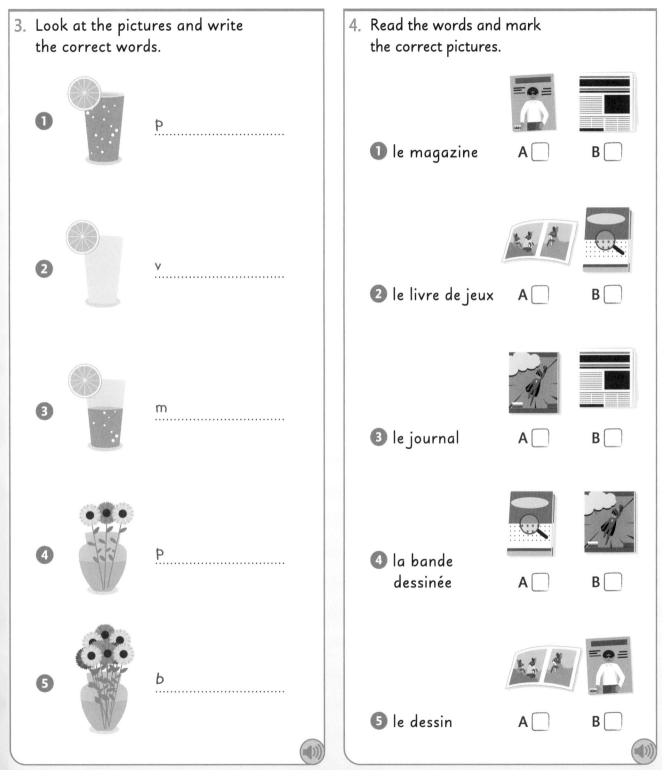

1  p.................................

2  v.................................

3  m.................................

4  p.................................

5  b.................................

4. Read the words and mark the correct pictures.

1 le magazine          A ☐          B ☐

2 le livre de jeux      A ☐          B ☐

3 le journal            A ☐          B ☐

4 la bande dessinée     A ☐          B ☐

5 le dessin             A ☐          B ☐

### Day 1

Listen, repeat, and copy.

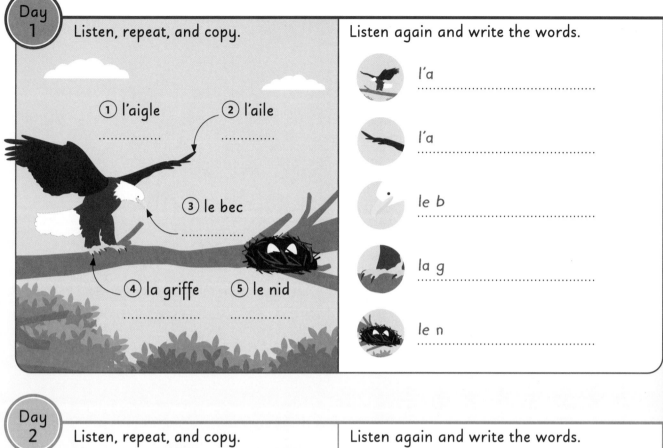

① l'aigle    ② l'aile
..............    ..............

③ le bec
..............

④ la griffe    ⑤ le nid
..............    ..............

Listen again and write the words.

l'a
...................................................

l'a
...................................................

le b
...................................................

la g
...................................................

le n
...................................................

### Day 2

Listen, repeat, and copy.

① s'ennuyer    ② bruyant    ③ silencieuse
..............    ..............    ..............

④ ordonné    ⑤ désordonnée
..............    ..............

Listen again and write the words.

s'
...................................................

b
...................................................

s
...................................................

o
...................................................

d
...................................................

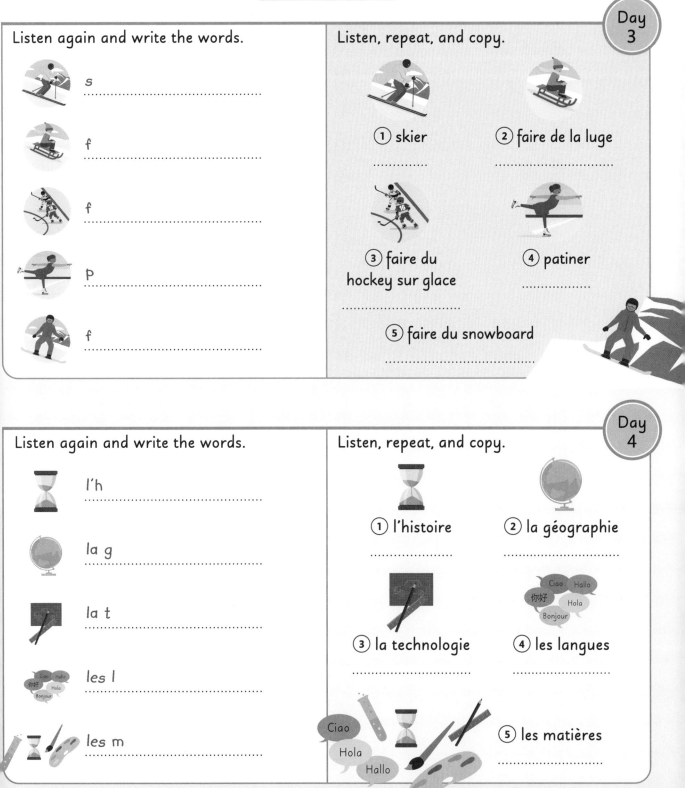

**Day 3**

Listen again and write the words.

s ...................................................

f ...................................................

f ...................................................

p ...................................................

f ...................................................

Listen, repeat, and copy.

① skier .................

② faire de la luge ...........................

③ faire du hockey sur glace ...........................

④ patiner .................

⑤ faire du snowboard ...........................

**Day 4**

Listen again and write the words.

l'h ...................................................

la g ...................................................

la t ...................................................

les l ...................................................

les m ...................................................

Listen, repeat, and copy.

① l'histoire .................

② la géographie ...........................

③ la technologie ...........................

④ les langues ...........................

⑤ les matières ...........................

**Day 5** What can you remember from this week?

**1.** Look at the pictures and mark the correct words.

1. la géographie ☐
   les matières ☐

2. les langues ☐
   la technologie ☐

3. l'histoire ☐
   la géographie ☐

4. les langues ☐
   l'histoire ☐

5. la technologie ☐
   les matières ☐

**2.** Look at the pictures and fill in the missing letters.

1. l _ _ n _ _ d

2. _ e _ _ _ e _

3. l' _ i _ e

4. _ a _ _ r _ f _ e _

5. l' _ _ i _ l _ _ _

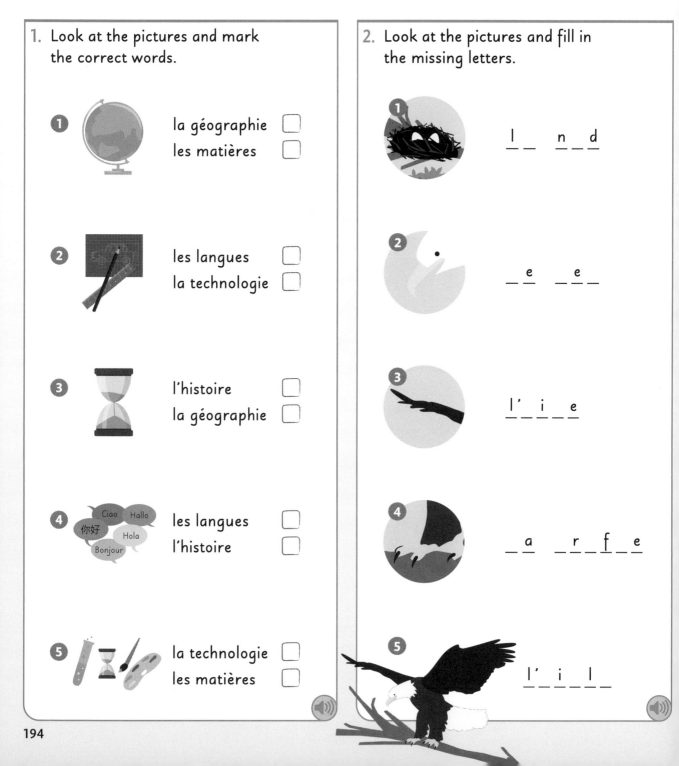

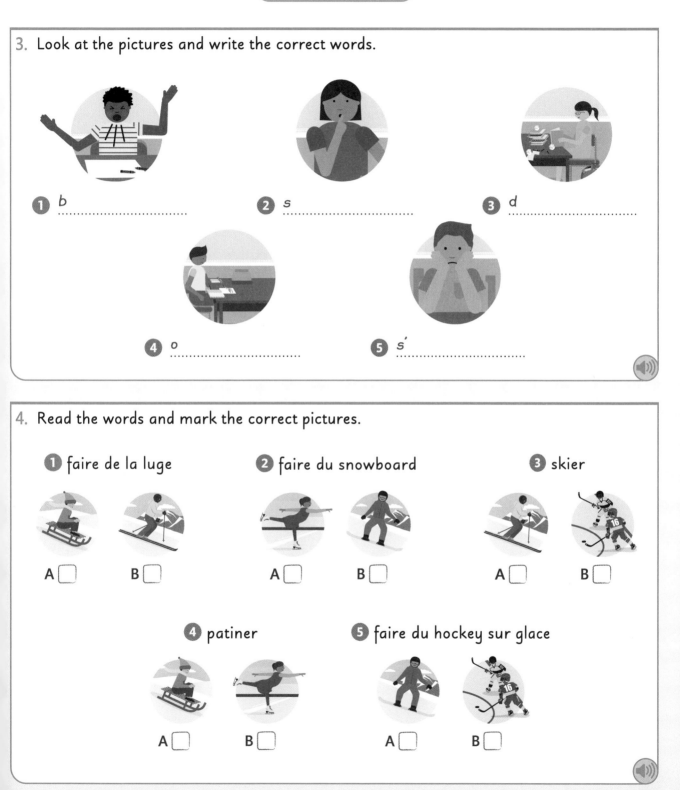

# Week 47

3. Look at the pictures and write the correct words.

1 b ......................................

2 s ......................................

3 d ......................................

4 o ......................................

5 s' ......................................

4. Read the words and mark the correct pictures.

1 faire de la luge

A ☐   B ☐

2 faire du snowboard

A ☐   B ☐

3 skier

A ☐   B ☐

4 patiner

A ☐   B ☐

5 faire du hockey sur glace

A ☐   B ☐

195

# Week 48

## Day 1

Listen, repeat, and copy.

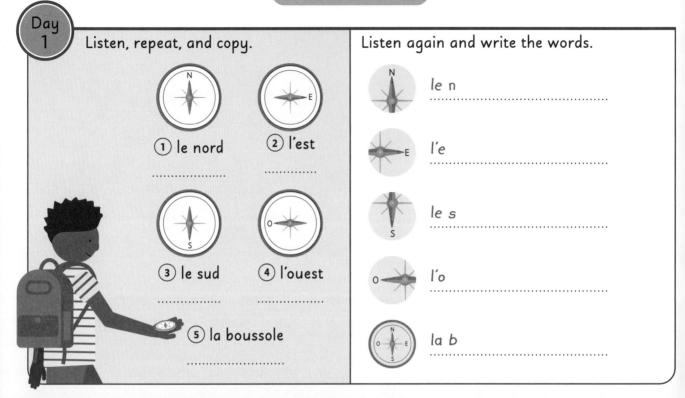

① le nord

② l'est

③ le sud

④ l'ouest

⑤ la boussole

Listen again and write the words.

le n .........................................

l'e .........................................

le s .........................................

l'o .........................................

la b .........................................

## Day 2

Listen, repeat, and copy.

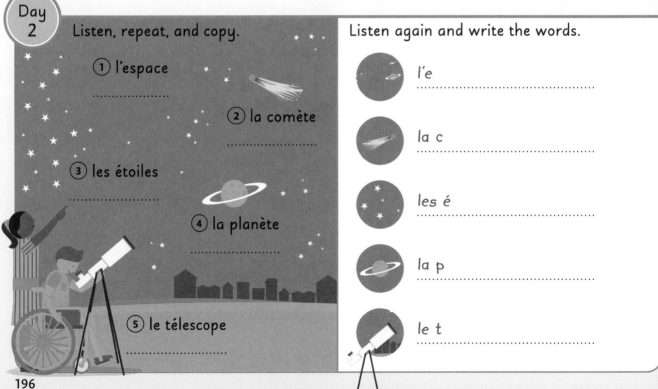

① l'espace

② la comète

③ les étoiles

④ la planète

⑤ le télescope

Listen again and write the words.

l'e .........................................

la c .........................................

les é .........................................

la p .........................................

le t .........................................

# Week 48

## Day 3

### Listen again and write the words.

le c

.................................

le s

.................................

la b

.................................

le b

.................................

la m

.................................

### Listen, repeat, and copy.

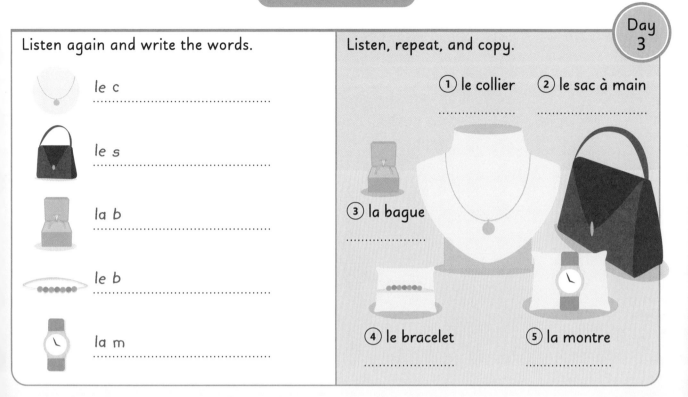

1. le collier

.................................

2. le sac à main

.................................

3. la bague

.................................

4. le bracelet

.................................

5. la montre

.................................

## Day 4

### Listen again and write the words.

le j

.................................

la s

.................................

l'a

.................................

la p

.................................

les e

.................................

### Listen, repeat, and copy.

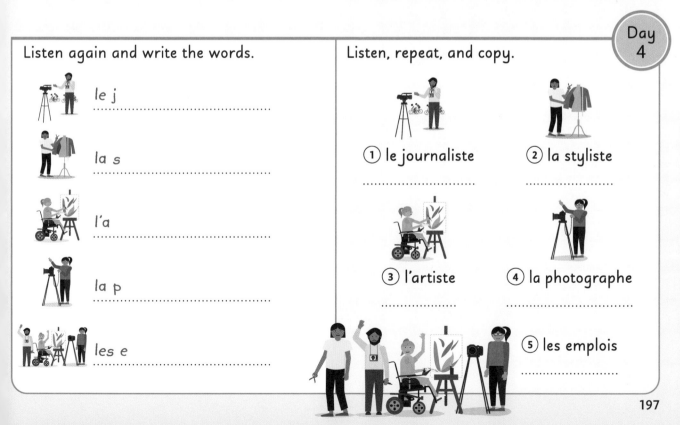

1. le journaliste

.................................

2. la styliste

.................................

3. l'artiste

.................................

4. la photographe

.................................

5. les emplois

.................................

197

Day 5

What can you remember from this week?

1. Look at the picture and write the correct words.

l'ouest

le nord

la boussole

le sud

l'est

1 la b _____

2 le n _____

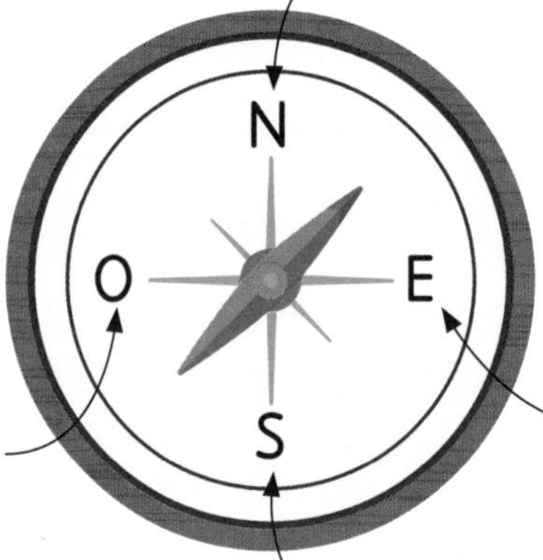

3 l'o _____

4 l'e _____

5 le s _____

N

O    E

S

2. Look at the pictures and circle the correct words.

1  les emplois
l'artiste

2  le photographe
la styliste

3  le journaliste
la styliste

4  l'artiste
le journaliste

5  les emplois
la photographe

3. Match the pictures to the correct words.

1   le sac à main

2   la bague

3   le bracelet

4   la montre

5   le collier

4. Look at the pictures and write the correct words.

les étoiles   la comète   la planète
l'espace   le télescope

1   la c ............................

2   l'e ............................

3   la p ............................

4   les é ............................

5   le t ............................

199

## Day 1

Listen, repeat, and copy.

① les moustaches
② le collier
③ la fourrure
④ la patte
⑤ la queue

Listen again and write the words.

les m ..................

le c ..................

la f ..................

la p ..................

la q ..................

## Day 2

Listen, repeat, and copy.

① inventer
② concevoir
③ penser
④ jouer
⑤ explorer

Listen again and write the words.

i ..................

c ..................

p ..................

j ..................

e ..................

**Listen again and write the words.**

le p .....................

le m .....................

la l .....................

le b .....................

la p .....................

**Listen, repeat, and copy.**

① le plastique .....................

② le métal .....................

③ la laine .....................

④ le bois .....................

⑤ la pierre .....................

**Listen again and write the words.**

les b .....................

le r .....................

le c .....................

la f .....................

la c .....................

**Listen, repeat, and copy.**

① les baguettes .....................

② le repas .....................

③ le couteau .....................

④ la fourchette .....................

⑤ la cuillère .....................

Day
5

## What can you remember from this week?

**1. Read the words and mark the correct pictures.**

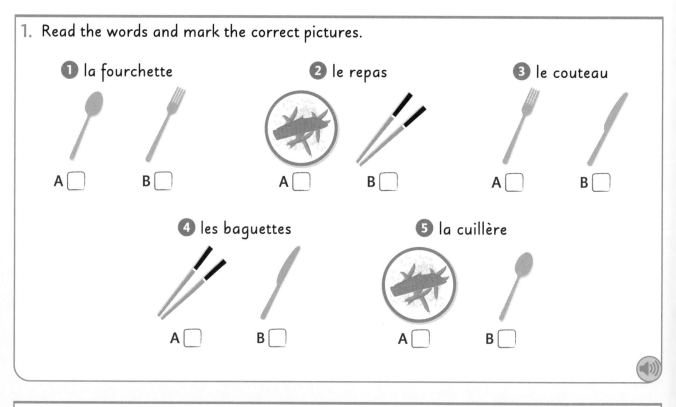

❶ la fourchette

A ☐   B ☐

❷ le repas

A ☐   B ☐

❸ le couteau

A ☐   B ☐

❹ les baguettes

A ☐   B ☐

❺ la cuillère

A ☐   B ☐

**2. Look at the pictures and fill in the missing letters.**

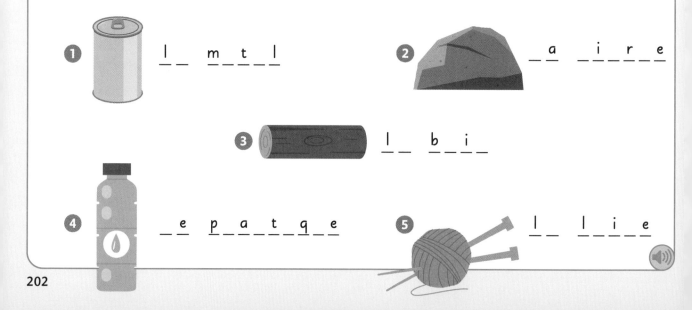

❶ l _ m t _ l

❷ _ a _ _ i _ r e

❸ l _ b i _

❹ _ e p a t q e

❺ l _ l _ i _ e

3. Look at the pictures and mark the correct words.

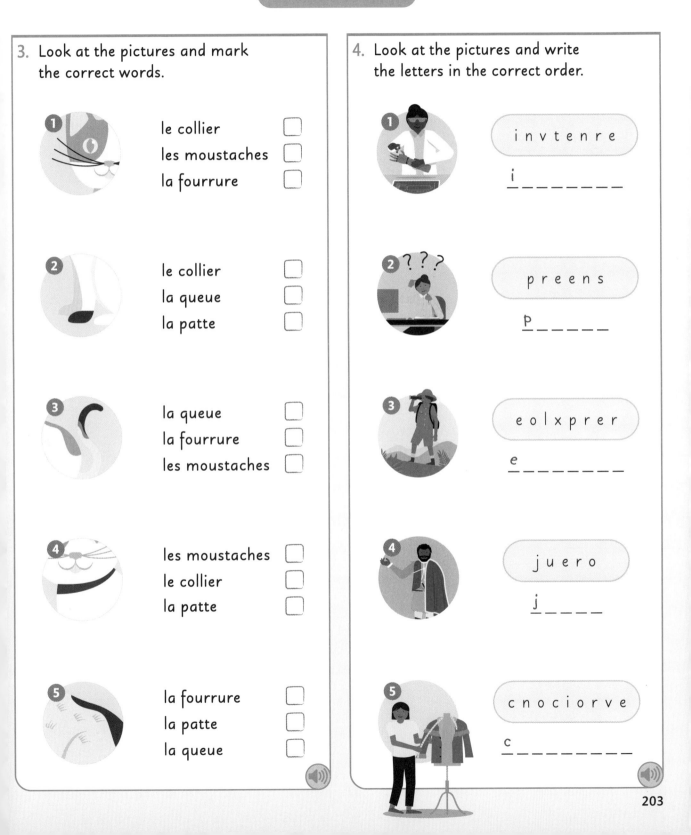

1.
le collier ☐
les moustaches ☐
la fourrure ☐

2.
le collier ☐
la queue ☐
la patte ☐

3.
la queue ☐
la fourrure ☐
les moustaches ☐

4.
les moustaches ☐
le collier ☐
la patte ☐

5.
la fourrure ☐
la patte ☐
la queue ☐

4. Look at the pictures and write the letters in the correct order.

1.
i n v t e n r e

i _ _ _ _ _ _ _

2.
p r e e n s

p _ _ _ _ _

3.
e o l x p r e r

e _ _ _ _ _ _ _

4.
j u e r o

j _ _ _ _

5.
c n o c i o r v e

c _ _ _ _ _ _ _ _

## Day 1

Listen, repeat, and copy.

① le prix

② première

③ deuxième

④ troisième

⑤ le concours

Listen again and write the words.

le p ........................

p ........................

d ........................

t ........................

le c ........................

## Day 2

Listen, repeat, and copy.

① tirer
..............

② pousser
..............

③ laisser tomber
..............

④ soulever
..............

⑤ tenir
..............

Listen again and write the words.

t ........................

p ........................

l ........................

s ........................

t ........................

## Day 3

**Listen again and write the words.**

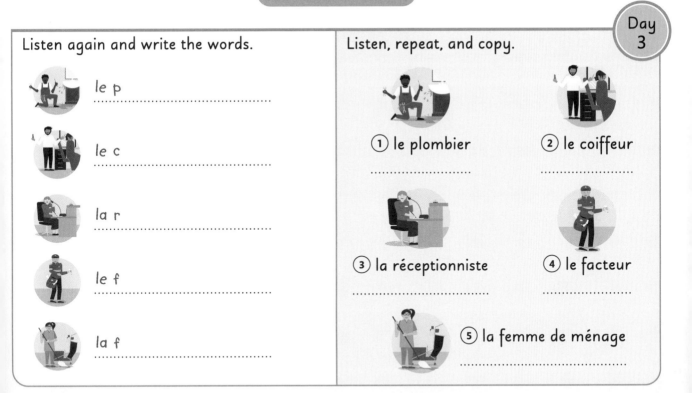

le p ......................................

le c ......................................

la r ......................................

le f ......................................

la f ......................................

**Listen, repeat, and copy.**

① le plombier ..................

② le coiffeur ..................

③ la réceptionniste ..................

④ le facteur ..................

⑤ la femme de ménage ..................

## Day 4

**Listen again and write the words.**

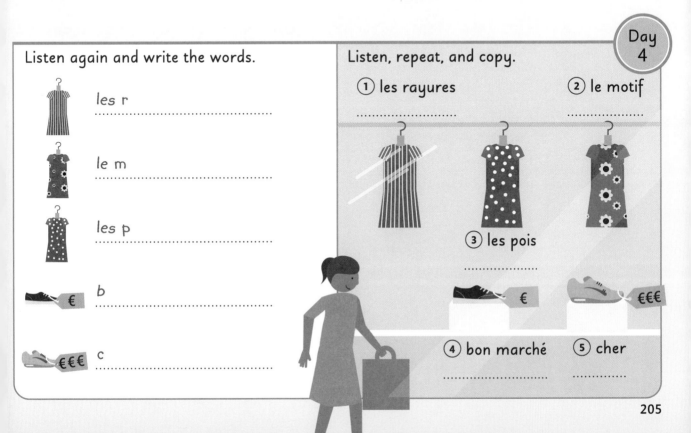

les r ......................................

le m ......................................

les p ......................................

b ......................................

c ......................................

**Listen, repeat, and copy.**

① les rayures ..................

② le motif ..................

③ les pois ..................

④ bon marché ..................

⑤ cher ..................

## What can you remember from this week?

**1.** Look at the pictures and circle the correct words.

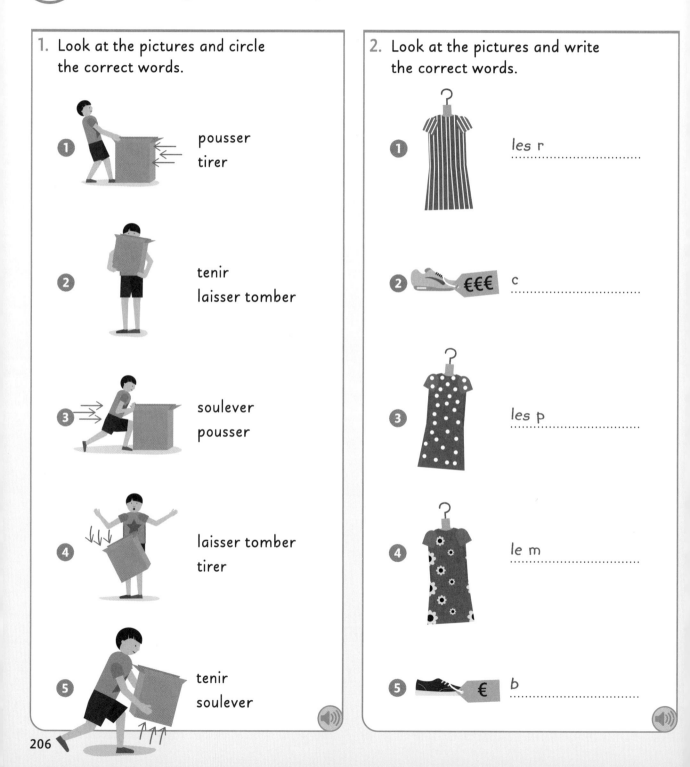

1. pousser / tirer

2. tenir / laisser tomber

3. soulever / pousser

4. laisser tomber / tirer

5. tenir / soulever

**2.** Look at the pictures and write the correct words.

1. les r ................................

2. c ................................

3. les p ................................

4. le m ................................

5. b ................................

3. Look at the pictures and write the correct words.

le prix   première   le concours   deuxième   troisième

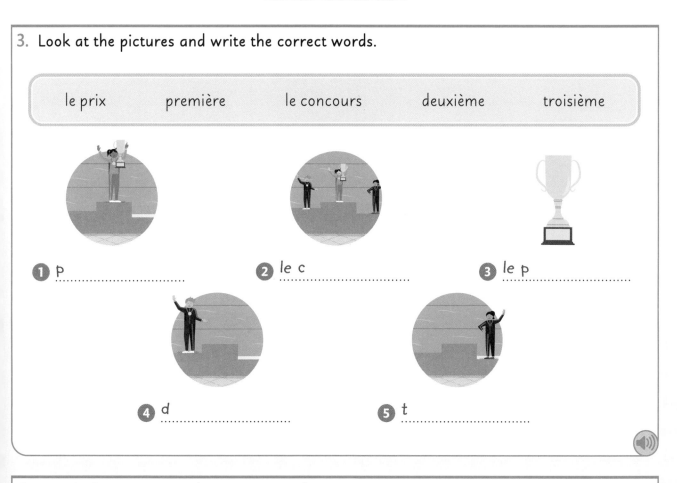

**1** p ..................................

**2** le c ..................................

**3** le p ..................................

**4** d ..................................

**5** t ..................................

4. Match the pictures to the correct words.

le coiffeur   le facteur   la femme de ménage   la réceptionniste   le plombier

## Day 1

Listen, repeat, and copy.

① la reine   ② le roi

.................... ....................

③ la princesse   ④ le prince

........................ ........................

⑤ la couronne

........................

Listen again and write the words.

la r ....................

le r ....................

la p ....................

le p ....................

la c ....................

## Day 2

Listen, repeat, and copy.

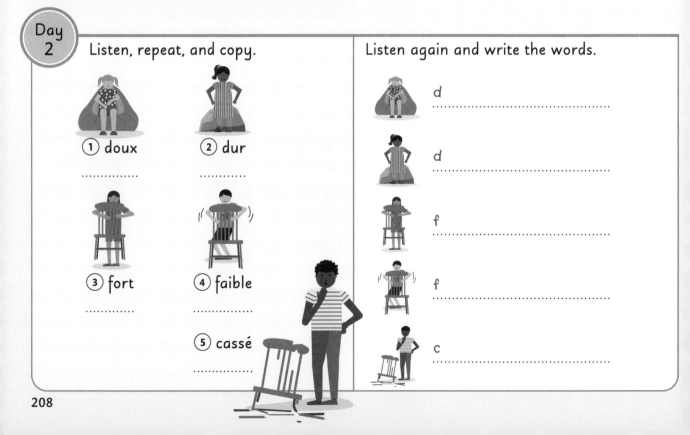

① doux   ② dur

............. .............

③ fort   ④ faible

............. .............

⑤ cassé

.............

Listen again and write the words.

d ....................

d ....................

f ....................

f ....................

c ....................

# Week 51

## Listen again and write the words.

c .....................................

r .....................................

a .....................................

é .....................................

c .....................................

## Listen, repeat, and copy.

① chercher
.....................

② réparer
.....................

③ allumer
.....................

④ éteindre
.....................

⑤ changer
.....................

## Listen again and write the words.

la c .....................................

la f .....................................

le b .....................................

la p .....................................

la c .....................................

## Listen, repeat, and copy.

① la cravate
.....................

② la fermeture éclair
.....................................

③ le bouton
.....................

④ la poche
.....................

⑤ la ceinture
.....................

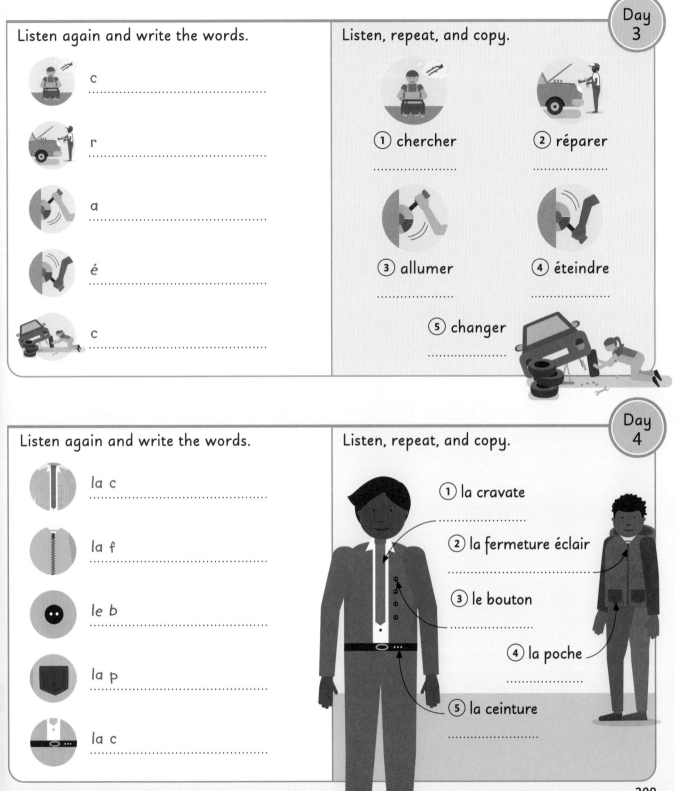

Day 5

What can you remember from this week?

1. Look at the pictures and fill in the missing letters.

1. c _ _ a _ g _ r

2. _ h _ r _ h _

3. a _ l _ m _ r

4. _ t _ i _ d _ e

5. r _ _ p _ r _ r

2. Look at the pictures and circle the correct words.

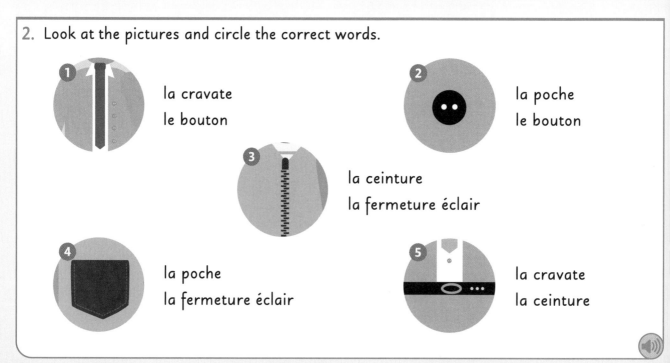

1. la cravate
   le bouton

2. la poche
   le bouton

3. la ceinture
   la fermeture éclair

4. la poche
   la fermeture éclair

5. la cravate
   la ceinture

3. Look at the pictures and write the letters in the correct order.

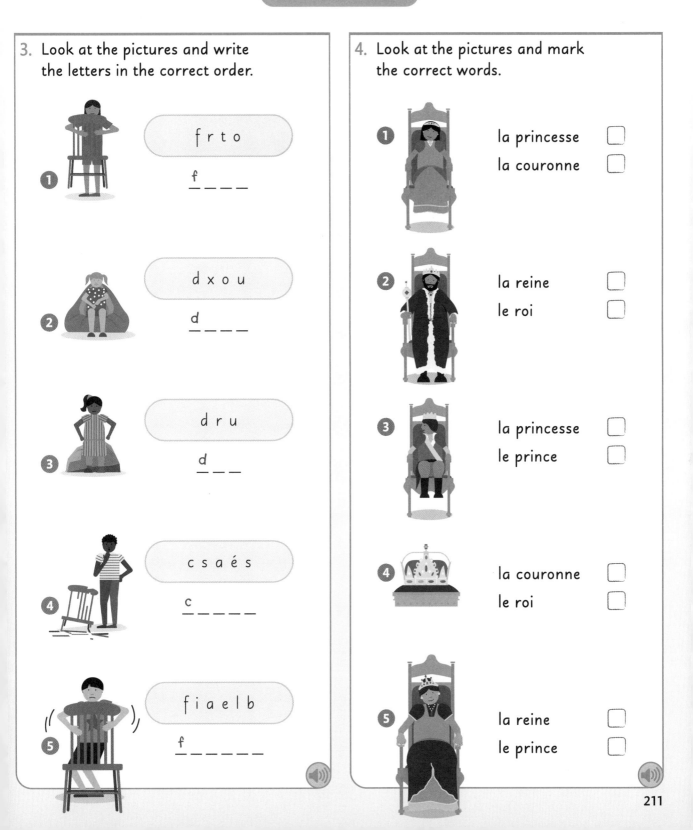

**f r t o**

1  f _ _ _ _

**d x o u**

2  d _ _ _ _

**d r u**

3  d _ _ _

**c s a é s**

4  c _ _ _ _ _

**f i a e l b**

5  f _ _ _ _ _

4. Look at the pictures and mark the correct words.

1  la princesse ☐
   la couronne ☐

2  la reine ☐
   le roi ☐

3  la princesse ☐
   le prince ☐

4  la couronne ☐
   le roi ☐

5  la reine ☐
   le prince ☐

**Day 1**

Listen, repeat, and copy.

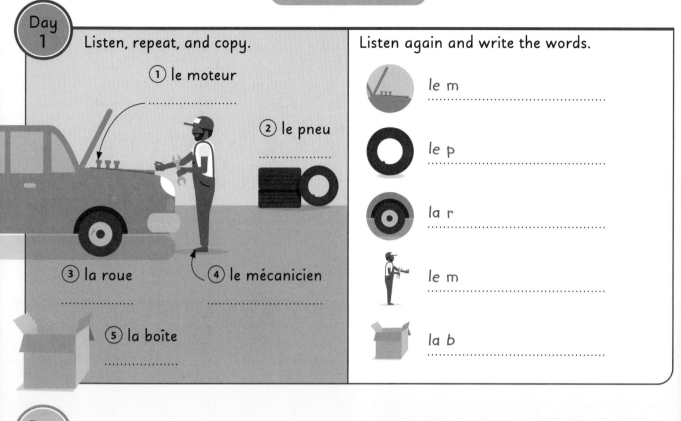

① le moteur

② le pneu

③ la roue

④ le mécanicien

⑤ la boîte

Listen again and write the words.

le m .....................

le p .....................

la r .....................

le m .....................

la b .....................

**Day 2**

Listen, repeat, and copy.

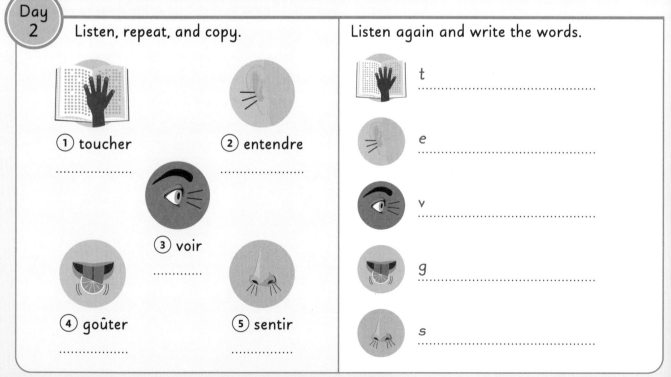

① toucher

② entendre

③ voir

④ goûter

⑤ sentir

Listen again and write the words.

t .....................

e .....................

v .....................

g .....................

s .....................

# Week 52

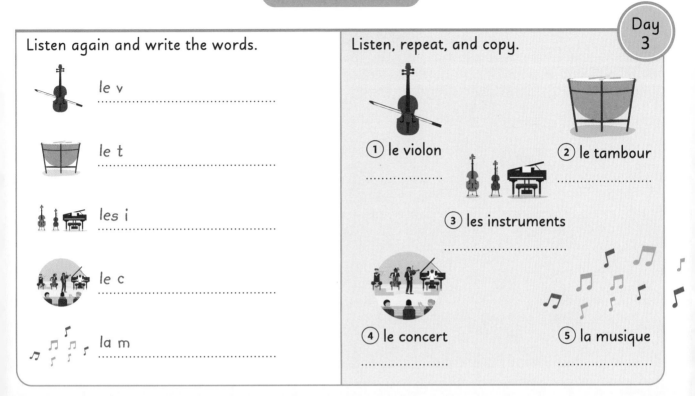

**Listen again and write the words.**

le v ......

le t ......

les i ......

le c ......

la m ......

**Listen, repeat, and copy.**

① le violon      ② le tambour

......

③ les instruments

......

④ le concert      ⑤ la musique

......      ......

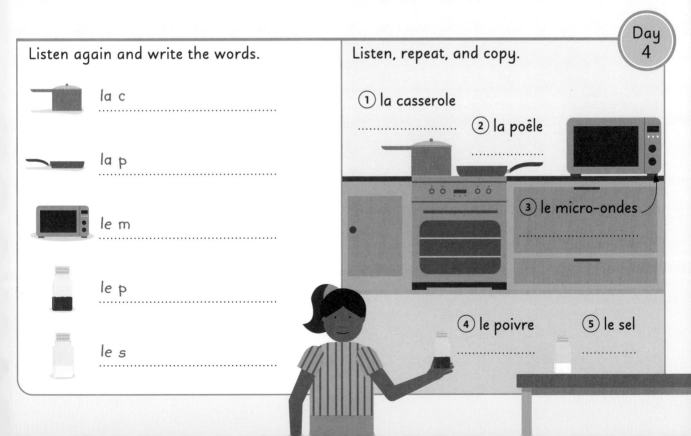

**Listen again and write the words.**

la c ......

la p ......

le m ......

le p ......

le s ......

**Listen, repeat, and copy.**

① la casserole

......      ② la poêle

......

③ le micro-ondes

......

④ le poivre      ⑤ le sel

......      ......

Day 5

## What can you remember from this week?

1. Look at the pictures and write the correct words.

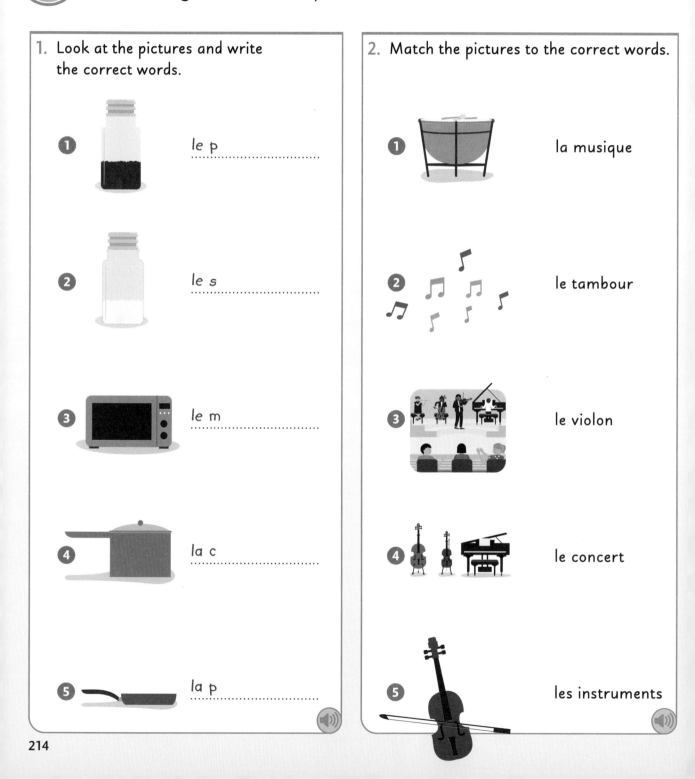

1　le p ........................................

2　le s ........................................

3　le m ........................................

4　la c ........................................

5　la p ........................................

2. Match the pictures to the correct words.

1　la musique

2　le tambour

3　le violon

4　le concert

5　les instruments

3. Look at the pictures and write the correct words.

| sentir | goûter | entendre | toucher | voir |

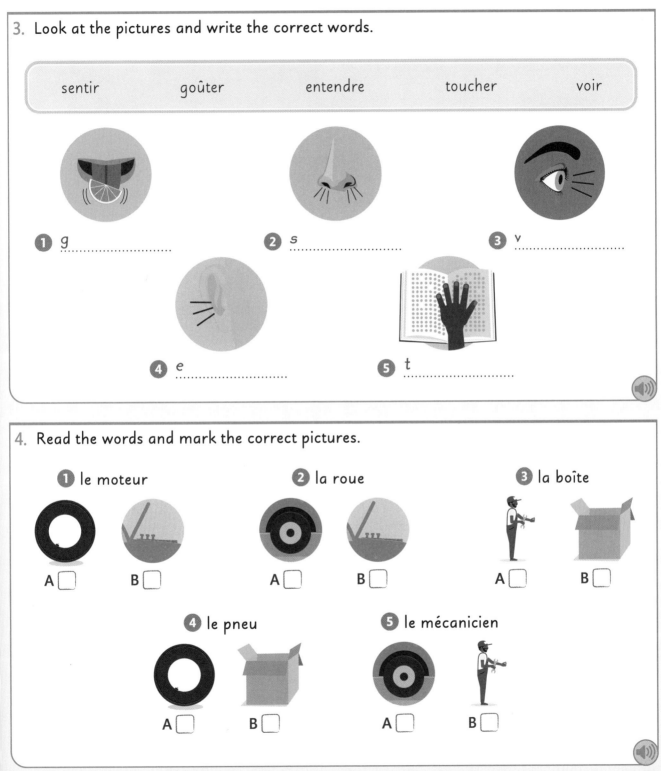

**1** g .........................................

**2** s .........................................

**3** v .........................................

**4** e .........................................

**5** t .........................................

4. Read the words and mark the correct pictures.

**1** le moteur     **2** la roue     **3** la boîte

A ☐     B ☐     A ☐     B ☐     A ☐     B ☐

**4** le pneu     **5** le mécanicien

A ☐     B ☐     A ☐     B ☐

# Numbers

Listen, repeat, and copy.

**0**
① zéro
...........

**10**
② dix
...........

**20**
③ vingt
...........

**30**
④ trente
...........

**40**
⑤ quarante
...........

**50**
⑥ cinquante
...........

**60**
⑦ soixante
...........

**70**
⑧ soixante-dix
...........

**80**
⑨ quatre-vingts
...........

**90**
⑩ quatre-vingt-dix
...........

**91**
⑪ quatre-vingt-onze
...........

**92**
⑫ quatre-vingt-douze
...........

**93**
⑬ quatre-vingt-treize
...........

**94**
⑭ quatre-vingt-quatorze
...........

**95**
⑮ quatre-vingt-quinze
...........

**96**
⑯ quatre-vingt-seize
...........

**97**
⑰ quatre-vingt-dix-sept
...........

**98**
⑱ quatre-vingt-dix-huit
...........

**99**
⑲ quatre-vingt-dix-neuf
...........

**100**
⑳ cent
...........

**1 000**
㉑ mille
...........

**1 000 000**
㉒ un million
...........

# Days

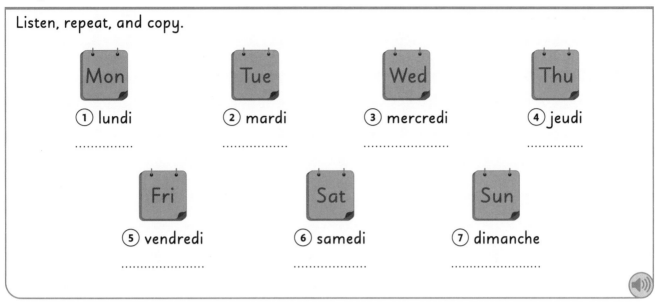

Listen, repeat, and copy.

Mon
① lundi
...............

Tue
② mardi
...............

Wed
③ mercredi
...............

Thu
④ jeudi
...............

Fri
⑤ vendredi
...............

Sat
⑥ samedi
...............

Sun
⑦ dimanche
...............

# Months

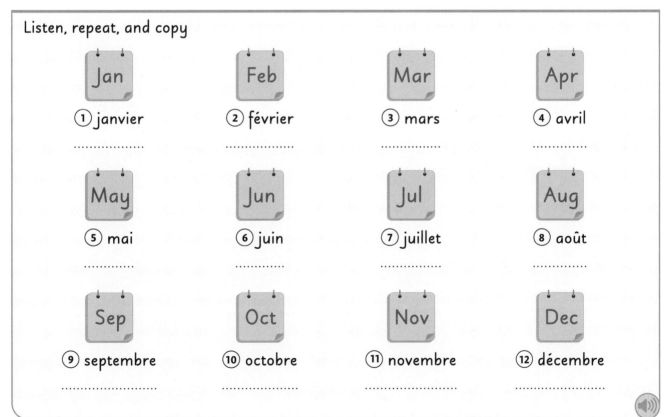

Listen, repeat, and copy

Jan
① janvier
...............

Feb
② février
...............

Mar
③ mars
...............

Apr
④ avril
...............

May
⑤ mai
...............

Jun
⑥ juin
...............

Jul
⑦ juillet
...............

Aug
⑧ août
...............

Sep
⑨ septembre
...............

Oct
⑩ octobre
...............

Nov
⑪ novembre
...............

Dec
⑫ décembre
...............

# English word list

Each word is followed by the number of the week it appears in. For words that are not in a weekly unit, a page number is given (for example, **p216**).

## KEY

| | |
|---|---|
| *adj* | adjective |
| *n* | noun |
| *num* | number |
| *prep* | preposition |
| *v* | verb |

## A

act *v* 49
action figure *n* 2
actor *n* 43
add *v* 10
address *n* 30
afraid *adj* 12
afternoon *n* 8
airplane *n* 38
airport *n* 38
alphabet *n* 2
ambulance *n* 25
angry *adj* 12
animals *n* 10
answer *v* 5
ant *n* 17
apartment *n* 12
apartment building *n* 12
apple *n* 1
apps *n* 21
April **p217**
arm *n* 6
armchair *n* 7
arrive *v* 38
art *n* 44
artist *n* 48
ask *v* 17
asleep *adj* 40

astronaut *n* 34
August *n* **p217**
aunt *n* 14
awake *adj* 40

## B

baby *n* 7
back *adj* 40
back *n* 23
backpack *n* 5
badminton *n* 6
balcony *n* 12
ball *n* 6
balloon *n* 16
banana *n* 1
band *n* 41
bandage *n* 45
band-aid *n* 45
bank *n* 35
barn *n* 10
baseball *n* 6
baseball cap *n* 11
basement *n* 22
basket *n* 33
basketball *n* 6
bat *n* 15
bathroom *n* 4
bathtub *n* 26
beach *n* 15
beach ball *n* 43
beak *n* 47
beans *n* 29
bear *n* 8
beard *n* 40
beautiful *adj* 11
bed *n* 8
bedroom *n* 4
bee *n* 17
beetle *n* 39
behind *prep* 12
belt *n* 51
bench *n* 21
between *prep* 28

bicycle *n* 21
big *adj* 11
bird *n* 19
birthday party *n* 19
black *adj* 38
black *n* 4
blanket *n* 34
blonde *adj* 38
blue *n* 1
board *n* 1
board game *n* 2
boat *n* 27
body *n* 6
book *n* 5
bookcase *n* 7
bookstore *n* 21
boots *n* 26
bored *adj* 47
borrow *v* 35
bottle *n* 33
bottom *adj* 35
bounce *v* 9
bowl *n* 33
box *n* 52
boy *n* 7
bracelet *n* 48
branch *n* 13
brave *adj* 39
bread *n* 14
break *v* 40
breakfast *n* 12
bridge *n* 34
bring *v* 38
broken *adj* 51
bronze *n* 36
brother *n* 14
brown *adj* 38
brown *n* 4
brush *n* 37
brush my teeth *v* 25
bucket *n* 43
build *v* 44
burger *n* 7
burn *v* 45
bus *n* 24
bus station *n* 24
bus stop *n* 32
butter *n* 44
butterfly *n* 39

button *n* 51
buy *v* 43

## C

cabbage *n* 23
cabinet *n* 31
café *n* 21
cake *n* 19
calendar *n* 8
camel *n* 24
camera *n* 34
camp *v* 45
candle *n* 19
candy *n* 16
car *n* 25
card *n* 19
carnival *n* 28
carpet *n* 19
carrot *n* 15
carry *v* 43
cart *n* 33
cartoon *n* 46
castle *n* 27
cat *n* 6, 16
catch *v* 9
catch a bus *v* 13
caterpillar *n* 17
cave *n* 23
ceiling *n* 30
cell phone *n* 31
center *n* 41
cereal *n* 12
chair *n* 16, 19
change *v* 51
charger *n* 31
chat *v* 45
cheap *adj* 50
check *v* 10
cheese *n* 38
chef *n* 32
cherry *n* 20
chess *n* 45
chest *n* 20
chicken *n* 4
chicken *n* 7
child *n* 18
children *n* 10
chin *n* 40

puzzle *n* 27
puzzle book *n* 46
pyramid *n* 24

# Q

quarter *n* 41
queen *n* 51
question *n* 22
quiet *adj* 47

# R

rabbit *n* 6
race *n* 36
race *v* 33
radio *n* 24
railcar *n* 39
railroad track *n* 39
rain *n* 13
rainbow *n* 13
read *v* 35
receptionist *n* 50
rectangle *n* 17
red *adj* 38
red *n* 1
refrigerator *n* 31
reindeer *n* 37
relax *v* 22
remote control *n* 24
repair *v* 51
restaurant *n* 32
rhino *n* 26
rice *n* 29
ride *n* 28
ride a bike *v* 20
right *adj* 40
ring *n* 48
river *n* 23
road *n* 32
robot *n* 10
rock *n* 31
rocket *n* 34
rocks *n* 46
roller skates *n* 15
roof *n* 14
rug *n* 7
ruler *n* 5
run *v* 13, 15

# S

sad *adj* 12
sail *v* 18
salad *n* 38
salt *n* 52
same *adj* 25
sand *n* 15
sandals *n* 9
sandcastle *n* 43
sandwich *n* 13
Saturday *n* p217
sauce *n* 14
sausage *n* 12
scared *adj* 27
scarf *n* 26
scary *adj* 9
school *n* 3
science *n* 44
scissors *n* 5
score *n* 39
score *v* 20
screen *n* 28
sea *n* 6
seagull *n* 6
seal *n* 37
search *v* 29, 35
seasons *n* 42
seat *n* 21
seaweed *n* 46
second *adj* 50
see *v* 52
seesaw *n* 21
sell *v* 43
send *v* 24
sentence *n* 22
September *n* p217
seven *num* 2
seventeen *num* 4
seventy *num* p216
shapes *n* 17
shark *n* 20
shed *n* 14
sheep *n* 4
shelf *n* 26
shell *n* 46
ship *n* 6
shirt *n* 11
shoes *n* 9
shop *v* 17

shopping *n* 33
shopping center *n* 45
short *adj* 18
shorts *n* 9
shoulder *n* 20
shout *v* 24
shovel *n* 43
show *v* 34
shower *n* 26
sick *adj* 39
silver *n* 36
sing *v* 11
singer *n* 43
sink *n* 27
sister *n* 14
sit down *v* 8
six *num* 2
sixteen *num* 4
sixty *num* p216
skate *v* 20
skateboard *n* 10
skateboard *v* 20
ski *v* 20
skiing *n* 47
skip *v* 15
skirt *n* 11
skis *n* 36
sky *n* 31
skyscraper *n* 33
sled *n* 36
sledding *n* 47
sleep *v* 45
slide *n* 21
slow *adj* 44
small *adj* 11
smell *v* 52
smile *n* 29
smoke *n* 42
snack *n* 13
snail *n* 39
snake *n* 24
sneakers *n* 15
snow *n* 32
snowball *n* 32
snowboard *n* 36
snowboarding *n* 47
snowflake *n* 32
snowman *n* 32
soap *n* 27

soccer *n* 23
socks *n* 7
soft *adj* 51
son *n* 3
sore *adj* 39
soup *n* 29
south *n* 48
space *n* 48
speak *v* 34
speakers *n* 24
spell *v* 3
spider *n* 39
spoon *n* 49
sports *n* 14
sports center *n* 35
spring *n* 42
square *n* 17
squirrel *n* 46
stable *n* 19
stadium *n* 31
stage *n* 43
stairs *n* 22
stamp *n* 30
stand up *v* 8
starfish *n* 46
stars *n* 48
start *v* 33
station *n* 39
step *n* 25
stomach *n* 23
stomachache *n* 30
stone *n* 49
stores *n* 45
storm *n* 13
story *n* 27
stove *n* 31
straight *adj* 18
strawberry *n* 20
stream *n* 34
street *n* 3
stripes *n* 50
strong *adj* 51
student *n* 45
study *v* 35
subjects *n* 47
sugar *n* 36
suitcase *n* 38
summer *n* 42
sun *n* 34

# French word list

Each word is followed by the number of the week it appears in. For words that are not in a weekly unit, a page number is given (for example, **p216**).

In French, all nouns (things or people) are either masculine or feminine (see p6). Adjectives (describing words) also change depending on whether the noun they are describing is masculine or feminine. When two options for nouns or adjectives are given in the following list (for example, âgé / âgée), the masculine is given first.

## KEY

| | |
|---|---|
| *adj* | adjective |
| *n* | noun |
| *num* | number |
| *prep* | preposition |
| *v* | verb |

## A

l'abeille *n* 17
l'abri de jardin *n* 14
acheter *v* 43
à côté de *prep* 12
l'acteur / l'actrice *n* 43
additionner *v* 10
l'adresse *n* 30
l'adulte *n* 18
l'aéroport *n* 38
à l'extérieur *prep* 28
âgé / âgée *adj* 9
l'agenda *n* 43
l'agent de police *n* 18
aider *v* 26
l'aigle *n* 47
l'ail *n* 23
l'aile *n* 47
aimer *v* 37
à l'intérieur *prep* 28
l'aire de jeux *n* 3
les algues *n* 46
aller chercher *v* 40
allumer *v* 51
l'alphabet *n* 2
l'ambulance *n* 25
les amis *n* 18
l'ananas *n* 1
l'âne *n* 19
les animaux *n* 10
les animaux de compagnie *n* 6
l'année *n* 43
août *n* **p217**
apeuré / apeurée *adj* 12
l'appareil photo *n* 34
l'appartement *n* 12
les applis *n* 21
apporter *v* 38
apprendre *v* 5

l'après-midi *n* 8
l'araignée *n* 39
l'arbre *n* 13
l'arc-en-ciel *n* 13
l'argent *n* 33
l'argent *n* 36
l'arrêt de bus *n* 32
arriver *v* 38
arroser *v* 41
l'art *n* 44
l'artiste *n* 48
l'ascenseur *n* 12
assembler *v* 29
l'assiette *n* 33
associer *v* 10
l'astronaute *n* 34
attendre *v* 17
atterrir *v* 36
attraper *v* 9
l'aubergine *n* 23
l'automne *n* 42
l'avion *n* 38
avoir faim *v* 27
avoir peur *v* 27
avoir soif *v* 27
avril *n* **p217**

## B

le badminton *n* 6
la bague *n* 48
les baguettes *n* 49
la baignoire *n* 26
la balançoire *n* 21
la balançoire à bascule *n* 21
le balcon *n* 12
la baleine *n* 20
la balle *n* 6
le ballon *n* 16
le ballon de plage *n* 43
la banane *n* 1
le banc *n* 21
le bandage *n* 45
la bande dessinée *n* 46
la banque *n* 35
la barbe *n* 40

la barque *n* 27
barrer *v* 10
le baseball *n* 6
le basket-ball *n* 6
le bâton de hockey *n* 36
la batte *n* 15
bavarder *v* 45
beau *adj* 11
beaucoup *adj* 46
le bébé *n* 7
le bec *n* 47
le beurre *n* 44
la bibliothèque *n* 7
la bibliothèque *n* 31
les bijoux *n* 37
le billet *n* 21
le biscuit *n* 36
blanc *n* 4
bleu *n* 1
blonds *adj* 38
boire *v* 16
le bois *n* 30
le bois *n* 49
les boissons *n* 17
la boîte *n* 52
la boîte à outils *n* 42
le bol *n* 33
les bonbons *n* 16
le bonhomme de neige *n* 32
bon marché *adj* 50
les bottes *n* 26
la bouche *n* 40
bouclés *adj* 18
la boule de neige *n* 32
bouger *v* 19
la bougie *n* 19
les boulettes de viande *n* 14
la boussole *n* 48
la bouteille *n* 33
le bouton *n* 51
le bracelet *n* 48
la branche *n* 13
le bras *n* 6
brave *adj* 39
le bronze *n* 36

# Common subjects

This is an index of common topics found in the book. Each subject is followed by the weeks it is taught in or the page number it appears on (for example, **p216**).

# Answers

## Week 1

**1**
1. l'enseignant
2. le tableau
3. les couleurs
4. les mots
5. la classe

**2**
1. violet
2. rouge
3. jaune
4. bleu
5. vert

**3**
1. deux
2. cinq
3. quatre
4. un
5. trois

**4**
1. l'ananas
2. le raisin
3. la pomme
4. la banane
5. l'orange

## Week 2

**1**
1. les chiffres
2. l'alphabet
3. les lettres
4. la camarade
5. la salle de classe

**2**
1. la poupée
2. la figurine
3. le nounours
4. le jeu de société
5. la marionnette

**3**
1. B  2. A  3. B  4. A
5. A

**4**
1. huit
2. six
3. neuf
4. sept
5. dix

## Week 3

**1**
1. dessiner
2. colorier
3. compter
4. épeler
5. écrire

**2**
1. l'école
2. la cour de récréation
3. le parc
4. la rue
5. la maison

**3**
1. onze
2. treize
3. quinze
4. quatorze
5. douze

**4**
1. la famille
2. le papa
3. la maman
4. le fils
5. la fille

## Week 4

**1**
1. marron
2. rose
3. orange
4. blanc
5. noir

**2**
1. B  2. A  3. B  4. A
5. A

**3**
1. la poule
2. la chèvre
3. le mouton
4. la vache
5. le cheval

**4**
1. dix-sept
2. vingt
3. dix-huit
4. seize
5. dix-neuf

## Week 5

**1**
1. le zèbre
2. l'hippopotame
3. le lion
4. la girafe
5. l'éléphant

**2**
1. les ciseaux
2. le livre
3. la règle
4. la gomme
5. le sac à dos

**3**
1. écouter
2. enseigner
3. apprendre
4. montrer du doigt
5. répondre

**4**
1. le kiwi
2. la poire
3. la pastèque
4. la noix de coco
5. la mangue

## Week 6

**1**
1. B  2. A  3. B  4. A
5. B

**2**
1. la tête
2. la jambe
3. le corps
4. le bras
5. le cou

**3**
1. le hockey
2. le tennis
3. le baseball
4. le basket-ball
5. le badminton

**4**
1. la mer
2. la mouette
3. le cerf-volant
4. le navire
5. la balle

## Week 7

**1**
1. la fille
2. l'homme
3. le garçon
4. le bébé
5. la femme

**2**
1. B  2. A  3. A  4. B
5. A

**3**
1. le canapé
2. le tapis
3. le fauteuil
4. la bibliothèque
5. la télévision

**4**
1. la pizza
2. les nouilles
3. le hamburger
4. les frites
5. le poulet

## Week 8

**1**
1. le tigre
2. la grenouille
3. le singe
4. la jungle
5. l'ours

**2**
1. A  2. B  3. A  4. A
5. B

**3**
1. s'assoir
2. ouvrir
3. fermer
4. ramasser
5. se lever

**4**
1. l'après-midi
2. la nuit
3. le matin
4. le soir
5. le jour

## Week 9

**1**
1. les grands-parents
2. la grand-mère
3. le grand-père
4. le petit-fils
5. la petite-fille

**2**
1. le t-shirt
2. la robe
3. les sandales
4. les chaussures
5. le short

**3**
1. joli
2. âgé
3. effrayant
4. jeune
5. gentil

**4**
1. attraper
2. taper
3. frapper
4. lancer
5. rebondir

## Week 10

**1**
1. la personne
2. les femmes
3. les enfants
4. les gens
5. les hommes

**2**
1. B  2. A  3. B  4. A
5. A

**3**
1. le tracteur
2. le champ
3. la ferme
4. les animaux
5. la grange

**4**
1. le dinosaure
2. le skateboard
3. le jeu vidéo
4. le robot
5. le monstre

## Week 11

**1**
1. l'œil
2. les lèvres
3. le nez
4. l'oreille
5. le visage

**2**
1. A  2. B  3. A  4. A
5. B

**3**
1. beau
2. propre
3. petit
4. sale
5. grand

**4**
1. la chemise
2. la casquette de baseball
3. la jupe
4. le pantalon
5. la veste

## Week 12

**1**
1. dedans
2. devant
3. derrière
4. à côté de
5. sur

**2**
1. les céréales
2. le petit déjeuner
3. l'œuf
4. la crêpe
5. la saucisse

**3**
1. le balcon
2. l'ascenseur
3. l'immeuble
4. le rez-de-chaussée
5. l'appartement

**4**
1. surprise
2. triste
3. apeuré
4. joyeux
5. en colère

## Week 13

**1**
1. A  2. A  3. B  4. A
5. B

**2**
1. la feuille
2. la branche
3. l'arbre
4. la plante
5. la fleur

**3**

1. la tempête
2. le vent
3. le brouillard
4. la pluie
5. l'arc-en-ciel

**4**

1. l'en-cas
2. le yaourt
3. les fruits
4. le sandwich
5. le déjeuner

## Week 14

**1**

1. le toit
2. la clôture
3. le jardin
4. l'abri de jardin
5. la maison

**2**

1. le dessin
2. la danse
3. la peinture
4. les sports
5. les loisirs

**3**

1. l'oncle
2. la tante
3. la cousine
4. le frère
5. la sœur

**4**

1. les pâtes
2. la sauce
3. le dîner
4. le pain
5. les boulettes de viande

## Week 15

**1**

1. la carotte
2. les petits pois
3. les légumes
4. la pomme de terre
5. le poivron

**2**

1. l'océan
2. la vague
3. la plage
4. le sable
5. l'île

**3**

1. le casque
2. les tennis
3. la batte
4. la raquette de tennis
5. les patins à roulettes

**4**

1. courir
2. sauter à la corde
3. jouer
4. escalader
5. sauter

## Week 16

**1**

1. les bonbons
2. la fête
3. le jeu
4. l'invitation
5. le ballon

**2**

1. cuisiner
2. manger
3. laver
4. sécher
5. boire

**3**

1. le chat
2. la souris
3. le chien
4. le chiot
5. le chaton

**4**

1. la lampe
2. l'horloge
3. le téléphone
4. le bureau
5. la chaise

## Week 17

**1**

1. demander
2. choisir
3. attendre
4. mettre
5. faire des courses

**2**

1. la coccinelle
2. l'abeille
3. la fourmi
4. la libellule
5. la chenille

**3**

1. le jus
2. les boissons
3. l'eau
4. la limonade
5. le milkshake

**4**

1. le triangle
2. le cercle
3. le rectangle
4. le carré
5. les formes

## Week 18

**1**

1. A   2. B   3. B   4. A
5. B

**2**

1. les cheveux
2. courts
3. longs
4. raides
5. bouclés

**3**

1. surfer
2. pêcher
3. voler
4. nager
5. naviguer

**4**

1. l'enfant
2. l'adulte
3. le parent
4. le groupe
5. les amis

## Week 19

**1**

1. bouger
2. marcher
3. toucher
4. frapper dans ses mains
5. faire signe de la main

**2**

1. l'oiseau
2. l'âne
3. l'étable
4. le cochon
5. le fermier

**3**

1. le cadeau
2. la carte
3. la fête d'anniversaire
4. la bougie
5. le gâteau

**4**

1. la moquette
2. le coussin
3. les lumières
4. la chaise
5. la table

## Week 20

**1**

1 A  2 B  3 A  4 B
5 A

**2**

1. le dauphin
2. la méduse
3. la pieuvre
4. le requin
5. la baleine

**3**

1. les doigts
2. l'épaule
3. le coude
4. la main
5. la poitrine

**4**

1. le citron
2. la cerise
3. la fraise
4. la pêche
5. le citron vert

## Week 21

**1**

1. la tablette
2. le livre numérique
3. le message
4. les applis
5. l'e-mail

**2**

1. la librairie
2. le bureau de poste
3. le magasin de jouets
4. le café
5. la ville

**3**

1. le siège
2. le cinéma
3. la star de cinéma
4. le billet
5. le film

**4**

1 A  2 B  3 A  4 A
5 B

## Week 22

**1**

1. l'entrée
2. en haut
3. en bas
4. l'escalier
5. le sous-sol

**2**

1. faire ses devoirs
2. ranger
3. s'entraîner
4. se détendre
5. nettoyer

**3**

1. la serviette
2. la piscine
3. le maillot de bain
4. les lunettes de natation
5. la natation

**4**

1. exact
2. la question
3. la date
4. l'erreur
5. la phrase

## Week 23

**1**

1. l'oignon
2. l'ail
3. le chou
4. le champignon
5. l'aubergine

**2**

1. la rivière
2. la cascade
3. la grotte
4. le lézard
5. la tortue

**3**

1. le golf
2. le volley
3. la gymnastique
4. le tennis de table
5. le foot

**4**

1. le dos
2. le ventre
3. le genou
4. le pied
5. les orteils

## Week 24

**1**

1 A  2 B  3 B  4 A
5 B

**2**

1. le chameau
2. la pyramide
3. le désert
4. le serpent
5. le crocodile

**3**

1. le taxi
2. le passager
3. le bus
4. le chauffeur
5. le gare routière

**4**

1. téléphoner
2. envoyer un e-mail
3. poster
4. crier
5. parler

## Week 25

**1**

1. la marche
2. le tapis
3. le mur
4. l'échelle
5. le portail

**2**

1. la voiture
2. le camion
3. la moto
4. le camion de pompiers
5. l'ambulance

**3**

1 B  2 A  3 A  4 B
5 A

**4**

1. pareil
2. différent
3. neuf
4. préféré
5. vieux

## Week 26

**1**

1. dire
2. pleurer
3. aider
4. se faire mal
5. tomber

**2**

1. le kangourou
2. le gorille
3. le rhinocéros
4. le panda
5. le perroquet

**3**

1. les bottes
2. le pull
3. l'écharpe
4. le manteau
5. les gants

**4**

1. la baignoire
2. les toilettes
3. le miroir
4. l'étagère
5. la douche

## Week 27

**1**

1. peur
2. excitée
3. amicale
4. soif
5. faim

**2**

1. le savon
2. le lavabo
3. le dentifrice
4. la brosse à dents
5. le robinet

**3**

1. le projet
2. le puzzle
3. l'image
4. l'histoire
5. la leçon

**4**

1. la forêt
2. la montagne
3. le château
4. le lac
5. la barque

## Week 28

**1**

1. A  2. B  3. B  4. A
5. B

**2**

1. brumeux
2. ensoleillé
3. la météo
4. venteux
5. nuageux

**3**

1. la souris
2. l'imprimante
3. l'ordinateur
4. l'écran
5. le clavier

**4**

1. le cirque
2. le manège
3. la glace
4. la fête foraine
5. le clown

## Week 29

**1**

1. chercher
2. trouver
3. assembler
4. terminer
5. essayer

**2**

1. le poisson
2. la pêche
3. la canne à pêche
4. le filet
5. le gilet de sauvetage

**3**

1. les dents
2. la langue
3. la dent
4. le sourire
5. la dentiste

**4**

1. les haricots
2. la viande
3. le riz
4. la soupe
5. la tarte

## Week 30

**1**

1. le village
2. les collines
3. la campagne
4. le bois
5. le marché

**2**

1. la lettre
2. l'adresse
3. l'enveloppe
4. le timbre
5. le nom

**3**

1. B  2. A  3. B  4. A
5. B

**4**

1. le plafond
2. la fenêtre
3. la porte
4. le sol
5. la clé

## Week 31

**1**

1. B  2. B  3. B  4. A
5. A

**2**

1. le bureau
2. la bibliothèque
3. le stade
4. la salle de sport
5. le supermarché

**3**

1. la cuisinière
2. la poubelle
3. le four
4. le placard
5. le réfrigérateur

**4**

1. la pierre
2. le ciel
3. le nuage
4. la terre
5. les insectes

## Week 32

**1**
1. B  2. A  3. A  4. A
5. B

**2**
1. le menu
2. le restaurant
3. la cheffe cuisinière
4. la nourriture
5. la serveuse

**3**
1. jouer
2. sautiller
3. tourner
4. se balancer
5. siffler

**4**
1. la route
2. l'arrêt de bus
3. la circulation
4. le passage piétons
5. les feux de signalisation

## Week 33

**1**
1. l'assiette
2. la bouteille
3. le verre
4. le bol
5. la tasse

**2**
1. A  2. B  3. A  4. A
5. B

**3**
1. le porte-monnaie
2. les courses
3. le panier
4. l'argent
5. le chariot

**4**
1. le zoo
2. la ville
3. le musée
4. l'université
5. le gratte-ciel

## Week 34

**1**
1. voyager
2. travailler
3. parler
4. rencontrer
5. montrer

**2**
1. l'astronaute
2. la terre
3. le soleil
4. la lune
5. la fusée

**3**
1. le pont
2. le ruisseau
3. le chemin
4. le pique-nique
5. la couverture

**4**
1. la photo
2. la vue
3. l'appareil photo
4. l'excursion
5. la carte postale

## Week 35

**1**
1. B  2. A  3. A  4. A
5. B

**2**
1. petite
2. bas
3. milieu
4. grand
5. haut

**3**
1. chaud
2. sèche
3. mouillée
4. froid
5. très chaud

**4**
1. étudier
2. chuchoter
3. chercher
4. lire
5. emprunter

## Week 36

**1**
1. le thé
2. le biscuit
3. le café
4. le lait
5. le sucre

**2**
1. l'or
2. le gagnant
3. l'argent
4. le bronze
5. la course

**3**
1. décoller
2. atterrir
3. se dépêcher
4. descendre
5. monter

**4**
1. B  2. A  3. A  4. B
5. A

## Week 37

**1**
1. aimer
2. ne pas aimer
3. payer
4. commander
5. préparer

**2**
1. le peigne
2. les lunettes
3. la brosse
4. le parfum
5. le bijou

**3**
1. le pingouin
2. l'ours polaire
3. le phoque
4. le renne
5. le morse

**4**
1. l'herbe
2. la grenouille
3. l'étang
4. le cygne
5. le canard

## Week 38

**1**
1. le pilote
2. l'aéroport
3. les vacances
4. la valise
5. l'avion

**2**
1. apporter
2. arriver
3. visiter
4. donner
5. accueillir

**3**

1. bruns
2. blonds
3. roux
4. noirs
5. gris

**4**

1. la salade
2. la laitue
3. la tomate
4. le fromage
5. les olives

## Week 39

**1**

1. le match
2. le coup de pied
3. l'équipe
4. le score
5. le joueur

**2**

1. le coléoptère
2. la mouche
3. le papillon
4. l'escargot
5. l'araignée

**3**

1. brave
2. nauséeuse
3. douloureuse
4. fatigué
5. malade

**4**

1. B  2. A  3. B  4. B
5. A

## Week 40

**1**

1. clair
2. réveillé
3. sombre
4. endormi
5. fort

**2**

1. cacher
2. aller chercher
3. nourrir
4. casser
5. s'occuper de

**3**

1. loin
2. gauche
3. derrière
4. droite
5. devant

**4**

1. la bouche
2. le menton
3. le sourcil
4. la moustache
5. la barbe

## Week 41

**1**

1. entier
2. le coin
3. la moitié
4. le centre
5. le quart

**2**

1. la piscine
2. le chapeau
3. l'hôtel
4. la chaise longue
5. les lunettes de soleil

**3**

1. B  2. A  3. B  4. A
5. A

**4**

1. cueillir
2. planter
3. arroser
4. faire pousser
5. couper

## Week 42

**1**

1. l'horloge
2. midi
3. la minute
4. minuit
5. l'heure

**2**

1. le feu
2. la caravane
3. la tente
4. la torche
5. la fumée

**3**

1. l'été
2. l'hiver
3. l'automne
4. le printemps
5. les saisons

**4**

1. la colle
2. l'ingénieure
3. la boîte à outils
4. les outils
5. la machine

## Week 43

**1**

1. peser
2. acheter
3. donner
4. vendre
5. porter

**2**

1. l'acteur
2. le rideau
3. la scène
4. la chanteuse
5. le théâtre

**3**

1. le drapeau
2. le ballon de plage
3. le seau
4. la pelle
5. le château de sable

**4**

1. le mois
2. la semaine
3. l'année
4. l'agenda
5. le week-end

## Week 44

**1**

1. l'art
2. les mathématiques
3. les sciences
4. le français
5. l'emploi du temps

**2**

1. construire
2. peindre
3. mélanger
4. réparer
5. coller

**3**

1 le beurre
2 la confiture
3 le chocolat
4 la farine
5 le miel

**4**

1 poilu
2 lent
3 gros
4 rapide
5 mince

## Week 45

**1**

1 la sortie
2 le parking
3 les magasins
4 l'entrée
5 le centre commercial

**2**

1 l'étudiant
2 la carte
3 les échecs
4 le dictionnaire
5 le cahier

**3**

1 le médicament
2 la radio
3 le bandage
4 le pansement
5 le masque

**4**

1 faire du feu
2 rire
3 bavarder
4 camper
5 dormir

## Week 46

**1**

1 le loup
2 le hibou
3 le cerf
4 l'écureuil
5 le renard

**2**

1 le crabe
2 le coquillage
3 les rochers
4 les algues
5 l'étoile de mer

**3**

1 plein
2 vide
3 moitié plein
4 peu
5 beaucoup

**4**

1 A  2 B  3 B  4 B
5 A

## Week 47

**1**

1 la géographie
2 la technologie
3 l'histoire
4 les langues
5 les matières

**2**

1 le nid
2 le bec
3 l'aile
4 la griffe
5 l'aigle

**3**

1 bruyant
2 silencieuse
3 désordonnée
4 ordonné
5 s'ennuyer

**4**

1 A  2 B  3 A  4 B
5 B

## Week 48

**1**

1 la boussole
2 nord
3 ouest
4 est
5 sud

**2**

1 les emplois
2 la styliste
3 le journaliste
4 l'artiste
5 la photographe

**3**

1 la bague
2 le bracelet
3 le sac à main
4 le collier
5 la montre

**4**

1 la comète
2 l'espace
3 la planète
4 les étoiles
5 le télescope

## Week 49

**1**

1 B  2 A  3 B  4 A
5 B

**2**

1 le métal
2 la pierre
3 le bois
4 le plastique
5 la laine

**3**

1 les moustaches
2 la patte
3 la queue
4 le collier
5 la fourrure

**4**

1 inventer
2 penser
3 explorer
4 jouer
5 concevoir

## Week 50

**1**

1 tirer
2 tenir
3 pousser
4 laisser tomber
5 soulever

**2**

1 les rayures
2 cher
3 les pois
4 le motif
5 bon marché

**3**

1 première
2 le concours
3 le prix
4 deuxième
5 troisième

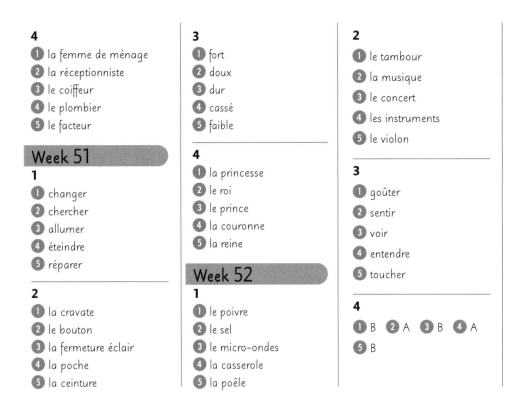

**4**
1. la femme de ménage
2. la réceptionniste
3. le coiffeur
4. le plombier
5. le facteur

**Week 51**

**1**
1. changer
2. chercher
3. allumer
4. éteindre
5. réparer

**2**
1. la cravate
2. le bouton
3. la fermeture éclair
4. la poche
5. la ceinture

**3**
1. fort
2. doux
3. dur
4. cassé
5. faible

**4**
1. la princesse
2. le roi
3. le prince
4. la couronne
5. la reine

**Week 52**

**1**
1. le poivre
2. le sel
3. le micro-ondes
4. la casserole
5. la poêle

**2**
1. le tambour
2. la musique
3. le concert
4. les instruments
5. le violon

**3**
1. goûter
2. sentir
3. voir
4. entendre
5. toucher

**4**
1. B 2. A 3. B 4. A
5. B

# Acknowledgments

The publisher would like to thank:

Adam Brackenbury for design and illustration assistance; Edwood Burn for illustration assistance; Ankita Awasthi Tröger and Andiamo! Language Services Ltd for proofreading; Abigail Ellis for indexing; ID Audio for audio recording and production; Sophie Adam, Sonia Charbonnier, and Christine Stroyan for audio recording management; and Rakesh Kumar, Priyanka Sharma, and Saloni Singh for jacket design assistance.

All images are copyright DK. For more information, please visit **www.dkimages.com**.